HELLENISTIC MAGIC
AND THE SYNOPTIC TRADITION

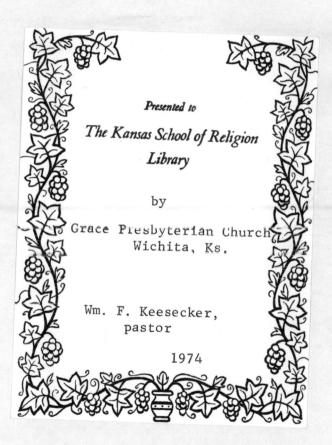

STUDIES IN BIBLICAL THEOLOGY

Second Series · 28

HELLENISTIC MAGIC
AND THE
SYNOPTIC TRADITION

JOHN M. HULL

ALEC R. ALLENSON INC.
635 EAST OGDEN AVENUE
NAPERVILLE, ILL.

© *SCM Press Ltd 1974*
ISBN 0-8401-3078-3
Library of Congress Catalog Card No. 73-77369

Published by Alec R. Allenson Inc.
Naperville, Ill.
Printed in Great Britain

TO DAPHNE AND IMOGEN

CONTENTS

PREFACE

This study is offered as a contribution to a neglected aspect of the history of the synoptic tradition. It also hopes to throw some light on the theology of the gospels, particularly Luke and Matthew, in so far as their theology has been modified by the encounter with magic.

I would like to express my thanks to Dr T. F. Glasson of New College, London, who encouraged me in the early stages of this work and to Dr J. N. Birdsall of the University of Birmingham, to whose advice and scholarly criticism, always given generously, I owe a great deal.

I am grateful to Mrs Helen Thompson of the University of Birmingham School of Education, and to Miss Jean Cunningham of the SCM Press, for their patient and careful work in preparing the material for publication.

JOHN M. HULL

ABBREVIATIONS

ANCL	Ante-Nicene Christian Library, Edinburgh 1867–72
Bab.	*The Babylonian Talmud,* ed. I. Epstein (Soncino ed.), 34 vols., London 1935–48
BZNW	Beihefte zur *Zeitschrift für die neutestamentliche Wissenschaft,* Giessen and Berlin
ET	English translation
FRLANT	Forschungen zur Religion und Literatur des Alten und Neuen Testaments, Göttingen
HTR	*Harvard Theological Review,* Cambridge, Mass.
ICC	International Critical Commentary, Edinburgh
JBL	*Journal of Biblical Literature,* Philadelphia
JEA	*Journal of Egyptian Archaeology,* London
JQR	*Jewish Quarterly Review,* London
JTS	*Journal of Theological Studies,* Oxford
LAE	*Light from the Ancient East*: see Bibliography under Deissmann
MNTC	Moffatt New Testament Commentary, London 1928–50
NT Apoc.	E. Hennecke and W. Schneemelcher, *New Testament Apocrypha* I–II, ET ed. R. McL. Wilson, London 1963, 1965
P	Papyrus
PBerol.	Berlin Papyrus (and similarly)
PEFQS	*Palestine Exploration Fund Quarterly Statement,* London
PGM	*Papyri Graecae Magicae*: see Bibliography under Preisendanz

Proc. Br. Acad.	Proceedings of the British Academy, London
TDNT	Theological Dictionary of the New Testament, ed. G. Kittel, ET ed. G. W. Bromiley, Grand Rapids, Michigan, 1964ff.
TLZ	Theologische Literaturzeitung, Leipzig
ZAW	Zeitschrift für die alttestamentliche Wissenschaft, Giessen and Berlin
ZNW	Zeitschrift fur die neutestamentliche Wissenschaft, Giessen and Berlin

I

INTRODUCTION

The rediscovery in modern times of the magic of the early Roman Empire has given us a new understanding of the beliefs of the ordinary people at that time. The possibility of a relationship between magic and the early Christian tradition has never been fully explored. Yet, if for no other reasons than the references in the Acts to the encounter between the Christian preachers and the magicians and the fact that Christianity and magic were both associated with the lower classes of society, it would not be surprising to find that the image of Jesus has been influenced by magical beliefs.

The belief that Jesus was a magician is an ancient one. It goes back at least as far as the middle of the first century, as is shown by the Beelzebub story in Mark. During the early Christian centuries it is found in a variety of traditions and became from time to time a subject of warm debate.

Jewish tradition attributes Jesus' miracles to his magical power[1] and he is said to have been executed as a sorcerer.[2] The Jewish objection to the healings on the sabbath was therefore, according to this tradition, not the sabbath activity itself but the magical techniques used by Jesus.[3]

Heretical and paganized forms of Christianity offer many examples of Jesus appearing as a master magician and as the giver of magical power or as occupying a role in a system which as a whole is conceived in magical and astrological terms. The system of the second-century gnostic heretic, Marcus, who was himself an outstandingly successful magician, is based on the magical powers of the alphabet and the mystic relationship between their numbers, names and sounds. Jesus as Alpha and Omega played an important role in the system.[4] The followers of the gnostic Carpocrates also in the second century used the name of Jesus to practise magical arts and believed that because the power of Jesus was in them they would have power over all archons and makers of this world.[5] Jesus is here the model of the supreme magician passing on his magical power to his initiates. The great Basilides taught that Jesus was subject to astrological predeterminism and referred to his saying 'Mine hour is not yet come' and to the visit of the magi.[6]

The early traditions about Jesus as a magician are often strikingly ambivalent, affirming and denying magic in almost the same breath. In *Pistis Sophia*, a product of third-century Christian Gnosticism, Jesus is described (ch. 102, §§255, 258) instructing his disciples to teach renunciation of magic and drugs and superstitious invocations. Yet the saving work of Jesus is set in a framework of acceptance of astrological powers and magical means of overcoming them (e.g. ch. 130, §§332–5) and those who know the power beyond the spheres, the 'mysteries of the magic of the thirteen aeons', may work marvels. Jesus is named in *Pistis Sophia* as *Aberamentho*, a magical name found both in the papyri and on engraved gems.[7]

It is not surprising, in view of the mixture of horror and fascination which magic aroused, to find within the Christian literature itself some of the clearest accounts of the accusation that Jesus was a magician. The apocryphal literature abounds in examples. In the *Acts of Pilate* 2.1 the Jews explain Pilate's wife's dream on the grounds that Jesus has bewitched her. 'Did we not tell you that he is a sorcerer? Behold, he has sent a dream to your wife.' In the *Clementine Recognitions* 1.42, the guards at the sepulchre say that Jesus was a magician and this is why they were unable to prevent his resurrection. The apostles are frequently accused of magic. In the *Acts of Thomas* (ch. 20) the Indian villagers say of Thomas, 'He teaches a new God and heals the sick and drives out demons and does many other wonderful things; and we think he is a magician.' The *Acts of Paul* (*c.* AD 190) describes (ch. 15) the crowd in Iconium accusing Paul of magic because their wives have taken vows of abstinence. In the *Pseudo-Clementines*[8] Simon the magician tries to turn the people of Berytus against Peter by saying that, having caused a recent earthquake, 'he is a magician'. Although the narrator adds, 'And many other false charges of this sort did Simon

. . . bring against Peter', when Peter himself speaks, far from denying the charge, he says, 'Ye men, I admit that, God willing, I am capable of doing what these men here say and in addition am ready, if you will not hear my words, to turn your whole city upside down.' The various infancy gospels are the richest store of magical works attributed to Christ and of these the Arabic Infancy Gospel is the most bizarre.

By the fourth century popular Christianity was thoroughly saturated with magical beliefs and practices.

> One is persuaded too, that all Christians with one consent attributed a magical force, exercised especially over demons, to the mere utterance of the name of Jesus and to the sign of the cross . . . one feels driven to conclude that Christianity has become a religion of magic, with its centre of gravity in the sacramental mysteries.[9]

That such deep inroads into Christian faith could be made is undoubtedly due in part to the fact that a magical interpretation of the synoptic miracles was possible, and that no clear distinction between the miracles of Christ and the wonders of magicians existed.

The belief that Jesus was a magician is often found in purely pagan circles. Celsus (*c.* AD 178) was familiar with the view, and used it to attack the church. Origen (*Contra Celsum* I) defends the Jews in general against the charge that they were addicted to sorcery, and Jesus in particular (I.38) against the charge that he learnt his supposed magic in Egypt and was enabled to perform his magic by means of these techniques. The embarrassment created by the apparent association in Matt. 2 of Jesus with astrology and with the magi is dealt with firmly by Origen in I.60, where he explains that the magi, who were on familiar terms with evil spirits, found their magic declining in power, since their demons had lost their strength. Knowing the prophecy of Balaam (Num. 24.17), they conjectured that the man whose appearance had been foretold along with that of the star had actually come into the world, and, having predetermined that he was superior in power to all demons and to all powers, they resolved to offer him homage. The charge of magic clearly ran through the whole of Celsus' work, and it is instructive to observe that Origen and Celsus agreed about the traits which a divine man would have. Origen's defence is, broadly, that in the first place the charge of magic will not stick and, secondly, that the attributes of the divine man, recognized by Celsus, were actually to be found in Jesus. The following of magicians such as Simon and Dositheus had not survived their death, but the community of Jesus had survived, grown and conquered.[10]

Tertullian was also aware of the fact that Matt. 2 was being used, whether by pagans or Christians, to defend astrology, and in his work *On Idolatry* (ch. 9) we have his rejection of this interpretation. Ignatius, nearly a century earlier, had already claimed the story of the star as indicating Christ's defeat of magic.

The *Koran*, V. 113, describes the miracles of Jesus, concluding: 'Such of them as believed not said, "This is nought but plain sorcery."' The miracles referred to are the making of birds from clay, the healing of blind men and lepers, and the raising of the dead. The *Hayât* of Ad-Damîrî[11] contains a Muslim tale of Jews who called Jesus 'an enchanter, son of an enchantress'. The Mandean sacred literature describes Jesus as a false prophet and a magician, emanating from the planet Mercury.[12]

The belief, accusation, or tradition that Jesus was a magician and that he passed magical power to his apostles and to the church as a whole is thus found in Judaism, gnosticism, Christian orthodoxy and heterodoxy, paganism, Islam and in Mandeanism. Is there any ground for this belief in the canonical scriptures? Are the synoptic gospels in particular aware of magic and do they lend support to the magical context against which such a strikingly wide range of circles interpreted Jesus? The question has been revived in modern times, partly because of the vast increase in our knowledge of ancient magic.

In the chapters which follow an account is given of the sources of our knowledge of Hellenistic magic and of the steps by which it was recovered and heard after centuries of silence in the strangeness of its original voice. The impact of this new knowledge on New Testament studies is described, and the main features of magic itself are outlined. In chapters V–VII an attempt is made to see if the synoptic gospels show any awareness of the world of magic and, if so, how they have reacted.

II

THE RECOVERY OF HELLENISTIC MAGIC

1. Sources

(i) *The magical papyri*

The main source of new knowledge in this field is that offered by
the Egyptian papyri. Before the discovery of the magical papyri,
the historian of ancient magic was mainly dependent upon works
such as the *Apology* of Apuleius,[1] written in the middle of the
second century AD, the *De Mysteriis* of Iamblichus (early fourth
century AD), and Pliny (died AD 79), in whose *Natural History*
there are a great number of magical recipes and exorcisms. Lucian
of Samosata however (born *c.* AD 120) provided the greatest fund
of knowledge of ancient magic, and remains an incomparable
source of illumination, even today after a century of work on the
papyri. Interest in ancient magic was stimulated by the first critical
editions of many of these works in the nineteenth century. The
Hermetic literature, for example, was edited by G. Parthey in
1854 and by L. Ménard in 1866, and 1857 saw the appearance of
Parthey's edition of the *De Mysteriis* of Iamblichus.

The older historical studies are of necessity based upon literary
sources such as these, and perusal of a work such as Alfred Maury's
La magie et l'astrologie dans l'antiquité et au moyen âge (1877) illustrates
the fairly high degree of detail which could be gathered from them.
Since the magical papyri are almost entirely in Greek, discussions
of Latin magic are still based primarily upon the literary sources[2]
and occasional works have appeared in this century which deliberately neglect the papyri to concentrate on the literary sources.[3]
Works of this sort provide a convenient way of assessing the
additional perspective on magic and the details of its procedure
which the papyri provide.

Although one or two imprecatory texts had already come to light, the first genuinely magical papyri were brought to Europe from Egypt in the late eighteen-twenties. This was largely due to the scholarly enthusiasm of Johann d'Anastasy, a Swedish diplomat stationed in Cairo from 1828 to 1859. d'Anastasy acquired a collection of papyri which had been discovered in a grave in Thebes some time earlier. The exact date and location of the find are unknown. The collection includes every type of ancient magic – love magic, apotropaic magic, revelation magic, exorcisms and so on – and the documents were written during the period *c*. AD 250–350.[4] They seem to form part of a library, perhaps with a single owner, who placed them in the tomb in the middle or late fourth century AD. Why he did so, we do not know. It may have been due to a desire to hide the manuscripts because of fear of the penalties for magical practices.[5] But the idea may have been to provide the dead man with magical expertise for use in the next life.[6] Provision of magical texts for such purposes is an extremely ancient Egyptian custom. The collector of the library, if such it was, may have been a bibliophile with exotic tastes, or he may have been a magician himself (many of the manuscripts are working copies).

Part of the d'Anastasy collection was acquired by the Leiden Museum of Antiquities in 1828. One of the papyri was incomplete; but the rest of this important document, together with a second, was secured by Leiden in 1830.[7] These were the subject of the first study of magical papyri, by C. J. C. Reuvens, which appeared in 1830 and is still worth reading, being at the time a brilliant example of insight and decipherment. Reuvens' *Lettres* were reviewed the following year by Carl Müller[8] and his reaction is interesting for the student of the papyri today. Müller recognized the importance of the newly published works for the progress of Demotic studies, and for the evolution of religion, but supremely for the history of magic, which (as Müller believed) could now be seen to have developed from the ancient religion of Egypt with the help of syncretistic additions. The papyri are also seen to be of significance to the student of ancient gems; Müller points out the appearance of the *Abraxas* formula, as well as others already familiar from the inscribed gem-stones. Müller's brief translations from these two papyri, intended to give his readers some idea of their style and general atmosphere, have the distinction of being the first translations into any modern European language of the magical papyri.

But the honour of presenting the first edited and fully translated text fell to an English scholar. At about the same time as the Leiden Museum acquired its samples from the d'Anastasy collection, others found their way to the British Museum, and in 1852 one of these, PLond. 46 (*PGM* V), was edited by the Cambridge scholar C. W. Goodwin. After more than a century, this work remains an important collection of parallels and suggestions about interpretation. Goodwin dated it no earlier than the second century AD on the grounds of its contents, and both Kenyon[9] and Preisendanz[10] date it to the fourth century on paleographical grounds.

It was natural that these early investigators should have compared their newly found texts with the references to magic in the other extant literature from antiquity. Because many of these were found in gnostic contexts, it was often thought that the magical papyri were gnostic documents. Reuvens had attributed PLond. 46 to the gnostic school of Marcus, partly because of the appearance in both Marcus and the papyrus of the seven vowels as a magical power-symbol, but *Pistis Sophia* had been published in 1851 and Goodwin pointed out that the link with this was closer than the link with Marcus, for *Pistis Sophia* contained not only the mystic associations of the vowels but also some of the mystical/magical names used in the papyrus. But Goodwin also noticed that the magical papyrus stresses the various gods of Egypt, Persia and Greece more than *Pistis Sophia* does, and is indeed a veritable jumble of syncretisms. Goodwin was thus the first to point out that the magical papyri are witnesses to the existence of a Hellenistic magic which, although entirely derivative, was not merely a part or an aspect of any other religion or sect, but had from all of them created a style and an ethos of its own. Even so, Goodwin, like Müller before him, underestimated the extent to which his document was a product of Hellenism, regarding its author as perhaps a priest of Isis or Sarapis and its ideas as being basically derived from the ancient Egyptian religion.

In 1857 the remainder of the d'Anastasy collection was auctioned in Paris.[11] Richard Lepsius bought two of the papyri for the museum in Berlin, the now justly famous PBerol. 5025 and 5026 (*PGM* I and II). The former is of the fourth or fifth century, whilst the latter is probably a little earlier, although still of the fourth century. About sixty papyri, some not even unrolled, were sold at the auction. A number were acquired by the British Museum, but lay unpublished for many years. An important one proved to be the first half of one already known at Leiden.[12] Another did not appear until 1931.[13] But the greatest treasure of the d'Anastasy collection, still the greatest of all the magical papyri, was purchased by the Bibliothèque Nationale in Paris. It is a fourth-century codex, of thirty-six sheets, written on both sides, having 3274 lines in all, and is usually known as the Great Paris Magical Papyrus (*PGM* IV).

These important discoveries of the early nineteenth century were followed by a steady stream of further new magical papyri. Most of the finds from the various villages and towns of Egypt have included magical specimens. A group found their way into the British Museum in 1888 and were published by Kenyon in 1893, the largest and oldest (third century AD) being PLond. 121 (*PGM* VII), the others being from the third and fourth centuries. Many examples have come from Oxyrhynchus, where B. P. Grenfell and A. S. Hunt began to excavate in 1896/7. From Eshmunein (Hermopolis) in 1903 came a roll of the fourth or fifth century (*PGM* XIXa), which, as its fifteenth line informs us, was intended to be placed as a magic charm in a mummy's mouth. The Norwegian scholar S. Eitrem bought a number of magical papyri in the Fayum in 1920, publishing them five years later. In 1889 in Hawara, Flinders Petrie discovered a mud figure wrapped in shreds of papyrus. The object was presented to the Ashmolean Museum in Oxford, remaining unexamined until 1928, when A. S. Hunt photographed it and published the text of the papyrus. It is a love charm, the mud figure being a model of the beloved.[14] These are of course, only a few illustrations of the constant stream of new discoveries and editions.

All the magical papyri discovered up to about 1930 were published in 1928 and 1931 in two volumes by Karl Preisendanz. This fine critical edition was the crowning achievement in this field and remains the standard handbook. Since 1931 however papyri have continued to come to light and many were included in the third volume of Preisendanz's collection, published in 1942, and almost immediately destroyed by an air raid. This concluding volume, containing indices to vocabulary as well as additional texts, has not therefore been easily accessible.[15]

A few examples of the more recent papyrological discoveries may be of interest. The Warren Papyri include a love charm from the late third century AD with many reminiscences of Egyptian mythology.[16] PErl. 37 is a fever amulet from the fourth century AD.[17] PBologn. 3 is a charm which uses verses from Homer, rather like PLond. 121, but it is at least a century older, coming from the second century AD. PBologn. 4 is a Christian amulet, referring to Mary and the Trinity.[18] A fourth-century protection against fever and demons to be used by parents in defending a sick child appears among the Lund papyri.[19]

At least one hundred and fifty magical papyri[20] have now been published. The number of unedited fragments in the various collections is unknown but is certainly quite considerable.

(ii) *The tabellae defixionum*

Although the most important, the papyri are not the only source of our new understanding of Hellenistic magic. Of great significance are the cursing tablets. Malevolent superstition suggested many ways of attempting to injure an enemy; one of the most popular, particularly amongst the lower and servile classes where such beliefs flourished, consisted of having inscribed upon some durable substance a prayer to a chthonic deity or a demon, invoking the infernal power to damage the hated enemy. The inscribed plaque would then be used in a ritual at the conclusion of which it would be cast into a grave or well or into a spot associated with a violent death, such as a place of execution, often with a nail driven through it. The prayers might be scratched on marble or other stone, or written on papyrus, but the majority, whether in Greek or Latin, are on thin sheets of lead. Because they were so frequently nailed they are known as *tabellae defixionum*.

Most of the large hoards were discovered in the course of the archaeological expeditions exploring Roman and Greek sites during the nineteenth century. The curses may be directed against thieves, faithless wives or husbands, personal enemies or business rivals. Those from Italy and Africa are often concerned with charioteering, and ask that the competing riders may be unable to move and may lose control of their horses. The 'Caerleon Curse', found in the Roman amphitheatre at Caerleon in Monmouthshire, is of this type. It is addressed to Nemesis against a fellow competitor who has apparently stolen the operator's boots and cloak.[21]

The *tabellae defixionum* discovered in the period up to the end of the century were gathered together by Wünsch[22] and Audollent.

What is the overall contribution to our knowledge of ancient magic made by these tablets? In the first place it is significant that they cover a wider range of time than do the papyri. None of the true magical papyri predate the Christian era; most of them come from the second to the sixth centuries AD. The oldest cursing tablets are of the fifth century BC, they become fairly common in the fourth century BC, and in the Hellenistic period they are extremely numerous. Like the papyri, the largest concentration comes from that high-water mark of magic, the third and fourth centuries AD. The tablets therefore witness to a thousand years of magic. It is possible to trace a distinct development. The earlier tablets are extremely simple. 'N. (a chthonic or subterranean god), bind N. son of N. (his mother's name)'. There are no formulae and no repetitions. The mere manufacture and deposition of the tablet is sufficient to effect the desired result. The later inscriptions become larger, they are adorned with magical diagrams to give added potency and replete with strings of vowels and magical names and sounds, often repetitive. Elaborate arrangements of the letters, especially wing-shaped figures and palindromes, are favoured. The growth of syncretism parallels the growth in complexity. The early Attic examples invoke the classic chthonic deities, Pluto, Kore, the Moirai, Hermes, Hecate and so on, but in later examples, both from Attica and elsewhere, we find Iao, El, Neptho, Ereshkigal, Serapis – a host of Oriental and Egyptian names. Since a somewhat similar process appears in the papyri as well, although the extremes are less evident, we are provided with a criterion for comparing the antiquity of various examples of magical practice, although our knowledge is still so fragmentary that it must be used with extreme caution.

On the other hand the tablets sometimes illustrate not only the evolution of magic but also its stability. A manuscript of the late sixteenth or early seventeenth century edited by Delatte contains an almost exact parallel to the words of a tablet from the third or fourth century (now in the museum of Reading University).[23] We have here a magical formula older than the fourth century AD (since the compiler of the inscription had copied it from his source) appearing almost unchanged thirteen centuries later.

Curse tablets have been found in every part of the empire from Britain to Egypt and from Africa to the Rhine. Everywhere the contents are broadly the same. Apart from the predominance of charioteering interests in the west, there is little or no regional character. The examples from Beisan in Palestine have no stronger element of Jewish influence than have those found elsewhere. This method of magic had established itself fairly uniformly wherever Greek was understood. This conclusion could not have been established from the papyri alone, for they are of Egyptian origin.

In this respect the tablets supplement the papyri. In other respects they corroborate them. The same magical names and formulae appear in both, often in the same order. It has sometimes been possible to correct the reading of a papyrus after comparison with a tablet bearing a similar inscription, and a fragmentary tablet will often be read with the aid of a papyrus. Often a common and much older source seems to lie behind the surviving remains.[24]

(iii) *Amulets*

Amulets are a third source of knowledge of ancient magic. An amulet, which gave its wearer special powers or protection from alien forces, might be of almost any material depending upon the occult sympathy which was believed to exist between the supernatural power in view and the material. Metals, minerals and precious stones were thought to be in particularly powerful bonds of sympathy with the spiritual world, and were popular as amulets. They have the added advantage from our point of view of durability and, whereas amulets of animal and vegetable products have largely perished, many thousands of carved gems with magical significance have survived.

Unlike the study of the papyri and the tablets, amulet study is by no means new. Examples have been known and collections acquired and studied for several centuries, although modern archaeological investigation has added considerably to the number. Several eighteenth- and even seventeenth-century works still contain valuable references.[25] The most complete standard modern work is that by Campbell Bonner.[26] But although the study of these remarkable antiquities is so long established, it is only in relatively recent times that their significance for the study of magic has been understood. This is due to the fact that only in the writings of the church fathers against the gnostic heretics did investigators find examples of the various inscriptions with which these gems are adorned. The most influential example was that of the word *Abraxas* which is found on many amulets and is said by Irenaeus and Hippolytus[27] to be the name given by the followers of Basilides to the ruler of the 365 heavens.[28] The first antiquarian who realized the distinction between magical amulets and genuine gnostic gems seems to have been Charles William King, whose work on the Gnostics, first published in 1864, is an instructive example of the insight provided by the new magical papyrus which had been published by his Cambridge contemporary C. W. Goodwin in 1852. King knew of only one magical papyrus – he refers to it as 'the magical papyrus' – so the scope for illustration was not very considerable. Nevertheless it was perfectly clear to him that the study of the amulets was not altogether relevant for the reconstruction of Gnosticism.

It sounds like a paradox to assert that our 'Gnostic' gems are not the work of the Gnostics; but taking that apellation in the strictest sense, the thing is perfectly true. The talismans we are considering never exhibit any traces of that admixture of Christian and Pagan doctrines which properly constitutes the Gnosis, that subject of the descriptions and the attacks of the Fathers of the Church. Their elements are drawn from the ancient religions of Babylon and Egypt, mixed at times with the formulae of the Jewish Kabbala. The 'Gnostic' stones are in reality the paraphernalia of magicians and dealers in charms . . . and only belong to the Ophites, Valentinians and other sub-divisions of the Christian Gnosis, in so far as those theosophists were especially given to the cultivation of the Black Art . . .[29]

The truth of the matter is probably that Gnosticism influenced magic rather less than it was influenced by magic. It now seems, for example, that while the early studies of the Coptic *Pistis Sophia* regarded its strange mixture of magical names and vowels sounds as indications of the gnostic character of the amulets, it is more probable that in the document and perhaps in the other gnostic literary remains we see the impact on later Egyptian Gnosticism of magical usages which, because they sprang from the ancient religions of Egypt and the Near East, were older and more revered.[30]

What then has the realization of the magical significance of the amulets contributed to our knowledge of ancient magic? Much of the answer has already been suggested. The magical amulets reproduce the formulae known to us from the papyri and the *tabellae defixionum* and thus provide corroborating evidence. Some of the diagrams found as illustrations of magical engravings in the papyri are found on the gems, no doubt copied from the papyri which would be the regular professional tools of the magicians. The various deities, demons and gods referred to in the papyri are here depicted, ready to do their fearful work on behalf of the fortunate possessor of the charm. A survey of the various influences of national religions on the amulets shows them to represent the same kind of international syncretism as is observed in the magical papyri.[31]

Sometimes an amulet will provide a detail not to be found elsewhere. This is particularly true of the relations between Christianity and magic, for, as is clear from the examples of papyrus amulets collected by Preisendanz in the second volume of *PGM*, Christians were not averse to using such lucky charms, nor were pagans slow to accept the remarkable powers of the Christian words.[32]

(iv) *Ostraca*

Broken pottery was rather like the scrap paper of ancient world. Large quantities of inscribed potsherds have been recovered, particularly from the rubbish dumps and domestic ruins of Hellenistic and Byzantine Egypt. The ostraca have yielded some magical examples but magical ostraca are very rare in comparison with the total number of these fragments,[33] most of which are receipts, lists of workmen, and schoolboys' exercises – day by day jottings. Five magical texts from ostraca have however been edited by Preisendanz. They range in date from the fourth century BC to Byzantine times. An interesting one is a 'wrath restrainer' from *c*. AD 300 which comes from Eshmunein in Egypt. Hor, the son of Mary, is to be restrained by Kronos 'who restrains the wrath of all men' and he is not to be allowed to speak at all to Hatros. Kronos is adjured by the finger of God.[34] 'Wrath restrainers' are fairly popular in the papyri; there was evidently a steady demand for this kind of protection.

Preisendanz's second ostracon is a second-century fragment from Oxyrhynchus discovered in 1928. It is rather a vicious little 'love' charm in which after a long series of vowel combinations and names of gods the operator seeks to separate Allous from her husband Apollonius and from his house and turn her affections towards himself.

Two or three Byzantine ostraca may be added to the magical group.³⁵ The first is listed as biblical, and so it is, but Ps. 68.1, 'Let God arise; let his enemies be scattered' is a suitable text for an apotropaic amulet and it is possible that that was the motive which led to its writing. The other two are described as liturgical or magical but they are almost indecipherable. They seem to be prayers or incantations, and the name of Jesus can be read in each of them. They are from the sixth or seventh century AD.

The ostraca are valuable as illustrations of practices advised by the authors of the magical papyri, as well as for the sake of their own contents. POslo.1 describes a love spell which is to be written upon an ostracon.³⁶ Later in the same papyrus the magician is to take a triangular potsherd from a place where three roads meet, hold it in his left hand, and having written the spell on it in ink of myrrh, to hide it. Use of a potsherd is advised in the fragmentary papyrus from the Rainer collection in Vienna.³⁷ It appears to be a 'silencer' or 'muzzler' from the fifth century AD.

(v) *Magical apparatus*

Finally, in this brief review of the sources of our knowledge of ancient magic, mention must be made of articles which can best be described as the professional equipment of the magician. The papyri often prescribe things such as laurel leaves, earthen altars and white garments, all of which have naturally perished. But we also read of tables, magical discs and plates made of metal, usually bronze or iron, and some of these have survived. PLond. 46 (*PGM* V) opens with details of a method for obtaining an oracle from a young boy (a medium), a lamp, a dish and a stand. In the Great Paris Papyrus the magician spins a top to Selene and in the same invocation he names the symbols of Selene which include an iron top, appropriate as a symbol of the moon, for epileptics were used as mediums, and the spinning of a top or a potter's wheel was believed to provoke a mantic frenzy.³⁸ The use of various kinds of metal rings was widespread. PLond. 46 describes the magical preparation of a Hermes ring. A number of these objects have been recovered. Delatte describes a magic sphere which is in the National Museum of Athens. It was found in the theatre of Dionysus in Athens in 1886, and is made of white marble, covered with figures and inscriptions in shallow relief. On epigraphical grounds Delatte dates it to the second or third century AD and shows that it issues from the same solar cult many traces of which remain in the gems and the papyri. It may have been in the theatre because of the superstitious beliefs of the actors, or the theatre may have been the appropriate venue for a magical ritual; we know of spells to be cast in a stadium and a circus.[39]

But the most remarkable discovery of this type was at Pergamon, where a large magician's kit from *c*. AD 200–250 has been discovered. It consists of a bronze table and base covered with magical signs, a dish similarly decorated, a long bronze nail with ten magical letters inscribed on its flat sides, two bronze rings and three black polished stones inscribed with angelic names, perhaps used in the casting of lots.[40]

Dolls for use in sympathetic magic have been recovered in quite large numbers. They are often in lead and seem to have been used with the leaden tablets, but dolls in clay and in bronze are also known. The name of the person they represent is sometimes inscribed on them.[41]

2. *Impact on New Testament studies*

In spite of the discovery of such a range and variety of first-hand sources for the study of magic in the Greek and Roman world, recognition of its importance for the study of ancient religion was long delayed. The turning point was the appearance in 1891 of Albrecht Dieterich's great study *Abraxas: Studien zur Religionsgeschichte des späteren Altertums*, the first work on Hellenistic magic to command the serious attention of classical philologists and historians of religion. Three years earlier the Viennese pioneer of papyrological studies, Carl Wessely, had published fine critical texts of a number of the newly discovered magical papyri, including the first complete edition of the Great Paris Magical Papyrus.[42] Dieterich's *Abraxas* was followed in 1903 by another work, if anything more influential, his famous *Mithrasliturgie*, in which lines 475–723 of the Paris papyrus were expounded as being an initiation hymn of a Mithraic cult.[43] Work of such scholars as F. C. Kenyon, F. Le. Griffith and H. Thompson in Britain and Adam Abt in Germany had established magic as a field worthy of serious attention.

Joseph Bidez and Franz Cumont presented in 1938 a masterly survey of the traditional mythological figures of Hellenistic magic and their impact on the occult tradition, while André Festugière, pursuing a similar line of thought, explored the magical literature associated with the name of Thoth-Hermes as a small part of his great work on the Hermetic literature.[44]

The work of Theodor Hopfner however stands out above all others as an interpretation of magic. *Griechisch-ägyptischer Offenbarungszauber*, of which the first volume appeared in 1921, is still the only full-scale history and exposition of Hellenistic magic. It is based upon study of all available sources, old and new, classical, papyrological and archaeological, and provides an authoritative and comprehensive treatment of the magical beliefs and practices of the period it covers.

At first and during the nineteenth century as a whole the magical discoveries had surprisingly little impact on New Testament studies. Philologists specializing in the religious sources were the first to use the papyri. H. Brugsch observed the significance of the Leiden d'Anastasy papyri in an article in 1852, and incorporated the results of his study in his Coptic grammar. The frequency of the $Ia\omega$ formula and variants attracted the notice of Semitic philologists investigating the origin and history of the sacred tetragrammaton. W. W. Graf Baudissin made use of the papyri then accessible in his *Studien zur semitischen Religionsgeschichte* in 1876, as did Ludwig Blau in *Das altjüdische Zauberwesen* in 1898. Blau's work illustrates another interesting point. It was Jewish scholars and historians of Judaism who, perhaps because of the striking Jewish elements in the papyri, were amongst the first to use them. Blau's work, still the standard study of ancient Jewish magic, is outstanding in this respect, making constant use of the papyri, and the later editions of Emil Schürer's 'History of the Jewish People in the Time of Christ' contained a number of references to the new discoveries.[45]

It was however the friendship between the great classical antiquarian Ulrich Wilcken and Adolf Deissmann, first Professor of Theology at Heidelberg and then Professor of New Testament exegesis at Berlin, which was to result in the first significant impact of the magical discoveries on New Testament studies. Deissmann incorporated the results of his investigations in his *Bibelstudien* and *Neue Bibelstudien* in 1895 and 1897, in a lecture course delivered in Frankfurt in 1905,[46] and finally in his epoch-making *Licht vom Osten* which appeared in 1908.[47]

The healing of the deaf mute (Mark 7.32–37) is discussed by Deissmann in the context of the binding conception in ancient magic.[48] James 2.19, where the devils are said to tremble at the very thought of God, is compared to the Great Paris Papyrus (*PGM* IV. 3016), which reads: 'Hang it round the sufferer; it is of every daemon a thing to be trembled at, which he fears.'[49] The exorcisms of the gospels are compared to line 3038: 'I adjure you, every demonic spirit, to say whatever you may be . . .'. Deissmann's comment is: 'To obtain complete power over the daemon, it is necessary to know his name; hence the question to the daemon in Mark 5.9 = Luke 8.30.'[50]. Concerning the burning of the magical books at Ephesus, described in Acts 19.19 Deissmann points out that τὰ περίεργα and πράσσειν are technical terms in the vocabulary of magic[51] and that the papyrus codices may in general be similar to those burnt by the Christians.[52] These few examples of Deissmann's work are amongst the earliest attempts to expound the New Testament in the context of ancient magic.

But the significance of Deissmann's work lay in the possibilities he suggested rather than the actual application of the documents in a systematic way. He did not attempt to interpret the development of Christian theology in part or as a whole in the light of the ancient parallels; his method was to take a point from here and there, and it must be remembered that his interest at this stage was philological rather than theological. Others were to use the rediscovery of ancient magic in a more far-reaching manner. Perhaps the first major study of this kind was *Im Namen Jesu* by Wilhelm Heitmüller of Göttingen, which appeared in 1905. Heitmüller places the early Christian use of the name of Jesus in the milieu of the use of names in Judaism and in syncretistic paganism and he concludes that there was no difference between the magical use of names in these circles and certain uses of the name of Jesus both in the apostolic period and beyond. The use of the name of Jesus in Christian baptism has its ultimate origin in name beliefs found in all parts of the ancient world contemporaneously with the rise of Christianity. The baptismal name was not merely symbolic or ideal, like the faith in Jesus as Messiah, but was full of literal, mystical, mysterious energy. When a person was baptized in the name he was occupied by the power of the name which drove out all alien powers; hence the association between baptism and exorcism leading to holiness and spirit-filling.[53]

In a small but important chapter of his study of the idea of 'Son of God' in John's gospel and in Hellenism, G. P. von Wetter contrasts the image of the magician who is possessed with diabolic power and the Son of God who is possessed with divine power.[54] It is this tension, this ambiguity between the nature of the two, which leads to Christian attacks on Simon, Dositheus, Menander and the rest of the magicians and false prophets. The work of Philostratus on Apollonius of Tyana is guided by motives similar to those which underlie all this Christian apologetic; they aim to show that their respective heroes are men of God and not wizards. Passages from John's gospel are interpreted against this background. The options facing the original reader of the gospel are that Jesus is a Samaritan (from the home of the prototype of the power-possessing magician, Simon) and demon-possessed, or he is the Son of God.[55]

The applications of ancient ideas of magic to the New Testament which we have been considering were prompted not only by the fact that the material was newly available, but also by the associated rise of the religious-historical school of biblical hermeneutics, which sought to place the biblical concepts in the setting of their contemporary religious trends. This prepared the way for the appearance of form criticism, which systematized the principles governing the impact of the original setting of the material and its context in the church upon the shape and meaning of the tradition itself. It is in the works of the form-critical school in the 1920s and 1930s that the magical impact receives its fullest and by now classical recognition. Bultmann, in his *Geschichte der synoptischen Tradition*, which first appeared in 1921, finds nearly a dozen traces of magic in the synoptics, mostly in the Marcan miracle stories, but he does not suggest that there is anything coherent, conscious or deliberate about these magical traces. They are either derived from folklore (like the magic sleep during the transfiguration or the idea that magic, when observed, loses its power)[56] or they are fragments of exorcist technique which have been almost submerged (like the roof incident in Mark 2) or overlaid by later theological motifs. He does not draw out any significant differences between Jesus and the other divine men of antiquity nor offer any explanation for the fact that the Christian tradition tended to obscure or forget or transform the magical implications of some of the material. He attaches no significance to any alleged anti-magic apologetic of the early church, the only exception to this being the temptation account. The magical traits of the synoptic tradition are, according to Bultmann, merely picked up as travel stains during the passage of the material through the Hellenistic milieu.

The approach of Martin Dibelius is similar, although in his book *From Tradition to Gospel* fewer examples are offered. The Marcan miracles are in general presented in a magical style, the disciples of Jesus acting rather like the magician's student in Lucian's *Philopseudes* 36. The healing miracles are interpreted against a magical background, the magical Aramaic words providing specific aid for the Christian healers.[57] But Dibelius believes that the miracles performed before select groups of disciples or in private (Jairus' daughter, the deaf mute and the blind man of Bethsaida) are not examples of magical display, but divine epiphany.[58]

For a reaction to the whole tendency to use magic in interpreting the New Testament, Vincent Taylor's commentary on Mark is instructive. On the Capernaum demoniac in Mark, the commentator remarks, 'Jesus shares the ideas of his time, but so far transcends them that by a commanding word alone, without the use of magical practices, He casts out the unclean spirit.'[59] The magical parallels to φιμόω are noted[60] without comment as to their applicability to the gospel stories. On Mark 7.33f. Vincent Taylor says,

Although sighing and groaning belong to the technique of mystical magic . . . , only a love for the bizarre rather than sober exegesis will find in the groaning of Jesus anything other than a sign of His deep feeling and compassion for the sufferer.[61]

Further specific quotations are difficult to find in a commentary which in spite of its immense learning and thoroughness is marked by an almost silent rejection of the sort of researches we have been describing, a rejection which is unacceptable, not because it is necessarily unjustified, but because it is done in silence.

So much for the rediscovery of ancient magic and its limited but significant impact on New Testament studies. Let us now take a closer look at these ancient magicians. What did they believe? What did they do?

III

THE MAIN FEATURES OF HELLENISTIC MAGIC

1. *The antiquity and persistence of magical traditions*

The most important witnesses of Hellenistic magic are, as we have seen, the papyri from Egypt. The most important of these date from the third and fourth centuries AD. Now, we may be able to show that the New Testament contains ideas similar to some which appeared later in these magical writings, but unless the originals of our third/fourth-century manuscripts are at least contemporaneous with the writing of the gospels (later middle first century AD) it will be difficult to show that the magical traditions represented in the papyri have also influenced the synoptic gospels.

There is no doubt at all that the existing magical papyri are not original compositions. They contain records of traditional forms of actions and words which to a large extent are copied from earlier manuscripts. As a small example of the persistence of the traditions we may take a case of Homer magic. Sacred texts, being writings which were believed to participate in the power of the spirit world of which they were revelations, and to contain the spirit force which had inspired them, have always been favourites when composing a magical prayer or spell of some kind. The Christians of the third and fourth centuries were already using texts from the gospels in amulets and spells,[1] and the pagans had been using verses from Homer for a long time. PLond. 121[2] opens with such a ʿΟμηρομαντεῖον, in which about 150 lines (some are lost) of verse, gathered from various parts of Homer, are set out. The idea was that each one was a sort of lucky message or oracle and you selected the one meant for you by throwing dice. Beside each line is marked the appropriate throw for the line. This part of the papyrus is from the third century AD. The same method of magic is now found in PBologn. 3[3] which comes from the second century AD, and thus represents Homer-magic one hundred years earlier than the London papyrus.

A hundred years however is not a very long span of time in the terms of magical traditions. Let us take a case[4] where the tradition can be shown to be more than a thousand years old. In PLond. 46[5] there is a method for getting an oracle from Serapis. It reads as follows:

A Sarapian divination, with a boy, a lamp, a bowl and a bench.

'I call upon you, Zeus-Helios-Mithras, Sarapis, unconquerable, Meliouchos, Melekertes, Meligenetor, . . . appear and pay heed to him who was manifest before fire and snow, Bainchooch, for you are the one who made light and snow appear, terrible-eyed-thunderer-and-lightning-giver . . .'

If he should say, 'I reveal', say, 'Let the throne of God enter, let the throne be brought in.'

If it is brought in by four men, then ask, 'With what are they crowned and what goes before the throne?'

If he says, 'They are crowned with olives and a censer goes before', then the boy is speaking the truth.

There follows a prayer for dismissing the god, a charm to protect the magician and his boy from harm, and some notes as to the most propitious time to carry out the whole process.

Now the main trend of the process is clear enough. The boy is a medium, the bench is for him to sit or lie on, the bowl or dish is to be filled with water or to have a polished surface and the purpose of the lamp or torch is to cast reflections on the surface of the water. The boy is questioned about what he thinks he sees in the reflections. He has to see a throne carried by four men wearing crowns of olive leaves with a censer going in front of the procession. If he says he sees all this, then he is indeed in a mantic trance and you may safely put to the god through the lad whatever question you want. The danger is not that the boy might lie, but he might be deceived by a demon. Careful tests guard against this.

E. W. Lane saw a similar ceremony carried out by an Egyptian magician in the early nineteenth century.[6] The magician wrote on strips of paper an invocation and a dismissal, and verses from the Koran. I continue in Lane's own words:

I had prepared, by the magician's direction, some frankincense and coriander-seed, and a chafing-dish with some live charcoal in it. These were now brought into the room, together with the boy who was to be employed: he had been called in, by my desire, from among some boys in the street, returning from a manufactory; and was about eight or nine years of age . . . The chafing-dish was placed before him and the boy; and the latter was placed on a seat. The magician now desired my servant to put some frankincense and coriander-seed into the chafing-dish; then taking hold of the boy's right hand, he drew in the palm of it a magic square . . . In the centre he poured a little ink, and desired the boy to look into it, and tell him if he could see his face reflected in it: the boy replied that he saw his face clearly. The magician, holding the boy's hand all the while, told him to continue looking intently into the ink, and not to raise his head.

He then took one of the little strips of paper inscribed with the forms of invocation, and dropped it into the chafing-dish, upon the burning coals and perfumes, which had already filled the room with their smoke; and as he did this, he commenced an indistinct muttering of words, which he continued during the whole process, excepting when he had to ask the boy a question, or to tell him what he was to say. . . . He then asked him if he saw anything in the ink, and was answered 'No', but about a minute after, the boy, trembling and seeming much frightened, said 'I see a man sweeping the ground.' 'When he has done sweeping', said the magician, 'tell me'. Presently the boy said, 'He had done.' The magician then . . . desired him to say, 'Bring a flag.' The boy did so, and soon said, 'He has brought a flag.' [A series of flags of various colours is then described by the boy.] . . . When the boy had described the seven flags as appearing to him, he was desired to say, 'Bring the Sultan's tent and pitch it.' This he did; and in about a minute after he said, 'Some men have brought a tent; a large green tent; they are pitching it.' . . . 'Now', said the magician, 'order the soldiers to come, and to pitch their camp around the tent of the Sultan.' . . . He now said 'Tell some of the people to bring a bull.' The boy gave the order required, and said, 'I see a bull: it is red; four men are dragging it along, and three are beating it.' He was told to desire them to kill it, and cut it up, and to put the meat in saucepans, and cook it . . . The magician then told him to call for the Sultan, and the boy, having done this, said 'I see the Sultan riding to his tent, on a bay horse, . . .'[7]

This done, the magician then asked Lane whom he wanted the boy to see, and a number of people were successfully described. 'Another boy was then brought in, and the magic square, etc. made in his hand, but he could see nothing. The magician said he was too old.'

Not only is the general outline of the magic the same but the introductory questions are strikingly similar. The god with his throne carried by bearers has become the Sultan with his tent and retinue. The censer accompanying the procession has become a full-fledged sacrifice of a red bull, brought by four men, and eaten. The man sweeping is not found in the papyrus, but is not an inappropriate figure in a temple scene. He corresponds to the temple attendant who would be busily at work before the arrival of the divine personage. The flags would be a development of the banners used in the ancient Egyptian ceremonies which throughout Lane's account are simply modified by the magician and the boy to suit the conditions of Islamic Egypt. The essence remains unaltered.

But how ancient was this little magic ritual at the time when our scribe recorded it in the third century AD? Was its life as long then as it has been since? In the papyrus a number of variants are written interlinear. In line 7 above one of the magic words (βαιβειζωθ) is written what looks like $\tilde{\eta}$ βαιβεβοθ (so Preisendanz reads). In line 13 we read, again interlinear, αλλ/αν which Preisendanz reads ἄλλως ἄνω. It is therefore not, as Goodwin thought, a correction or later addition but a variant reading. Our scribe has before him at least two copies of the document he is transcribing. In line 15, after the magical word μεθομηνως there is a little sign, a bit like an S with sharpened corners. Preisendanz, to whom the sign is new, suggests that it may indicate another variant. Yet a further variant is enclosed in brackets by the scribe. There are therefore in lines 14ff. no less than three variant forms of the magic words. May we suppose then at least three recensions of the text? That the scribe was indeed using written documents and not referring to oral traditions is made clear in line 54 where an alternative propitious time is introduced with the words 'But in other copies it was written that . . .'. We see that our manuscript stands at the end of a long process of written tradition, which must include several generations of manuscripts.

The tradition itself was no doubt a good deal older than the first written instructions. In *Apology* 42, Apuleius is charged with magic of just this sort:

They asserted that I had taken a boy apart to a secret place with a small altar and a lantern . . . and there so bewitched him with a magical incantation that he fell in the very spot where I pronounced the

charm . . . they should have added that the boy uttered many prophecies.

Apuleius refers in the same chapter to having read in the
philosopher Varro (116–27 BC) a similar story.

Inquiry was being made at Tralles by means of magic into the
probable issue of the Mithridatic war, and a boy who was gazing at an
image of Mercury reflected in a bowl of water foretold the future in a
hundred and sixty lines of verse.

He also records a similar incident involving Nigidius and Marcus
Cato. With these persons and with the Mithridatic wars (88–*c*. 72
BC) we are now dealing with the first half of the first century BC.
But the practice of divination through water (hydromancy) is
much older than that.[8] The Egyptian rituals can be traced back for
centuries, although we do not know that they were used in exactly
this sort of magic. Only a general similarity may be looked for.
The Serapis cult was itself a newcomer in Ptolemaic Egypt.
Herodotus (II.38f.) describes the sacrifice of a bull which must
not have a single black hair. The bull is flayed, then eaten. Lane's
boy saw soldiers beating and then eating a red bull. Herodotus
also describes (II.63) the procession with the image of the god
drawn in a four-wheeled cart by a huge crowd from one temple to
another. The questions the magician asks are clearly intended to
exclude any false demon, who would be exposed by his ignorance
of the inner secrets of the Serapis mysteries, which are described in
the question and answer sequence.

There are of course some late elements in our papyrus. No
doubt the magical incantations grew steadily longer with the
addition of new combinations. But there seems little reason to
doubt that in its main outlines this passage is several centuries
earlier than our surviving papyrus of the third century AD.

The signs of their secondary and dependent nature appear in
most of the longer magical papyri. Eitrem believed that POslo.1
(fourth century AD) was by no means a first-generation papyrus.
The fact that it is copied is clear from the state of the text. The
recipe in col. VIII is in a corrupt state. The scribe did not understand a good deal of what he was copying; there are omissions,
and he has failed to complete a number of important words in a
manner not consistent with the behaviour of someone writing an
original work. This can be seen particularly in the diagrams which

accompany the text, for the guidance of the amulet maker. These
are in some cases almost non-existent; the scribe has been unable to
decipher them in his working copy.[9]

This is also true of the Great Paris Papyrus. Many corruptions,
repetitions and variants testify to its secondary nature.[10] The
papyrus itself is early fourth century, probably coming from about
the time of Constantine, but its origin is some two hundred years
earlier. The type of Gnosticism represented in the papyrus is still
purely pagan,[11] but it cannot antedate the rise of Neoplatonism.
There are quite a number of similarities between this papyrus and
the *Chaldean Logia* which appear to have originated about AD 200.
The influence of Mithraism, which is prominent, indicates a period
after AD 100, since the rapid expansion and influence of Mithras
did not really get going until then. We have therefore to reconcile
the contents of the document with its signs of textual tradition.
Dieterich thought the section he calls a Mithras liturgy had its
origin *c*. AD 100–150, was taken into use by a Mithraic cult *c*. 150–
200, succumbed to the magical tradition *c*. 200 when it was adopted
for magical use, and reached its present form in this actual manuscript *c*. 300.[12] Festugière agrees that the second century rather
than the third suits its contents best.[13]

The extreme difficulty of determining the date of the contents
of these jumbled documents is well illustrated by study of the
London–Leiden Demotic papyrus edited by Griffith and Thompson. The papyrus itself is from the third century AD, probably the
first half of the third century, and is written in hieratic, demotic
and in Greek with Coptic glosses. The work is probably a translation from the Greek. But behind the Greek lay an even older
Egyptian original, in oral if not written form, although since
Egyptian written magic is so ancient (e.g. the Pyramid Texts) we
are not obliged to believe it was oral. The influence of Greek
mythology is slight in comparison with the other magical papyri,
and the Greek names which are found have probably come from
Alexandrian Judaism. But references to Egyptian gods are very
numerous indeed. Of course, even pure Egyptian elements could
exist without being ancient. Max Müller thought however that
some of the formulae are as old as the Eighteenth or Twentieth
Dynasty, and Griffith and Thompson agree that this could be true
of a few odd phrases. In general the linguistic evidence assembled
by Griffith and Thompson indicates the first century of our era,

for even the hieratic is a strange jumble and seems intended to imitate the ancient style rather than truly representing it. The written forms lying behind the present redaction of the papyrus are therefore roughly late first century AD with older fragments, and the magical procedures are very much older in some cases.[14]

Some of the actual papyri are of course older than the third and fourth centuries. A Greek magical cryptogram deciphered by A. S. Hunt[15] has been strengthened by having a strip of papyrus stuck to it down one side. This reinforcing strip is covered with cursive Greek from the time of Hadrian, and the papyrus itself is similarly dated (*PGM* LVII). A love charm in the Louvre (*PGM* XVI) is on palaeographical grounds dated to the first century AD, and the prayer for an oracle revelation found in the Temple of Bachias in the Fayum is also from the same century.[16] Another brief prayer for an oracle, addressed this time to Serapis-Helios and found in Oxyrhynchus,[17] is also from the first century, while PRainer 26 (*PGM* XXXb) actually includes a note of date equivalent to AD 6.

By examining the contents of these and other magical remains, it is possible to build a picture of the evolution of magic and so within broad limits to date the type of magic practice which is dealt with. Greek magic is already well established by the time of Homer. In the *Iliad* and particularly the *Odyssey* we find plant-magic and magic potions used by Circe (already at that stage a fully developed witch-figure) and belief in the power of incantations to perform miracles and to summon and dismiss spirits. Figures such as Hecate, Hermes, Orpheus, and Medea testify to the widespread power of magic over the Greek imagination.

Comparison of the magical papyri with these classical sources reveals in some cases very little difference. Festugière remarks that the fourth-century BC curse (*PGM* XL) 'is in the purest tradition of Greek religion'.[18] The prayers for oracular response from the first century AD which were mentioned above are very similar to the leaden tablets from the fifth to the second centuries BC which appear in Michel's collection. It looks as if a change came over the magical tradition in the second and third centuries of our era. Before then, the formulae are relatively brief, exact, pure; but from about the second century AD the texts become much more complex while influence from gnosticism, Christianity and the mystery cults is more obvious. We may well believe that a magical practice like the ἀπαθανατισμός in *PGM* IV. 475–834, which has so many connecting links with the Hermetic literature and with *Pistis Sophia*, is not much earlier than the fourth-century document which now contains it.

We may conclude that although the more bizarre and complex features of later Hellenistic magic will be much too late to have had any impact at all on the canonical Christian literature, the main features of magic were well developed by the early and middle first century AD if not before, and we may safely use selections from the magical papyri if cautious attention is given to these problems.[19]

2. *Syncretism in the magical traditions*

Perhaps the most immediately striking feature of the magic of the period we are considering is its syncretism. Elements may be found of the older national religions, and of the newly born international faiths. Religious truth being less of a recommendation than utility, almost any name and formula could be accepted and subjected, even if it was not already saturated with magic, to the ideals and attitudes which lay behind international magic. Examination of some of the aspects of this syncretistic tendency is perhaps the most convenient way to approach the understanding of the atmosphere of magic.

Hellenistic magic was a product of the Greek spirit. Of the many tributaries the Egyptian was the greatest. From Egypt comes that element which is often thought to be the most central characteristic of magic, the desire to compel the gods to do one's will.

> But whereas the magic of every other nation of the ancient East was directed entirely against the powers of darkness, and was invented in order to frustrate their fell designs by invoking a class of benevolent beings to their aid, the Egyptians aimed at being able to command their gods to work for them, and to compel them to appear at their desire.[20]

Teta, King of Egypt *c.* 3266 BC, possessed a book which 'hath effect upon the heart of the gods',[21] and the desire of the magician of the fourth century AD was not very different when he prayed,

> Come to me, such-and-such a god, be revealed to me in this present hour and do not startle my eyes. Come to me, such-and-such a god, be heard by me, for thus wills and commands Achchor Achchor Achachach.[22]

The very common magical device of pretending to be the god, more a mystical and power-producing identification than naive trickery, is Egyptian in origin. 'I am Horus' cries the magician, 'the son of Isis, and I have come to see my father Osiris.'²³ 'I am the headless demon', echoes the later follower, 'I am the truth, . . . I am the lightning and thunder, . . . I am the begetter and the destroyer.'²⁴

The word of power is almost certainly older in Egypt than anywhere else in the ancient East. The conception is a natural one in magic and has evolved independently in many cultures, but it is Egyptian influence which has done most to form this all-pervading feature of Hellenistic magic. The custom of writing these words of power on gems, on stone and on papyrus is extremely ancient. The inscriptions from the tomb of the Pharaoh Unas (c. 3300 BC) tell us that a book with words of magical power had been buried with the monarch.²⁵ The Amulet of the Buckle, a familiar type, usually has upon it an inscription, words from the *Book of the Dead*, ch. 156:

The blood of Isis and the strength of Isis, and the words of power of Isis shall be mighty to act as powers to protect this great and divine being, and to guard him from him that would do unto him anything that he holdeth in abomination.²⁶

The idea of foreign, meaningless and repetitive magic words, the idea of the power of a word which is the name of a god – these are Egyptian both in ultimate origin and in their fullest development. A charm for opening a door, from the fourth century AD, instructs the magician to pronounce certain magic words in Coptic which are then translated and enforced with magical identification and implied threat.

This is the formula: *Auon nei auon nei tkelli*, that is, be opened, be opened, bar, for I am the great Horus Archephrenepsu phirinch, the son of Osiris and Isis; I want to get away from the godless Typhon now! now! quick! quick!²⁷

There are so many examples of Egyptian influence and so many illustrations available of each type of influence that it would be wearisome to list them all. Suffice to say that Egypt provided the belief that the magic words gained additional power if written on a gem; she provided the monstrous beings, half animal and half human, which decorate the papyri, and also the very significant belief that magic, while allowing man to control the gods, is at the same time the gracious gift and revelation of the gods to man; and, lastly, she provided the impressive antiquity which gave figures such as Seth and Thoth and Osiris a unique authority, figures seized upon and assimilated into their own native art by the Greek magicians.[28]

Persia is the second important homeland of Hellenistic magic, important more for the prestige of the magic associated with its religion by reputation than for the particular influence which can be traced back to genuinely Persian sources. But the reputation existed and proved extraordinarily fertile. The prestige of the magi is well known. The members of this priestly class were in Greek and Roman times famed as the exponents of sacerdotal magic and as the supreme representatives of its lore. They were believed to have inherited the yet more venerable secrets of Assyrian and Babylonian magic[29] and hence to be the heirs of the Chaldeans.[30] The greatest of them, and indeed their teacher, was Zoroaster. The proportion of his reputation is indicated by the fact that works of some two million lines, or ten million words, were ascribed to him,[31] dealing with astrology, magic, natural science and religion. Other great names such as Oromazes, Omanos, Ostanes, and Mithras, in an enormous variety of garbled and half understood forms, shared in the mystic prestige.

Some of the more specific Persian influences upon Hellenistic magic will be briefly listed. The impact of demonology was extremely important. The idea of magic as a means of defence against evil spirits, rather than as a pressure upon the high gods, is originally Assyrian–Babylonian–Zoroastrian, not Egyptian. Devils were, of course, a familiar feature of Egyptian religion, but they did not constitute the same daily terror as in the Mesopotamian cults, nor was the activity of the priests so concerned with their exclusion. Egyptian magic was directed towards the gods, against death and the spirits of the dead and against dangers and illnesses of every kind, but rarely against evil spirits as such. Egyptian magic cast a cloak of sacred protection over the lives of gods and man, but it was not primarily apotropaic or exorcistic. The growth of Egyptian demonology during the Ptolemaic period was partly a natural development and partly an influence from the East which arrived with astrology. But by the early centuries of our era demonology was ubiquitous, and what had once distinguished

Egypt and Babylon no longer did so. The greatest contribution of Egyptian demonology to Hellenistic magic was the formidable figure of Seth-Typhon.[32]

The dualism of the Zoroastrian system lent itself readily to the techniques of the magicians who thus found a theological justification for their superstitions and a further extension of their art in the vivid fears of the uneducated Hellenistic masses. With the cult of demonology appears the supreme object of apotropaic magic, exorcism. This aspect of Persian religion was easily assimilated to the belief in Greek chthonic deities.

The doctrine which lay behind the magical use of animals, plants and stones, the belief that all nature was linked together by invisible bonds of sympathy and antipathy, is a further contribution of those who looked to the names of the Persian magi for their inspiration.[33] In the magical literature which gradually developed, the name of Ostanes, the Persian magus who had accompanied Xerxes on his campaigns, is prominent.[34] He was believed to have been the teacher of Democritus (*c.* 400 BC), by whom the chief ideas of Persian magic later reached the West *c.* 260 BC. Bolos of Mendes, working in Egypt, had collected the works ascribed to Ostanes by *c.* 200 BC, and it is not surprising that the doctrine of sympathy was easily combined with Egyptian beliefs about the magical value of various substances. So arose the magical pseudo-sciences of alchemy and pharmacology.[35]

But possibly the most important Persian contribution to magic was astrology. This was originally oriental, not Egyptian, having roots in Babylonian and Assyrian superstition, and having been transmitted to the West both directly, after the conquests of Alexander, and indirectly through Egypt, where it had been naturalized about the sixth century BC. The leading ideas matured slowly, and the first extant horoscope is only as old as 410 BC.[36] The instructions regarding the propitious moments at which various rituals were to be carried out, which stand at the end of most of such rituals, are a sufficient indication of the part played by astrology in the formation of Hellenistic magic.[37]

Heir of the traditions of both Egypt and Babylon, the third great contribution to the formation of Hellenistic magic was that of Israel. The reputation of the Jews for magical practices was almost as considerable as that of the other two nations we have considered.[38]

In the opinion of Justin Martyr Jewish exorcists are successful because of their possession of the name of God, but in their method they use the same sort of magical techniques as the Gentiles:

> But though you exorcise any demon in the name of any of those who were among you – either kings, or righteous men, or prophets, or patriarchs – it will not be subject to you. But if any of you exorcise it in [the name of] the God of Abraham, and the God of Isaac, and the God of Jacob, it will perhaps be subject to you. Now, assuredly your exorcists . . . make use of craft when they exorcise, even as the Gentiles do, and employ fumigations and incantations.[39]

Celsus shares the universal opinion that the Jews were a race expert in the magic art: 'They worship angels, and are addicted to sorcery of which Moses was their teacher.'[40]

With Jewish magic, as with Persian, we are dealing both with the actual behaviour of Jews and (perhaps rather more) with their reputation and with the use of Jewish features by pagans. The Jewish response to the accusation of magic was complex. It consisted partly in returning the accusation upon the accusers (we have noted the strong Jewish tradition that Jesus himself was a magician) and also of attacking the principles of magic itself. But, because of the difficulty of drawing a distinction between harmful and beneficial magic, the result was equivocation. Josephus hails the magic of Solomon as a boon to mankind,[41] and in the Talmud we find both approval and condemnation of magic.[42]

The greatest contribution of Judaism to international magic was the name of the living God. Use of *Ia*, *Iaω* and all sorts of variants, of Sabaoth, Adonai, and Jahweh appear on almost every page of the magical papyri. It is easy to see how this would arise. To the natives of Egypt, the practices of the Jewish colonies, especially the large one in Alexandria, must have seemed full of esoteric power, and a monotheistic religion which refused to pronounce the name of its secret and all-powerful deity was bound to be appropriated, whether understood or not, by those in constant search of still more mighty magical names. We may thus consider the use made of the divine name in pagan magic as the revenge of syncretistic pantheism upon Jewish monotheism, as well as indicating a sound appreciation of an ancient characteristic of Semitic religion.

As well as the great name, Judaism provided other names to

conjure with. That of Moses is almost as highly revered as Thoth
and Zoroaster. Indeed, as early as the second century BC Moses was
identified with Thoth–Hermes in the writings of Artapanus, one
of the originators of Jewish–Hellenistic syncretism. Moses is
regarded as the teacher of mankind, the inventor of philosophy,
writing and religion, especially the originator of Egyptian animal
worship, and the interpreter of hieroglyphics.⁴³ The account of his
successful contest in magic with the Egyptian priests dominates
the tradition. Moses becomes the master magician, the possessor
of the powerful name of the Hebrew God.⁴⁴ Moses' reception of
the law becomes the model for the magician in search of a divine
oracle. Did not Moses know God face to face? So in the Demotic
Magical Papyrus the magician desiring a dream-oracle lies down
on a rush mat beside a lamp and, after a formula of invocation,
prays,

> Reveal thyself to me here today in the fashion of thy revelation to
> Moses which thou didst make upon the mountain, before whom thou
> thyself didst create darkness and light.⁴⁵

The relationship between Moses and his God becomes the model
for all kinds of relationships between the magician and the object
of his desire. In a love spell in the same papyrus we read,

> The longing such as a she-cat feels for a male cat, a longing such as
> a she-wolf feels for a he-wolf, a longing such as a bitch feels for a dog,
> the longing which the god, the son of Sopd, felt for Moses going to
> the hill of Ninaretos to offer water unto his god, his lord, his Yaho,
> Sabaho, his Glemura-muse, Plerube . . . Abrasax . . . Let N.
> daughter of N. feel it for N. son of N. . . . the fury of Yaho, Sabaho . . .
> Pantokrátor: . . . I cast fury upon you.⁴⁶

As in the case of Hermes-Thoth and Ostanes-Zoroaster, a
magical literature developed around the name of Moses. Deut.
33.29 refers to 'the shield of thy help, and the sword of thy excel-
lency'. The sword was believed to be the piercing name of Yahweh
possessed by Moses and used by him to destroy evil magic and
demons. The sword is the symbol of authority over the angelic
hosts of the Lord and thus the guarantee of victory. The medieval
Aramaic and Hebrew text 'The Sword of Moses' is clearly inspired
by these words.⁴⁷ PLond. 121 (*PGM* VII. 620), contains a charm
which will make the user invisible to everyone and yet without
any disadvantage to his love life. It is said to be from the 'Diadem

of Moses'. This would appear to be another magical book of some repute from which the compiler of the papyrus has taken material.

The inspiration for the title 'Diadem' is probably from Lev. 8, where Moses dresses Aaron with his high priestly attire, including breastplate and (v. 9) 'the holy crown'. An object associated with the Jewish High Priest, conferred by Moses at the direct command of Yahweh, would possess in the highest degree the qualities looked for in a magical archetype. A Leiden papyrus (*PGM* XIII. 21, 31 etc.), refers to a work called the 'Key of Moses', and another, Moses' 'Archangel', is also quoted in line 970. The association between the giving of the law and angels was well known, and so was that between Moses himself and archangels, the account of Moses and Michael in Jude 9 being the most influential.[48] Traditions of this sort have undoubtedly provided the inspiration for the 'Key' and the 'Archangel' of Moses.

The most famous example of a magical book attributed to Moses in the papyri is provided by this same Leiden papyrus (*PGM* XIII) in which appears the 'Eighth Book of Moses'. This is an interesting case of the attribution to Moses for purposes of prestige of material not particularly Jewish in content.[49] The papyrus concludes with a prayer to the moon attributed to Moses (lines 1059ff.) and the papyrus breaks off with the title only of yet another Mosaic item, 'The Secret Tenth Book of Moses', of which we have no further knowledge.

We saw earlier how the Egyptian wizards identified themselves with one of the gods in order to absorb the power and the essence of the god and to terrify the enemy. In PLond. 47 (*PGM* VI. 110) in a prayer addressed to the composite deity, the Akephalos Creator, Osiris-Yahweh, the magician says, 'I am Moses your prophet to whom you delivered your mysteries, which are celebrated by Israel.' Two amulet gems inscribed with the name of Moses offer additional evidence of the acceptance of the name into Egyptian and solar pantheism.[50]

Solomon is perhaps an even more popular figure in magic. His prayer for wisdom was interpreted as bestowing upon him magical σοφία, and the tradition of his magical skill was well established before the coming of Christ. In the Wisdom of Solomon (first century BC) 7.17–21 the sage is reported as saying:

For it is he who gave me unerring knowledge of what exists, to know the structure of the world and the activity of the elements; the beginning and end and middle of times, the alternations of the solstices and the changes of the seasons, the cycles of years and the constellations of the stars; the natures of animals and the tempers of wild beasts, the powers of spirits and the reasonings of men, the varieties of plants and the virtues of roots; I learned both what is secret and what is manifest.

Solomon is here acquainted with astrology and fate; he has insight into divination and supernatural knowledge; he is the controller of spiritual powers and the dispenser of herbal remedies. Behind the passage is the conception of sympathy. The one who through his insight and divinely granted revelation perceives the nature of the mystic bonds which tie everything from the lofty stars down to the earth-bound roots in one throbbing unity, he is at once saint, seer, philosopher, and magus.[51]

It is in Josephus that the Solomonic demonological tradition is first clearly witnessed. 'God granted him knowledge of the art used against demons for the benefit and healing of men.'[52] Solomon not only received this beneficial knowledge; he passed it on, and here we have perhaps the earliest reference to Solomon as the author of magical remedies: 'he left behind forms of exorcisms with which those possessed by demons drive them out never to return.' Josephus goes on to say that this is still a living tradition of great therapeutic power.

Of the large store of magical literature in the name of Solomon, the most important work to have survived is the Testament of Solomon. This is extant in a dozen or so fifteenth- and sixteenth-century manuscripts and since 1922 has been available for convenient study in the excellent critical text provided by Chester Charlton McCown. The date of the document is uncertain; estimates vary from the Middle Ages to the very early Christian centuries. McCown's conclusion, that the early third century AD provides the conditions which suit the Testament best, is justified. It is difficult to overestimate the importance of this conclusion for the study of ancient magic. If it is sound, then we have here, in a fairly corrupt but still recognizable form, an example from the Hellenistic period of the kind of magic most deeply impressed with the Jewish spirit, and the kind which would be most familiar to the early Christians.[53]

The ring by which Solomon was able to control the evil spirits, described in his Testament, is well known in the papyri. In the 'Tested Recipe of Pibeches' in the Great Paris Papyrus we read:

'I adjure you, by the seal which Solomon placed upon the tongue of Jeremiah and he spoke' (*PGM* IV. 3039f.). This particular recipe is outstanding for its strongly Jewish content. The great God and his seal are the content of the power of an amulet prescribed in PLond. 121 (*PGM* VII). 582ff.

As with Moses, some items are ascribed to Solomon which have little sign of Jewish influence. So in *PGM* IV. 850, we read of 'Solomon's Trance-Inducer, working both with children and adults' but, unless the magical words beginning Ἀμοῦν with which the spell closes represent Amen, there is no trace of Jewish influence.

Further important evidence of Solomon's influence is provided by the scores of amulets on which Solomon is portrayed as a mighty king, mounted on horseback and spearing a female figure, perhaps the Lilith of Jewish superstition.[54]

The question which is of particular significance to the study of the New Testament Christology is whether the magical aura of Moses and Solomon has passed over to Jesus. Jesus was the greater Moses and the greater Solomon. The image of Solomon as the wise and powerful healer of the possessed could not be allowed to overshadow the ministry of Jesus.

The Jewish contribution to syncretistic magic also included the names of the patriarchs and of angels. PBerol. 13895 (*PGM* XXIIb) is entitled 'Prayer of Jacob'. The general exorcism in *PGM* XXXV. 14 is in the names of Abram, Isaac and Jacob. Sometimes these names appear in lists of otherwise unintelligible words where they are evidently regarded as powerful traditional formulae with no knowledge of their original and literal significance. In PBerol. 5025 (*PGM* I. 216) the magician, having said that he is about to call upon the secret name of the Lord, recites amongst other things, Ἀβραμι Ἀβρααμ θαλχιλθοε . . . Ἰσακ χωηῖουρθασιω Ἰωσια . . . Strings of angelic or pseudo-angelic names, constructed on the Hebrew model ending with -el, are extremely common.

Finally we may observe that the Hebrew language was itself appropriated to magical use. Its use in the sacred literature of the Jews, its peculiar shape and its associations with the great names of Jewish power, all contributed to the prestige of the language. The one who performs the 'Recipe of Pibeches' (*PGM* IV. 3009) is to keep himself pure and not to eat, 'for the prayer is Hebraic, and is preserved by pure men'.[55]

In our survey of national influence we come finally to the Greeks. Greek heroes and sacred authors are mentioned quite often in the papyri. A magical formula is described as a logos of Orpheus in *PGM* VII. 451, and Apollonius of Tyana is the authority for a recipe in PLond. 125 (*PGM* XIa. 1).

Of the gods, Hermes was by far the most significant. This was largely because of his identification with Thoth, but the Greek Hermes is also fairly common. Olympian Hermes is the subject of an invocation in *PGM* V. 174, and in *PGM* IV. 2290, the moon is invoked as 'venerable Hermes'. He is often associated with magical herbs. PLond. 46 (*PGM* V). 212 describes the preparation of a Hermes ring. He is not only a world-ruling deity and a healing god but above all a dream-giving and oracle-granting god.[56]

The other Greek deities with magical and/or chthonic associations also figure prominently in the papyri.[57] Selene, often associated with Hecate, the most ancient Greek goddess of magic, appears less often than one would expect, but there are a number of allusions to her. Aphrodite and Eros are naturally found as granting the delights of love. In *PGM* IV. 2891, there is a famous example of a threat against a god. Aphrodite is warned that if she does not bring the desired woman to the door of the magician's house she will never see Adonis again. Apollo, as god of the oracle, is a familiar figure always associated with his sacred plant the laurel. In *PGM* I. 298f., he is summoned to forsake the Parnassian mount and the Delphic Python. Zeus seldom appears alone; usually he is added to lists of important gods, but now and then he appears in his own right, as in *PGM* IV. 825, where he stands on a mountain with a golden calf and a silver sword. Kronos is found fairly often.[58] Pan, Dionysus, Bacchus, Ares, Athena, Asclepius, Hestia, Hera and others also appear.

The old Greek ghosts are found now and then. Megaira and Allekto are mentioned with Persephone in *PGM* IV. 2798. Typhon is usually identified with the Egyptian Seth. Agathos Daimon, of Greek origin but especially revered in Alexandria, is found frequently.

Greek religion is the foundation of Hellenistic magic. All the borrowed names and conceptions are built upon the Greek basis. The gods of Egypt, Persia and Israel are modified by the Greek view, adapted for the magical purpose and identified with native Greek deities. The Greek deities are the presupposed realities upon which the other national elements are added as exotic, fearful, prestigious, power-creating growths.

This accumulation of religious fragments from all sources (and only a few of the more significant have been mentioned) leads in magic to the most extraordinary mixture. PLond. 46 (*PGM* V) begins by calling upon Zeus, Helios, Mithras and Sarapis. The prayer to Apollo in PPar. 2391 (*PGM* III. 211ff.) calls upon the 'fiery angel of Zeus, divine Iao, and you, Raphael, who maintains the heavenly frame', followed by Michael, Σαβαώθ and Ἀδωναί hailed as Lord of the world, and then the magician adjures by the 'seal of God, before which all the immortal gods of Olympia tremble' and then by the great god Apollo. Just a few lines before, in the same papyrus, is a prayer to the sun in which the magician, having summoned the sun, announces that he is Adam, the original father, and proceeds to exorcize the sun in the name of the God Iao, the God Adonai, the God Michael, the God Souriel, the God Gabriel, the God Raphael, the God Abraxas and so on (lines 146ff). In *PGM* XIII. 335, Helios is described as sitting between the two cherubim, as being the archangel of God, and in the 'Prayer of Jacob', *PGM* XXIIb. 11, Iao sits upon Helios. Naturally, this syncretism is not systematic, and the papyri are full of inconsistencies. These few remarks must serve to convey the general atmosphere of this kind of magic.

3. *The system of magical belief*

But is there any kind of system behind it all? Are there any principles by which this bubbling brew with its weird assortment of ingredients is cooked and served?

The basis of the system is a belief in non-human, superhuman, usually invisible powers, including the gods themselves, the angelic beings, demons of various orders and the souls of heroes and men. But the distinctive development is a belief that these superhuman, supernatural entities are linked by invisible bonds of sympathy to visible and material things which are thus 'symbols' of the power to which they adhere – plants, minerals, animals, times and seasons, human beings. A further development leads to the theory that by knowledge of the powers, their sympathies and antipathies and their symbols, it is possible to influence the supernatural world. The art of magic is to collect such knowledge and apply it correctly so as to swing the enormous forces of the universe in the desired direction.

(i) *Angels*

Angels occupy a special place in the intermediate world because of their special essence which is of the most perfect nature next to that of the gods themselves.[59] God appears in Semitic thought as the oriental monarch surrounded by a host of angels through whom man approaches him and whom he must first influence if God is to be influenced. In Jewish thought[60] the angels are responsible for everything, for the years, the weather, the changes in animal, plant and human life; the whole universe is filled with them.

The association of angels with planets and stars[61] created a bridge between Semitic angelology and pagan demonology. Not only were both angels and demons heavenly messengers, but both were stellar powers. Planetary angel worship is a familiar problem in Judaism as well as early Christianity. The association of angels with seven planets and seven days of the week, with minerals and with plants, naturally follows. There is thus a direct link between angelology, astrology and magic, and this is why the early Christians looked upon the Jewish feasts fixed by reference to heavenly bodies as demonic.[62]

So the mere names of both angels and planets had in themselves magical power. Gnosticism provides the richest store of examples,[63] but early association between Christians and the magical names is shown in the belief, hotly denied by Arnobius, that Jesus 'from the shrines of the Egyptians stole the names of angels of might',[64] thus indicating the popular belief which is no doubt correct that angelic magic arose out of Babylonian astrology which migrated into Egypt, fused with the Egyptian 'word of power' idea and finally attached itself to the Jewish angels as the figures nearest the throne of the mysterious Yahweh.

(ii) *Demons*

Turning to demons we find a wide range of conceptions,[65] but their place may be defined by reference to three groups of spiritual powers. God and the angels were in heaven; demons and heroes were in the air; men were on earth. The moon was an important boundary. God occupied the aether as far as the moon, demons below the moon, and heroes and souls of dead men were nearer the earth, some souls being under the earth.

. . . they say that the heaven, and the ether as far down as the moon, are assigned to gods; and the parts about the moon and the atmosphere to daemons; and the region of the earth and parts beneath the earth to souls. And . . . we ought to worship first of all the gods of heaven and of the ether, secondly the good daemons, thirdly the souls of the heroes, and fourthly to propitiate the bad and wicked daemons.[66]

There were many views regarding their origin but the essential point is that they were under the dominion of the higher essences, especially the gods. At the great voice of the mighty God, demons trembled and fled. The gods had power not only to drive the demons away but to summon them as well. The magician prayed that the god would send a demon under his command at the midnight hour by force.[67] Inscriptions to this effect engraved on gems are extremely common: for example, 'Iao, Abrasas, Adonai, holy name, favourable powers, guard O. Paulina from every evil demon.'[68] Diseases are urged to flee, for such and such a god is chasing them, or often there is the simple acclamation 'So and So (i.e. a god) conquers!'; 'Nemesis, help!'; 'Plague and fever, flee from the wearer of this amulet.'[69]

This conception of the innate superiority of the gods was a fundamental one in magic and especially in exorcism. Angels also controlled the demons, as is seen frequently in the Testament of Solomon. In Test.Sol. 5.5 Asmodeus looks forward to the day when men shall again revere the demons as gods, 'since men do not know the names of the angels set over us'. Asmodeus is then adjured to disclose the name of the angel who frustrates him.

The demons themselves were of almost infinite variety. Some were weak, others strong, some superior, others inferior, some bad, some good. Many lists of demonic varieties exist in magic spells, the object being to include them all in the scope of the power. So in *PGM* IV. 2700ff., we read: 'Protect me from every demon, of the air and the earth and under the earth, and every angel and phantom and shade and ghostly visitation, me, so and so.'

In general the lower the demon the thicker his substance and the more dangerous and malevolent his nature. It was because of the coarseness of their essence that the demons were unable to remain in the higher realms with the finer ethereal spirits. Solomon asked Ornias how the demons knew the future of men. He replied:

We demons ascend into heaven, and fly about among the stars, and we hear the sentences which go forth upon the souls of men. . . . And having no ground on which to alight and rest, we lose strength and fall . . . and men, seeing us, imagine that the stars are falling from heaven. . . . But we fall because of our weakness, and because we have nowhere anything to lay hold of.[70]

The subterranean and light-hating demons were the most dangerous to men because, unable to bear the light, they tried to possess men or animals, to hide in their bodies, and thus caused illness and disease. Indeed this idea is probably the root of the conception of demons as causing disease. When the material demons were in cold and dry places their gaseous but still material bodies thickened and condensed and they wanted to retreat into places of warmth such as inside animals, in hot steaming baths, into the protection of pits and holes in the ground or graves.

Demons could become visible, but Iamblichus[71] says it is easier for them to manifest their activities than their substance. This is why magicians were usually content to notice some sign that the demon had departed and did not normally expect to see the actual demon leaving.[72] They were not disembodied, however, but possessed a body, the exact nature of which was a subject of speculation amongst the ancients.[73] A striking case from the papyri is *PGM* XII. 141, where the magician says that if the demon does not obey him he will give his flesh to the mangy dogs to eat. But the voice of a demon could be heard – Pythagoras, Democritus, Socrates, Plato, Plotinus all agree on this.[74] Demons were susceptible to smells and noises. They needed nourishment, the good requiring the sweet odour of incense offerings and the evil the blood and fat of a sacrifice.[75] The drama of the Testament of Solomon begins because Ornias sucks blood each day from a child's thumb. Philostratus recounts an amusing and instructive story about the ghost of an Ethiopian satyr who was a passionate lover and pestered the women in the village. Apollonius with his customary wisdom trapped him into drinking a trough of wine. 'He . . . called the satyr by means of some secret rebuke or threat; and though as yet the latter was not visible, the wine sensibly diminished as if it was being drunk up.' So the satyr was caught and his frolics were ended.[76] A spirit if driven from its home in an animal's body would be angry and would seek to vent its rage on the one who had expelled it. Aelian describes how a husbandman by accident cut a snake in half. It was a sacred asp, the phantom of which drove the poor man insane until Serapis had mercy and in reply to prayer removed and abolished the wandering spirit.[77]

It is against this background that the magician had to operate. Only force would work on demons and, because demons disliked force, magic was a dangerous business. The art of black magic consisted in arousing the anger of a demon and then diverting it away from oneself to the enemy. This was a hazardous activity fraught with possibilities of disaster. The demon would try to kill the magician and protective measures had to be adopted. The Great Paris Papyrus (*PGM* IV. 2505ff.) describes the serious dangers of working without protection. Magical beliefs could exist in the absence of a demonology, but *it is extremely doubtful whether demonology has ever existed in a developed form in any race or religion without being associated with magical methods of control and protection.*[78]

(iii) *Sympathy and antipathy*

High on the list of the magician's weapons was his understanding of the sympathy and antipathy of the universe. In a famous passage on the efficacy of magical theurgy, Iamblichus says that it does not depend upon the will, intention, thought or intellect of the operator, but is on the contrary the result of an ineffable activity surpassing the mind of man, working through mute symbols known fully only by the gods. Thus the unity which is the aim of the theurgist is attained.[79]

Hence the divinity of the magician who can achieve that which the philosopher can only meditate upon. The mystic knowledge of stones and plants, to use, to open and to close the powers, is conferred by the gods and is realized in ecstasy coming from beyond the magician himself.[80] The divine breath, the spirit of power, can only come upon man through the symbols.[81] Having described the sympathetic forces flowing to the earth from the stars, Plotinus remarks that the aim of all magical art is to establish contact with those things affected by this dynamic sympathy.[82] So ancient and revered was this belief that in the Hermetic literature Isis is described as telling Horus how the gods had revealed the sacred secret of Hermes-Thoth. He, being a spirit in the line of sympathy with the heavenly mysteries, learned the sacred symbols

of the elements of the cosmos and passed the secrets on to others.[83]
Eusebius provides a vivid description of the system.

> For there are many kinds of roots, and herbs, and plants, and fruits,
> and stones, and other powers, both solid and liquid of every kind of
> matter in the natural world; some of them fit to drive off and expel
> certain diseases; others of a nature to attract and superinduce them;
> some again with power to secrete and disperse, or to harden and to
> bind . . . some things occur by physical necessities, and wax and wane
> together with the moon, and . . . there are countless antipathies of
> animals and roots and plants . . .[84]

The whole process was a ladder of knowledge beginning with
the humblest stone and leading up to knowledge of the gods themselves. The association between a material object and a god might
be established because of some odd or striking quality which
caught the attention. Often the vagaries of supposed etymological
connection gave rise to belief in sympathy; so Hermes was of
sweet speech (λαροῦ λόγου) and the sea-gull (λάρος) is thus his
sacred symbol.[85] Each hour is sacred to a god and each animal is
created to be sacred to a particular hour, so the sun moved
through the sacred animals (the Zodiac) shedding its radiant power
through them. There are twenty-four hours in the day and twenty-
four letters in the Greek alphabet. Every letter equals an hour and
is therefore an image of divinity. The alpha-omega, like the sum
of the hours, represents the power of God in his totality. This is the
idea behind number mysticism.[86]

4. *The practice of magic*

How did the magician actually put all his knowledge to work?
The normal magical ceremony consisted of two parts, first the
κλῆσις or ἐπίκλησις in which the power, god or demon was summoned; secondly the πρᾶξις, the ritual itself. Often in the papyri
the details of the ritual are given first, as one might list the apparatus
for an experiment.

The invocation usually conformed to a cultic tradition which
required the following sections, found in Greek and oriental
hymns as well. (i) The invocation proper, beginning 'I call upon
you, I summon you, come to me, help me' and so on. (ii) The name
of the god would be uttered. Often the name is omitted from the
papyrus either to guard its secret power or to allow the magician

to insert the name of his choice. (iii) Epithets describing the god would follow. 'Hecate, Hecate, three-formed, the seal of everything . . .'[87] (iv) Next would come descriptions of the god, to increase the benevolence of the one invoked.

Hail to thee, who art appointed to rule over the East, and the world, to whom all gods are the bodyguard, in thy good hour, in thy good day, the Agathodemon of the world, the crown of the inhabited lands, thou who risest from the abyss, thou who every day art born anew as a child and settest like an old man . . .[88]

(v) Remembrances would follow in which the god was reminded of what he had done in the past, deeds similar to what he was being asked to do. This was often mixed with the predications of stage three, since both stages often consisted of a recital of the mythological exploits of the god. So, in a love-spell from the same papyrus, myrrh, a sacred substance often used for erotic purposes, is sprinkled on the fire while the magician personifies it, calling upon the myrrh spirit and reminding it of its glorious past.

Myrrh, Myrrh, thou who art a servant of the gods, thou who didst stir up the mountains, who didst inflame the marsh of Achalda, who didst burn the goddess Typhon, the fellow-combatant of Horus, the protector of Anubis, the guide of Isis.[89]

Reminders are particularly striking in Jewish and Christian charms where, because of the greater scope given by the biblical records, the possible parallels to the type of divine intervention now sought for are greater.[90] (vi) Finally, the request itself is uttered. The prayer to the sun, referred to above, continues after the reference to its setting like an old man:

I pray to thee, Lord, that I may not fail, nor be the object of plots, nor take any noxious potion, nor fall into embarrassments or troubles of subsistence, but receive and obtain from thee life, health, fame, riches, power, strength, good luck, loveliness, favour with all men and all women, victory over all men and all women.[91]

The fact that these prayers are modelled on the cultic liturgies of Greece, and especially of Egypt, illustrates not only the antiquity of the style but the fact that the magician was ready to use in the first instance the normal prayers and offerings of religion, steadily increasing the pressure on the divinity until at last, with the operation of the symbolic substances in the ritual, the god was forced to succumb to the will of the operator.[92]

Sometimes the structure of the more elaborate pieces of magic is very complex, and might include details of an amulet to be made and worn during the ceremony and a whole series of prayers and sacrifices, each to be prepared and offered at the right moment. A piece of magic as complex as this could take several days. *PGM* IV. 2675 mentions the first and second days of a ceremony and line 2685 the third day.

POslo. 1 (*PGM* XXXVI) describes various rituals. One could be a burnt offering such as the lumps of sulphur thrown on a fire of vine-wood (prescribed in line 295). Various ingredients might be mixed to the accompaniment of incantations. Lines 283–4 instruct the magician to mix a crow's egg and the juice of the crowfoot plant and the gall of a fish pounded together in a dish with honey. It might be necessary to write upon some special material in special ink. Another recipe in the same papyrus requires a donkey's skin, with ink made from a certain fish and from juice of a herb sacred to Serapis (lines 361–3), and another a libation of myrrh and vinegar in a wine-cup thrown on the front door at the third hour of the night (lines 134–7). It was a question of what sympathies and antipathies were needed for the particular task in hand. Sympathetic substances are of course used in the sacrifice to attract the desired spirit, antipathetical substances are used in the ἀπόλυσις when the god or spirit is forced to depart.

These then are the leading features of Hellenistic magic. At first sight there might seem to be little prospect of much rapport with the New Testament. This seems particularly true when lists of the items used in magic are drawn up as indicated in the previous paragraph. But the papyri were the professional property of the magicians, not popular works which anyone might read. In its broad outline and ethos this kind of magic brings us closer to the ordinary beliefs of the uneducated first-century man than does study of the mystery religions or the philosophical systems. Since Christianity was also a religion of slaves and working people, it is at least worth asking if any impact was made by the magical world-view on Christian ideas, especially on Christology. This is what we propose now to consider.

IV

MIRACLE AND MAGIC

1. *The Jewish tradition of magical miracle*

It is not easy to make a clear distinction between magic and miracle. The fundamental miracle of biblical thought is the creation of the world,[1] and although in Genesis this has already become a vehicle of theological meditation it is also connected with magic. In the Egyptian and Babylonian creation legends which lie behind the Hebrew myths, the magical association was expressed most clearly in the idea of creation by means of a word of power.[2] In Canaanite religion the miraculous rebirth of nature was connected with the performance of magical rituals, as in the ancient Near East generally.[3] The Hebrew attitude to nature and history is such that everything is pregnant with magical-miracle.[4] In prophetic miracle, including the miracles of blessing and cursing, of prediction and of symbolic creation of the future, as well as the nature and healing miracles performed by the prophets, the magical associations are always prominent.[5] One only has to remember Moses' brazen serpent,[6] the raising of the dead carried out by Elijah and Elisha and the events associated with the capture of the ark in Judges to see that they are thoroughly magical in their approach and method. The Exodus events are specifically magical, portrayed as a battle by one thaumaturge against less potent ones. Miracles in the Old Testament are also associated with eschatological theology, especially in the later books. Both the magical influence and the eschatological influence are seen in operation in the miracles of Jesus.[7]

In Judaism we find a similar situation. Eschatological miracles were still common, but by no means all miracles in Judaism of the period immediately preceding and accompanying the birth of

Christianity were eschatological. Paul Fiebig provides a selection of eighteen 'Rabbinic Miracle-Stories' and they are various standard types, such as stilling a storm, exorcisms, blindings and so on, and are in no way connected with eschatology. Grant points out that most of Fiebig's examples come from the period after the destruction of the temple and represent Judaism purged of apocalyptic hope; he claims that they are therefore not typical of Jewish miracle stories. Grant continues: 'We have already found in Josephus a reliable witness for the linking of miracles with apocalyptic hopes.'[8] The miracles Grant refers to are those associated by Josephus with events leading up to the outbreak of the Jewish-Roman war and he points out correctly that this type of miracle represents an eschatological understanding of the Old Testament. But miracles are used by Josephus for many different purposes and not only as eschatological portents. They appear as a proof of divine authenticity[9] and as illustrating God's providence and power. Other miracles are clearly displays of magic, such as the battle between Moses and the Egyptian wizards (*Ant.* II.284ff.). It is true that there Moses says,

I assert that the deeds wrought by me so far surpass their magic and their art as things divine are remote from what is human. And I will show that it is from no witchcraft or deception of true judgement, but from God's providence and power that my miracles proceed.

But what he then does is exactly the same as what the Egyptian wizards have done only better. When Josephus has Moses deny that his methods are magical, all he means is that Moses is really and truly doing the miracles, whereas the Egyptians only make sticks *seem* to look like snakes.

Josephus' distinction is based on apologetics, not on objective criteria. For, to see the situation fairly, the Egyptians work a miracle which turns sticks into snakes by the power (let us say) of Thoth, while Moses does it through the power of Yahweh, whose power is greater. It is clearly not eschatological, but a contest of magic. The pictures of Moses striking the Red Sea so that it recoils and springs away (*Ant.* II.338), of the Philistines using sympathy to get rid of the ark (VI.8–12), the wonders of Solomon's art (VIII.42–49) and many others are certainly tainted with magic, and Josephus' rather non-committal asides, his occasional rationalizations and his omission of some of the more obviously magical feats seem to suggest a sentitivity to the reaction of a world where such things were all too familiar and from quarters sufficiently notorious. When Grant therefore refers to miracles associated with an obvious eschatological event such as the destruction of Jerusalem, and associates this with miracles in apocalyptic writings, concluding that 'the kind of belief which passes into early Christianity is given its impetus by eschatology',[10] it seems reasonably clear that he is too narrowly restricting the Jewish conception of miracle and therefore the possible kinds of influence on the synoptic miracles. It may even be possible that we are too ready to see an eschatological miracle where its eschatological aspect is more apparent to the modern Christian than to the ancient Jew. Miracles in the apocalyptic literature associated with the Messiah are eschatological by virtue of their context. But not all miracles associated with Messiah are eschatological merely because the Messiah concept itself happens to be an eschatological category. Rabbinic Judaism did not look upon Messiah as a demi god, and 'if the Messiah wrought miracles, that was no more than Moses had done, and Elijah, and many others'.[11]

Of miracles in Judaism in general, the two most prominent categories in which there is any kind of human stimulus for the miracle are wrought either in response to prayer or in response to the divine name being used.[12] Miracles of the latter type are certainly magical; the ones in response to prayer may be magical in certain cases.

Miracles of healing have a notable tendency to be associated with magic. The book of healing herbs described in Jubilees 10.12f. as having been committed to Noah and passed on to his sons is magical. The angels say,

We explained to Noah all the medicines of their diseases . . . how he might heal them with herbs of the earth. And Noah wrote down all things in a book as we instructed him concerning every kind of medicine. Thus the evil spirits were precluded from hurting the sons of Noah.

In I Enoch 8.1–10.16, plague as well as law-breaking is the result of the introduction of magic by the fallen angels and the plague is healed when the angels are bound by the mighty power of Uriel, Raphael, Gabriel and Michael. Here is a situation quite similar to that found later in the Testament of Solomon, where the angels of magic and sickness are frustrated by the angels of the

divine presence. In Tobit 11.8–13 the old man's blindness is healed
by the gall of a fish on the instruction of Raphael. In these examples
we see clear evidence of magical, non-eschatological miracles from
the period well before Christ. In view of the fact that it is in the
healing stories of the gospels that magical traces are said to appear,
it would be worthwhile, in order to understand of the miracles of
Jesus, to consider the possibility that *the magical tradition of miracle
as well as the eschatological tradition of miracle has been influential in
creating the form of the synoptic tradition.*

2. *The Greek tradition of magical miracle*

In Greek literature we find that the tradition of the magical miracle
is if anything stronger than in Judaism. Erland Ehnmark points
out that in the majority of the Homeric miracles we are not told
how the wonder is brought about except that it is through the
will of the god. But there is also a large number of miracles where
the method used is described and these miracles are magical.[13] The
use of the wand, particularly in controlling and transforming
matter, is in this class, as is also the use of articles of their attire by
the gods.[14] Even when no account is given of the method, the
gods still have the mystical power that produces magical effects
such as the power to make themselves and others invisible, particularly by enveloping themselves in a cloud, or the power to do something merely by raising a hand.[15] Zeus in particular has the magical
power to produce miracles at a distance.

Magical miracle being an unsatisfactory way of conceptualizing
the divine activity, we find as early as Homer but more clearly in
Herodotus the attempt to rationalize the miraculous, thus alienat-
ing it from its roots in magic. Herodotus (II.55–57) describes how
talking doves had announced the establishment of the oracles of
Zeus in Dodona and Libya, but then explains this as a misunderstanding arising from the fact that the shrines were actually founded
by foreign women whose language sounded like the chattering of
doves.[16] But the ability of the gods to protect their sanctuaries, as
in the case of Apollo's protection of his shrine at Delphi (Herod.
VIII. 36–39), seems to indicate belief in a relationship between the
gods and the physical conditions of the areas in which their shrines
were set which is rather similar to a magical view of the sympathy
between deity and its earthly symbols.[17]

It was in the Hellenistic period that the ancient connection between magic and miracle came to flower. It was no accident that the period which saw the rapid growth and development of Hellenistic magic also saw a growth in love of the miraculous. In his history of Greek religion Martin Nilsson deals with faith in miracle and faith in magic in the same section,[18] pointing out that faith in oracles and faith in miracles were indistinguishable, that omens are to be classed as wonders and that omens are obtained by magical arts. The many paradoxographical works of the period testify equally loudly to the same connection, and to the love of the marvellous which was such a feature of the period 200 BC–AD 200.[19]

In the *Philopseudes* of Lucian, members of various philosophical schools are mocked for their desire to tell tales of wonder. In the tales of healing miracles and in the stories which follow, Lucian assumes that faith in magical methods goes along with faith in miracles. Reitzenstein and Weinreich[20] both point out that, for Lucian, magic and miracle had become identical. To cure sickness by means of holy names is regarded by Deinomachus as an act of religious reverence, but Lucian (in the person of Tychiades) associating this with magical techniques, insists (ch. 9) on being shown some rational connection, however slight, between the god and the cure:

If , , , you do not first convince me by logical proof that it takes place in this way naturally, because the fever or the inflammation is afraid of a holy name or a foreign phrase and so takes flight from the swelling, your stories still remain old wives' fables.

Lucian is willing to agree that drugs and doctoring can heal the sick and that the gods as the benefactors of mankind have given the knowledge of such arts to men, but he will not accept healing by contact with lions' skins and weasels or incantations or holy names.

The examples Lucian offers are most instructive. Midas, a vine-dresser, having been bitten by a snake, was healed by a Babylonian who drove the poison out by means of a spell and bound upon the injured foot 'a fragment which he broke from the tombstone of a dead maiden'. 'Midas himself picked up the litter on which he had been carried and went off to the farm.' Here we see the formal technique of the miracle story being parodied. The feature of the story where the healed man picks up his bed and walks away in proof of his cure is common in such stories. The Babylonian then demonstrates his power over snakes, asps, vipers and toads, summoning them all by repeating seven sacred names out of an old book and destroying them by breathing upon them. The same wonder-working divine flies through the air, walks on water and goes slowly on foot through a fire. The wonder-worker also summons supernatural beings to his side and brings mouldy corpses to life (chs. 11–13).

Exorcism figures prominently in many accounts of magical miracles. Ion asks Lucian what he had to say 'to those who free possessed men from their terrors by exorcising the spirits so manifestly' and goes on (ch. 16):

Everyone knows about the Syrian from Palestine, the adept in it, how many he takes in hand who fall down in the light of the moon and roll their eyes and fill their mouths with foam; neveitheless, he restores them to health and sends them away normal in mind. . . . When he stands beside them as they lie there and asks: 'Whence came you into his body?' the patient himself is silent, but the spirit answers . . . , telling how and whence he entered into the man; whereupon, by adjuring the spirit and if he does not obey, threatening him, he drives him out.

Another speaker, Eucrates, is no longer afraid of evil spirits, for an Arab gave him a ring made of iron from crosses and taught him the spell of many names.[21]

Reitzenstein shows how the story in *Philopseudes* 25, about a man sick with fever who dreamed of his stay of execution and awoke to find himself well again, but that his neighbour had died in the night, comes from a source older than Lucian. It survived in a variety of traditions until it was adopted by the Christians and transferred by St Augustine to his own times.[22] Like the magic with which they were associated, such healing stories were truly international and passed with ease from one nation and age and faith to another.

It seems to make little difference to Lucian's attitude whether particular magical means are described or not. In *Philopseudes* 26 Antigonus testifies simply to knowing of a man who came back to life after being more than twenty days dead. There is no mention of magic words, herbs, spells, incantations or touchings. It is still magic.

So close is the connection between exorcism, magic and demonology that even to believe in the existence of demons amounts to a superstitious inclination towards the magic inevitably associated with such a belief. So Lucian, in the person of Tychiades, refuses to believe in spirits and phantoms and the appearance of dead men's souls. His denial is refuted by the Pythagorean philosopher Arignotus who, having a great number of Egyptian works about magic and exorcism, exorcized a demon from a house by adjuring him in the Egyptian language.[23] These beliefs and prophecies, oracles and 'verses uttered by a maiden who foretells the future' are all to be regarded as superstitious. Against all such poisons, truth and a sound reason provide a sure antidote.[24]

The association of magic and miracle could be illustrated from many other sources. Clement of Alexandria[25] seeks to show that the Gentiles have no reason for denying the biblical miracles, since miracles of the same sort are accepted in their own circles. He cites the breaking of a drought brought about by the advice of the Delphic oracle. Aeacus ascended the hill, stretched out ritually pure hands to heaven and invoked Zeus, and as he prayed there was a heavy thunderstorm brought about by 'the husbandry of the prayers of Aeacus'. On another occasion Aristaeus had summoned the winds by offering sacrifice to Zeus. Empedocles, on the other hand, made the wind cease and was called 'Checker of Winds'. Clement continues, 'And they say that he was followed by some that used divination, and some that had been long vexed by sore diseases.' He then remarks, 'If certain powers move the winds and dispense showers, let them hear the psalmist', who praises God as the ultimate producer and actor in everything. He goes on to speak even more clearly of those amongst the pagans who believe that 'plagues, and hailstorms, and tempests . . . take place . . . through anger of demons and bad angels.' He describes how the magi avert disaster by incantations and sacrifices or, if they have no animal, they bleed a finger instead of sacrificing. And the souls of the dead have been invoked by those expert in the art of consecrating statues and then these invoked daemonic spirits have 'received the power of wandering about the space around the earth in order to minister to men'. The whole passage concludes with a statement about the greatness of God who, without a medium, can perform wonders both outwardly and in the soul to convert men to the truth. In this eloquent apology the unspoken assumption is that magic and miracle are intertwined and both are used and at the same time transcended by the one God.

Iamblichus' *Life of Pythagoras* speaks of a not entirely dissimilar faith. By their perfect sympathy with all nature and their mysterious knowledge Pythagoras and his followers performed many wonders such as 'infallible predictions of earthquakes, rapid expulsions of pestilence and violent winds, instantaneous cessations of the effusion of hail, and a tranquillization of the waves of rivers and seas, in order that his disciples might easily pass over them'. His followers 'receiving the power of effecting [them], performed certain miracles of this kind in many places.' One of them, Abaris, was called 'a walker on air, because being carried on the dart which was given to him by the Hyperborean Apollo, he passed over rivers and seas and inaccessible places, like one walking on the air' (ch. 28). In the Pythagorean healing miracles no distinction is made between those which take place by sheer act of the will, those which are the result of technical magic and those which are performed by means of herbs and ointments and the soothing power of music (ch. 29). All alike spring from the wisdom and power of their mysterious skills. Many stories describe the supernatural knowledge which Pythagoras achieved by his grasp of the sympathies. Tasting the well-water of a certain region he was able to predict not only an earthquake in the area but that a ship, just then sailing before a prosperous wind, would be lost at sea (ch. 28). The following story from ch. 8 must be set in this general context.

At that time also, when he was journeying from Sybaris to Crotona, he met near the shore with some fishermen, who were then drawing their nets heavily laden with fishes from the deep, and told them he knew the exact number of the fish they had caught. But the fishermen promising they would perform whatever he should order them to do, if the event corresponded with his prediction, he ordered them, after they had accurately numbered the fish, to return them alive to the sea: and what is yet more wonderful, not one of the fish died while he stood on the shore, though they had been detained from the waters a considerable time. Having therefore paid the fishermen the price of their fish, he departed for Crotona. But they everywhere divulged the fact, and having learnt his name from some children, they told it to all men.

Further examples, which are found in abundance in Pliny, in Apuleius, in Philostratus and in the many miracles predicted in the

magical papyri, need hardly be given here.[26] But it is worth re-
membering the intimate association between miracle and magic
which is also found in the Christian apocryphal literature of the
first two centuries, and the great miracles attributed to magicians
such as Simon Magus, who flies through the air, makes statues
walk, and turns stones into bread.[27] Indeed, the whole history of
the use of miracles in Christian apologetic in the first few centuries
indicates the difficulty of distinguishing miracle and magic. In the
Clementine Recognitions Niceta asks Peter,

In what respect did the Egyptians sin in not believing Moses, since
the magicians wrought like signs, even although they were done rather
in appearance than in truth? For if I had been there then, should I not
have thought, from the fact that the magicians did like things to those
which Moses did, either that Moses was a magician, or that the magicians wrought their signs by divine commission? For I should not have
thought it likely that the same things could be effected by magicians,
even in appearance, which he who was sent by God performed. And
now, in what respect do they sin who believe Simon, since they see
him do so great marvels? . . . But if he sins who believes those who
do signs, how shall it appear that he also does not sin who has believed
our Lord for His signs and works of power?[28]

That the problem of distinguishing the true Saviour's miracles
from the magic of Antichrist was an old one in the church is
evident from the places in the New Testament itself where the
faithful are warned against accepting the apparent testimony of
such miracles.[29] Patristic apologetic betrays the same difficulty in
the use of miracles.[30]

In making these observations about the tradition of miracles in
Hebrew and Greek thought, my purpose is not to suggest any
literary or oral dependence of particular Christian canonical
miracles on non-Christian ones or the reverse. Such influences may
have been at work in both directions; that is not the concern of
this study. My purpose is to show the sort of atmosphere which
surrounded the miracle story in the Hellenistic world, an atmosphere which it would have regardless of the more detailed
question of the factors governing the evolution of particular
miracle stories, an atmosphere which would amongst other aspects
include the magical. It seems, in view of the conception of the
magical-miracle which we have been considering, not unreasonable
to suppose that it has played some part in the later development of

the synoptic miracle tradition, and may have been present from the very beginning in the ministry of Jesus.

3. *The relationship between miracle and magic*

Before we look more closely at the synoptic tradition and its formation we must ask what the exact significance is of this relationship between magic and miracle. Why are they associated? Do the two realms coincide completely or do they merely intersect at certain points? Is there non-miraculous magic and non-magical miracle?

A miracle is partly or wholly magical if it possesses any or all of the following characteristics.

(i) The miracle has no cause but the will of the miracle worker.

(ii) If cause and effect are indicated, their connection is based upon a theory of sympathetic bonds or *mana* or something similar.

(iii) The cause of the miracle is believed to be the performance of certain rituals which, whether explicated in terms of any general theory or not, are efficacious in themselves; in other words, the miracle is brought about by human effort acting through a ritual.

Let us examine these criteria. It is often supposed[31] that if a wonderful event contrary to all normal human experience were to take place not by means of a spell, a wand, or even a nod, but by simply happening, that this would be a 'pure' miracle, free because of its simplicity and absence of technique from any suggestion of magic.[32]

This supposition is based however upon a theory of magic, that set out for example by J. G. Frazer in *The Golden Bough*, this particular part of which is now largely discredited.[33] Frazer believed that magic is essentially an error of reasoning in which causes and effects are wrongly connected. Certain rituals, being associated with certain results, are thought to be the cause of those results, and so magic is a kind of misplaced science. The tribe sacrifices a cock before sunrise, therefore the sacrifice is thought to be the cause of the sun's rising. If an event takes place which is caused by nothing, if it is not the final result of a series of operations, it cannot be magical. This view of magic is, however, too mechanical; it does not allow sufficient weight to the fact that magic is a personal, charismatic operation springing from the will of the magician. So Marett writes of the 'ground-idea' of magic, 'namely, the view that it is an inter-personal, inter-subjective transaction, an affair between wills'.[34] A magical act does not require means, although it will often have them. So far from the 'simple' miracle being therefore not magical the reverse may be the case. The strongest magic seems often to be that effect caused merely by the will of the operator; so strong is that will that it needs no extra help; it defies opposition since a magician who can work without his wand cannot be incapacitated by its theft; it cannot be interrupted or delayed because its triumph is its immediate attainment of its objective.

When the gods act in a magical way, their actions can only to a certain extent be described in graphic terms. Indeed, it is an essential characteristic of a magical act that its workings cannot be clearly apprehended. Nobody knows exactly what happens when a magical effect is produced.[35]

Many examples could be given of magical miracles which occurred simply because of the will of the god or the human actor.[36]

Effects caused by a mere act of the will or by a word are frequently met with in magic, and when manipulations occur they do not as a rule serve to make the miracle itself more credible.[37]

When Apollo is described as ἐκηβόλος the reference may be to his 'magical will-power', 'Apollon "who strikes what he wills"',[38] and the references to the βουλή or βουλαί of Zeus may also 'imply the will-power characteristic of the magician-king'.[39] It may be that magic had its origin in the need to express a will that such and such an action should come about, a will which is violently expressed when there seems nothing that can be actually done about it, but that should not lead us to the belief that magic expressed through acts of will-power alone is necessarily older or more primitive in any given case, although it may sometimes indicate an attempt to return to the naked power which archaic magic is always supposed to have possessed.

Sometimes relatively simple miracles are performed by use of the voice alone with a magical prayer or, simpler still, by a direct imperative without further elaboration.

The natives have a special expression for such acts; they say that the formula is recited 'by the mouth only'. . . . This form of magic with such a rudimentary rite is, however, relatively uncommon. Although one could say that there is no rite at all in such cases, for the magician does not manipulate anything or perform any action beyond speaking, yet from another point of view, the whole performance is ritual in so far as he has always to cast his voice towards the element, or being, which he addresses.[40]

This point is emphasized by Malinowski, who denies that magic is based on observation of the laws of nature but says it is a personal power passed on to individuals through the magical traditions, 'a force unique of its kind, residing exclusively in man, let loose only by his magical art, gushing out with his voice, conveyed by the casting forth of the rite'.[41]

Any attempt to introduce rational cause and effect into the event removes it from both magic and miracle simultaneously. In a famous passage at the end of the Wisdom of Solomon (19.18–21), one of the earliest attempts to explain miracles on scientific or philosophical grounds, the sage employs the Stoic conception of the transmutation of elements. This treatment is sometimes called a 'theory of miracle'[42] but what 'Solomon' suggests is not a theory of miracles but a scientific theory. There can be no theory of miracles in the sense of explaining how they take place because the essential feature of the miracles is its very inexplicability. The religious instinct is to preserve the mystery which shrouds the god's miraculous act. It is the absence of any theory of cause and effect which made miracle and magic equal options for the Hebrew people. So when attempts are made to rationalize the miracle, like those in Wisdom or Philo's allegorical approach,[43] they deal with the problem of credibility and the problem of magic at the same time. Sometimes one factor will dominate the mind of the apologist, sometimes the other.[44]

Is belief in the divine omnipotence indistinguishable from belief in magic?[45] The problem for the church fathers was created by the fact that originally in the Christian tradition miracle was also connected with eschatology. With the fading of eschatology as a living part of the faith of the church, miracle was removed from its interpretative context and inevitably fell into its only other context, magic. Magic is the charge laid by the non-Christian world against the isolated fragments of the church's faith in the last things. Magic is in some respects an attempt to explain how the gods act: they do what the magicians do.[46] When one says that

Zeus does it by nodding his head or by holding up his finger this is a sort of rationalization. Of course it need not be magic in this case; it could be anthropomorphism. And indeed, anthropomorphism ('God does it the way a big man does it') and magic ('God does it the way a magician does it') were the two main alternatives confronting the ancient philosopher of religion in attempting to give some account of the nature of the divine activity. Broadly speaking, Greece adopted the former method and explained the gods by humanizing them. Egypt and Israel, then Christianity and Islam, rejecting the humanization of God for theological reasons, laid themselves open to the magical explication of the divine acts. Transcendental monotheism finds magic an odd bedfellow but the alternative is worse. The problem for the believer today is to conceive of the divine activity in a form other than anthropomorphic realism and magical miracle.[47]

On the second criterion for recognizing a magical miracle, it is only necessary to point out that to say that a miracle is worked by a mysterious universal power is not the same as saying that it is worked by a ritual which acts of its own accord (which is the third criterion). For the power residing in a great magician can, as we have seen, work without technique, and, on the other hand, mastery of the technique does not mean that you will be able necessarily to make the magic because you may not have the power.

Thus only last week a correspondent wrote to me from Simbo in the Solomon Islands to say that a native has no objection to imparting to you the words of a *mana* song. The mere knowledge will not enable you to perform miracles. You must pay him money, and then *ipso facto* he will transmit the *mana* to you – as we should say, the 'good-will' of the concern.[48]

On the other hand, one of the sages in Lucian's *Philosopseudes* (ch. 36) says that he overheard a spell of three syllables by which a pestle could be made to pick up a jar of water and carry it. He tried the syllables and they worked. But he could not stop the magical pestle and was flooded.

It all depends where the power is thought to reside, in the person or in the spell and apparatus. It may be in the one or the other. If it is in the person, the person can voluntarily pass it on to someone else; if it is in the apparatus, anyone who uses the apparatus can perform the magic.[49] In the absence of apparatus and technique, where a theory of power is nevertheless present, to tell if it is a magical miracle one must ask if the power is different in kind from that possessed by ordinary men. If Zeus shoots his enemy with an arrow he exerts no power different in kind from that possessed by men; the difference is merely one of degree. And there would in that case be no miracle, magical or otherwise, for anthropomorphism would have swallowed up both. But if Zeus makes a man invisible, or if a man flies through the air, a power is present different in kind from that possessed by ordinary men. These would then be magical miracles.

Having discussed the most debatable aspects of our criteria we must now face another difficulty. Is there any such thing as a non-magical, *religious* miracle? Or do the three criteria sweep the board clean? There are a number of possibilities here. A religious miracle could be one which took place according to the foreknowledge of God. So we might say that the miracle in the crossing of the Jordan river consisted in the fact that the Israelites happened to arrive just as the river, because of a landslide further upstream, was drying up anyway. This category is common in Josephus.[50] In this case the integrity of cause and effect is safeguarded and therefore there would be no magic. But there would be no miracle either, since miracle would be transformed into providence and, instead of the antithesis of natural law versus miracle, you would have chance versus providence. This, by the way, leads us directly into the significance for miracle of prophecy. Origen argues that the credibility and therefore the usefulness of the miracles as divine attestation is enhanced by the fact that the Old Testament predicts them.[51] Prophecy has the added advantage of showing that the miracle does not come from the will of man, that it is not the consequence of some magician forcing the deity to act, for it is the deity himself who foretells the wonders in his own scriptures. This eliminates the third criterion which involves human initiative using techniques to compel miracles – an important asset, since this criterion was one of the most widely recognized signs of a magical miracle in the ancient world.

Religious miracle might also take the form of an epiphany which might take place in dream or vision and might still (in the light of modern knowledge at any rate) preserve cause and effect intact and therefore be free of magic. Indeed, most biblical miracles are epiphanies and, by concentrating attention upon the element of personal confrontation with God which takes place during the miracle, it is possible to reduce the atmosphere of magical miracle. 'Jesus manifested his glory and his disciples believed in him' (John 2.11). But he had only changed water into wine. A magical miracle has been transformed into theophany.

A third possibility is that miracle might take place in answer to prayer. Here we must make some careful distinctions. If the miracle comes as a response of the grace of God to the prayer it is not magical unless it involves the additional factor of suspending normal cause and effect. Even here, it might be possible to argue that both the prayer and its answer were within the foreknowledge of God. But if the prayer *compels* the response, if the response comes *because of* the prayer rather than because of grace, then it is becoming magical. Here are two illustrations. Hanina ben Dosa (end of first century AD) was asked to pray for a son of Gamaliel II.

Hanina at once went up to the chamber on the roof and prayed for him; when he came down, he said to the messengers, Go, for the fever has left him. They asked, Are you a prophet? He replied, I am neither a prophet nor the son of a prophet, but I have learned that if I have freedom in prayer, I know that it is accepted; if not, I know that it is rejected.

The servants, arriving home, found that the fever had left him at the very same hour. The next illustration is as follows:

Hanina's prayers once caused a shower of rain to hold up for his own convenience, and then to fall again. His prayer on that occasion seemed to countervail that of the high priest.[52]

In the second case, since the prayer is a technique which creates a divine intervention, and since there is the concept of a struggle between two powerful prayers, it is magic. In the first case, the miracle is wrought by God, and all the praying man does is to find out what God had decreed. Since it is based on knowledge of God's foreknowledge, it is even *less* magical.

We must also distinguish between the circumstances of one age and of another. Since the ancient Hebrews had little appreciation of cause and effect, we may suppose that a prayer, the result of which was a fall of rain, was not necessarily conceived of as being magical by them. But for us, since we can fully account for the fall of rain without recourse to prayer as an explanation, such a prayer would be magical. Compare the situation regarding belief in

astrology. A Roman aristocrat of the first century was not superstitious when he accepted astrological advice, for astrology was in
harmony with the best scientific and mathematical knowledge of
the period. But in our day we rightly regard a person who accepts
astrology as being superstitious. Growth in knowledge turns
science into pseudo-science, and the divine mysteries into magic.
In other words, when considering if an activity is magical, one
must consider the state of mind of the actor and also the context of
that mind in relation to other minds. Magic is part of a world-
view.

In conclusion and summary, we may say that the category of
miracle, although an indispensable form in the mythological expressions of faith found in the ancient world, was for the ancients
difficult to separate from the category of magic. For us today it is
impossible to separate magic from miracle without seriously modi-
fying the strictly miraculous part of the miracle. Lucian of Samosata
was nearly two thousand years before his time.

The criteria by which the magical miracle was detected in the
Hellenistic world were rather different from the ones suggested
here, and much confusion in the discussion of magic would be
avoided if the two sets of criteria were kept clearly in mind. The
three factors looked for by the church fathers were:

(i) Lack of reality. The magical act was in appearance only.
(ii) Operation by evil powers.
(iii) Use of physical helps.

The charge of magic implied then that the miracle had not
happened, or, if it had, it was worked by demons. It is easy to see
how such criteria, with their lack of objectivity and their failure
to make essential distinctions, would lead to a hopeless confusion
about the location of the magical. The third criterion is the only
really useful one.

Thus Lactantius, defending the 'wonderful works' of Christ, 'on
account of which, though they were signs of heavenly powers, the
Jews esteemed him a magician', says that these miracles were performed

not by magical tricks, which display nothing true and substantial, but
by heavenly strength and power, which were foretold even long ago.
And he performed all these things not by His hands, or the application
of any remedy, but by His word and command.

Lactantius is here wide of the mark, since both use of the hands in a variety of ways and the application of remedies are found in Christ's miracles. It is interesting to see that Lactantius uses Isa. 35. 3–6, 'Then shall the eyes of the blind be opened, and the ears of the deaf shall hear', to show that the Jews must be mistaken in thinking that the miracles were performed by demonic power. The argument is simply: God works miracles, demons work magic. Like most of the ancients, Lactantius was more interested in who did miracles than in exploring the characteristics of what was done. Magic may look the same but (because it is done by devils) it cannot possibly be the same. The only conclusion is that it is deceptive. The similarity is a fraud.

I ask, therefore, what the art of magic could have contrived in this case [the feeding of the five thousand], the skill of which is of no avail but for deceiving the eyes ?[53]

You can deceive people's eyes but not their stomachs.

We have shown that, whether because of the operation of criteria such as these or because of a more sophisticated use of argument, as in the case of Lucian, or because of the general atmosphere and archaic associations of such deeds, miracles were often regarded as being tainted (or glorified) by association with magic.

4. *Exorcism*

Let us turn now to a particular class of miracle, the exorcism of a demon. What sort of thing was Jesus believed to have done when he was reported as having exorcized demons? Into what category does this kind of healing fall? Examination of extra-biblical stories of demonic possession is one way of understanding the impact which the stories about Jesus would make on the early communities. Such stories from the period before Christ are very few indeed. An early case from Egypt is an exorcism by a mother of her child's sickness, where the sickness is spoken to and rebuked and told to flee and escape, in a manner not unlike Christ's rebuke of the fever in the Lucan version of the healing of Simon's mother-in-law (Luke 4.38f.).

I drive away the sickness which is in your body, and the weakness which is in your body, and the weakness which is in your limbs, like

the crocodile travelling up the Nile, like the snake secreting venom. . . .
Drain away, swelling, and go down![54]

From the thirteenth century BC comes what is probably the
oldest extant case of individual possession and exorcism. It is an
inscription from the period of Rameses II (1292–1225 BC) describing how when the Pharaoh was in Mesopotamia he met and married
the daughter of the Prince of Bekhten, whose younger sister Bent-
ent-resht was later heard to be ill. Upon arriving at Bekhten, the
Pharaoh's learned priest found that the lady was 'possessed of a
demon or spirit over which he was powerless'. Exorcism was
effected by imparting 'a fourfold measure of magical power' to the
statue of the god Khonsu, which was transported to the spot, and
'having performed a magical ceremony over her, the demon
departed from her and she was cured straightway.' The demon and
the god later became good friends.[55] Although there are no similar
stories of individuals being cured of demon possession from
Mesopotamia itself,[56] demons did cause sickness and were exorcized, and we may reasonably believe that there were many tales of
outstanding cures which have not survived. R. Campbell Thompson published an invocation to the Headache Demon, and describes
how the god Marduk learned from Ea to take water from the
confluence of two streams, to sprinkle it over the attacked man
and perform certain rituals.[57]

Possession of individuals and subsequent exorcism is unknown
in ancient and classical Greece, but the seed of the idea is already
present in the *Odyssey* (V.396), where the hateful demon causes
wasting sickness, and in the *Eumenides* of Aeschylus the Erinyes are
like vampires sucking the blood of men.

> Thyself shalt yield instead,
> Living, from every vein,
> Thine own blood, rich and red,
> For our parched mouths to drain.[58]

Men are destined to become shadows, 'flung to devils for their
food'. The conception of possession is a good deal earlier than
that of specifically demonic possession, but the simple possession
idea prepared the way. E. R. Dodds draws attention to Corybantic
possession and to the method of ascertaining which divinity was
troubling a disturbed person by seeing to which divine ritual he
reacted. Diagnosis was based on the patient's response to music,

the idea being that the appropriate sacrifice could be offered once the origin of the possession was isolated. Dodds compares the technique with later Hellenistic and Christian exorcism.[59]

Magical exorcism in Ptolemaic Egypt is detailed by Franz Cumont; here it is well on the way to the fully developed technique.[60] But the first occurrence of ἐξορκιστής in Greek literature appears to be in an epigram attributed to Lucian.[61]

The earliest specific case of demon exorcism in Jewish literature is in Tobit, where magical means are used to protect the hero from the attacks of the demon Asmodeus. From Jewish sources roughly contemporary with the birth of the New Testament we have two accounts of clear cases of exorcism, both from the *Antiquities* of Josephus. The first is that of Saul.

He was beset by strange disorders and evil spirits which caused him such suffocation and strangling that the physicians could devise no other remedy save to order search to be made for one with power to charm away spirits and to play upon the harp, and, whensoever the evil spirits should assail and torment Saul, to have him stand over the king, and strike the strings and chant his songs.[62]

David was appointed and drove the evil spirits away by means of his music. The other case in Josephus is the well known story of Eleazar and King Solomon's ring.[63]

This then, as far as we can reconstruct it, was the state of the exorcist tradition when the gospels were written. It amounts to four actual stories of individual cases and a good deal of suggestive but not conclusive evidence from Greece, together with the considerable weight of information (but no case histories) from Hellenistic Egypt and more ancient Babylonia and Assyria. The curse tablets can be ignored because, although exorcistic in general intention,[64] they do not deal with possession. Evidence taken from the magical papyri is not helpful at this point because, although there is good reason to see older traditions in them, there is no single case of individual exorcism which can without doubt predate the Christian era.

Examination of this exorcist tradition reveals that even in this still embryonic stage it is saturated with magical ideas. There does not seem to be a single reference in pre-Christian or first-century literature to the expulsion of demons troubling the mind or causing disease which is not associated with magic. Several important passages in the Jewish pseudepigraphical apocalypses deal not with the *expulsion* of demons of sickness or oppression but with their defeat and overthrow in a more general sense.[65] Only one of them[66] refers to healing, and this seems to be spiritual healing leading to truth and salvation, not physical healing of a demon-oppressed body or mind.

When, about the third quarter of the first century or a little later, certain Graeco-Jewish works appeared which contained two or three particularly vivid and memorable additions to the now rapidly growing number of such stories, their literary genre and their associations would be immediately recognized. C. K. Barrett, pointing out that Jesus' exorcisms were not unique, remarks:

It is true that Jesus must have presented a 'demonic', a 'pneumatic' figure as with authority he rebuked the unclean spirits, but so did the legendary Solomon, and the half-legendary Apollonius of the *Life*; and so too did the perfectly real Rabbis who exorcised demons, and the equally real magicians who hawked the magical spells which we have considered.[67]

This then was the sort of figure the demon-mastering Christ would appear to be.

The nature of exorcism is made still clearer if we include the evidence from sources a little later than the gospels. Lucian's three cases[68] have been mentioned already and there are five further cases in Philostratus' *Life of Apollonius of Tyana*. In II.4 the sage meets a ghost which flies screaming as he abuses and rails at it. In III.38 a demonic boy is healed. His age is given as sixteen; he has been affected for two years. He is 'with a demon' who is described as mocking or teasing and lying. On being asked by one of the Brahmin sages why she described it in this way the boy's mother gives an account of the demon's characteristics:

(i) He interferes with the boy's life, driving him into the desert places; the devil desires and loves him.

(ii) The boy has lost his own voice but speaks in a deep and hollow tone and has a strange look in his eyes.

(iii) He is unresponsive to tears and threats.

(iv) The demon using the child as a mask has said he is the ghost of a man killed in battle. Infuriated by the unseemly haste with which his wife has married, he is now attaching himself to this lad in a rebound.

(v) The demon has pleaded not to be reported to the sages.

(vi) The woman has not brought the boy himself because the

demon has threatened her with steep places and precipices and declared that he would kill her son.

Healing is accomplished by means of a letter which the sage produces, already written, which contains 'threats of an alarming kind'.

Note the form of the story, which includes the usual details of age and so on but has a more detailed description of the case than is usually found. The healing is carried out at a distance and is told very briefly. Indeed we are not actually told if the letter was effective and the sage does not actually promise a cure, merely that the demon will not kill the boy when he has read the letter. The sage tells the woman to 'take courage'.

The third Apollonian case (IV.10) describes the recognition of a plague spirit by Apollonius in Ephesus. An old beggar is stoned to death on the wonder-worker's orders. His eyes are full of fire and so he is recognized to be a demon. The removal of the stones reveals the demon in the form of a huge mad dog.

The fourth case (IV.20) is a healing of a demonic youth who interrupts Apollonius' lecture with laughter. Apollonius recognizes this as a case of possession; the youth's odd behaviour shows him, although he does not realize it himself, to be a mouthpiece of the devil. As Apollonius gazes on him the ghost utters cries of fear and rage, as from tortured people, swearing he will leave the young man and never take possession of anyone again. Apollonius however angrily orders him to come out and, to make sure, to create a sign of his exit. The devil says he will throw down a certain statue, which then falls over. The people are amazed, clapping their hands with wonder, but the young man is like one who has just woken up; he changes his clothes and his way of life and models himself in future upon Apollonius.

This story was not invented by Philostratus, but is a popular story which circulated at least as early as the second half of the second century AD and can be assumed therefore to express popular opinions about the nature of possession and the behaviour of exorcized demons. A similar tale appears in the apocryphal *Acts of Peter* 11.[69] Peter is disturbed by a laugh from the crowd, and exorcizes the young joker in the name of Jesus Christ. A marble statue of Caesar is broken to pieces but reassembles when sprinkled with holy water. The Petrine version of the story may be later, since the miraculous restoration of the statue indicates further growth.

Reitzenstein traces the story back to the temple cult in Egypt, in the custom of lustrating the idol of the god each day to bring him to life again.[70]

The fifth and final exorcism of Apollonius is the detection of a vampire who, in the form of a beautiful woman, is seeking to prey on Menippus (IV.25).

From these examples in Lucian and Philostratus we can see that the exorcism tradition continued as it had begun, thoroughly magical. The Jewish accounts continue in the same manner as well, most of the stories involving the use of magic, although for the first time exorcisms appear which are less clearly magical. They are based upon prayer and are gracious gifts of God.[71] The enormous number of exorcisms in the apocryphal writings and in the lives of the saints betray the same general features. Some are religious, the great majority are magical. To illustrate the difference let us take some examples of Coptic religious exorcism.

A man who was possessed by the devil, and suffered a great deal, in frothing at the mouth, struck an old anchorite on the cheek. The sage offered him the other cheek, and the demon, unable to endure the presence of his humility, came out of him.[72]

Another story tells how a demon-possessed man came to an old saint at Thebes, to be healed. The sage, having prayed, cried out, 'Come out of the divine creation!' The demon replied with a question, 'Who are the sheep and who are the goats?' The saint answered, 'The goats – that's me! But the sheep, God alone knows them.' The demon, when he heard that, said, 'Because of your humility, I will come out.'[73]

A possessed man was brought to Father Longinus who said, 'I am unable to help; go to Father Zeno.' When Father Zeno had prayed the demon cried out, 'Do you think I am coming out because of you? Look, it is Father Longinus who is praying and who exorcizes me. I believe his prayers and am coming out, but to you I will reply not a word!'[74]

The quality of stories such as these is strikingly different from those in Lucian and Philostratus. They are in fact not miracle-exorcism stories but hagiography, the interest being in the sanctity of the father, his humility, or in the way the fathers literally obeyed the scripture (turning the other cheek), or the stories may be illustrations of the greatness of one particular saint. The demono-

logy exists merely as a vehicle for these features; they are not
practical models since no help by way of method or advice is given
to the church's professional exorcists.[75] The lack of interest in the
exorcism itself is illustrated by the fact that in the first example there
is no will on the part of the sage to exorcize at all. The departure
of the demon takes place simply as an evidence of character. Reading the exorcisms in Mark's gospel serves to increase awareness of
the fact that they are not of this hagiographical type.

Examination of the parallels between the synoptic stories and
the magical papyri deepens the impression.[76] In Mark 1.24 the
demon cries out to Christ, 'I know who you are' continuing with
the holy name as proof of recognition. This is a magical formula
well attested in the papyri. Compare *PGM* VIII.13, 'I know you,
Hermes, who you are and whence you come and which your city
is'.[77] The demons cry out the names, 'The Holy One of God'
(Mark 1.24), 'Son of God' (Mark 3.11), 'Son of the Most High
God' (Mark 5.7) and in a similar fashion the demon-possessed
mystically-united magicians cry out to the spirits they seek to
control invoking the holy name of the god.[78] The 'You are (name)'
formula is as common as the 'I know you' formula.[79]

The description of God as 'most high' is occasionally found in
magical adjuration. In the Testament of Solomon the God who
gave Solomon the ring is described (1.6) as 'The Lord God most
high, Sabaoth', and in 11.6 we read 'I adjure you by the great
name of the most high God'.[80] In astrological and magical texts
not under Jewish influence the expression 'most high god' is
used to describe the one who is supreme in the celestial spheres.[81]
In *PGM* IV.1067f. the god who has given an oracle is described
as the 'good and holy light of the most high god'. A departure-
prayer in *PGM* V.46 also exhorts the spirit to leave, and not to
harm the magician or his medium 'in the name of the most high
god'. In *PGM* XII.63f., a ritual directed at Eros, the magician
commands the god to make sure that everyone loves him and to
do it right away, 'by order of the most high God Iao Adoneai'.
This example is preceded and followed by strings of sentences
beginning 'You are . . .' and a few lines later the magician describes himself as a servant of the most high God (*PGM* XII.72).
This is rather similar to the girl with the oracular spirit in Acts
16.17 who greets Paul and his friends with the warning exclama-
tion, 'These men are servants of the most high God' just before

the spirit is exorcized. Similarly in Mark 5.7 the madman addresses Jesus as 'Son of the Most High' just before the exorcism takes place. The expression 'I adjure you by God' (Mark 5.7) naturally has many parallels. Hecate is adjured in a love spell, 'I adjure you by the great name of Ablathana' (*PGM* XXXVI.189f.) and in *PGM* IV.3205, we read 'I adjure you, who are hidden in the magic virtue of the plant. . . .' The bilingual magical papyrus in the British Museum uses the expression, 'I adjure thee by the great god on the roof of heaven.'[82]

The command of Jesus to the spirits is 'Come out of him' (Mark 1.25; 5.8; 9.25). This is the usual form of address in the magical papyri. Thus 'Come out, whatever demon you be, and depart from so and so . . . come out, demon, for I will bind you with adamantine bonds . . . and I will deliver you up to the black chaos in perdition' (*PGM* IV.1243ff.). Compare this threat with the cry of the legion (Mark 5.7) 'Torment me not' and of the Capernaeum demon 'Have you come to destroy us?'[83]

The demons when they see Christ or when they are being expelled cry out and scream (Mark 1.23, 26; 3.11; 5.7; 9.26). This is common in the Testament of Solomon. When he was captured the demon gave a great scream and in spite of his protests he was dragged before Solomon crying out with a loud voice (1.14). When the prince of the demons was hit by the ring, he screamed (3.4), and a female demon confessed the power which destroyed her with a loud cry (4.11). Grundmann remarks that in the Greek world κράζω and ἀνακράζω have religious significance in the sphere of the demonic and, speaking of the demonic cries in the New Testament, he says,

> In these sayings of demons, which are magical incantations, we have demonic resistance to Jesus, who on His way attacks the realm of the demons . . . Even the magical arts of this kingdom have no power in face of Him.[84]

As well as these verbal links, the general technique of exorcism in Mark's gospel is that of magical exorcism, although there is in Mark a striking absence of use of rings, holy water, herbs and similar aids. Campbell Bonner[85] describes three aspects of the technique. First the demon must be made to speak.[86] In PGM IV.3038ff. there is an interesting example. The magician adjures the demon, whoever he may be, to speak, and adds that the exorcism is by Solomon's ring, which he placed on Jeremiah's tongue. Bonner argues that the mention of Solomon's ring, the effect of which upon Jeremiah was simply to make him speak, shows that here the demon is commanded merely to speak and not necessarily to utter his name. The main point is to break his silence. The problem with a deaf and dumb demon is that, being deaf, he will not be moved by threats since he will not hear them, and, being dumb, he will not respond by disclosing his true identity. To Bonner's illustrations may be added the demons in Test. Sol. 13.2 who react with resentment when Solomon orders them to speak. So when a limbless female spirit is asked, 'Who are you?', she replies, 'No, but who are you? And why do you wish to learn about me?' When Asmodeus is summoned and asked about his identity he replies, with a look of fury, 'Who are you?' Solomon says, 'Punished as you are, do you answer me back?' But the demon, still raging, says, 'But how can I answer you, for you are a son of man, but I was born of angel's seed?' (Test. Sol. 5.2ff.).

The second feature of exorcism mentioned by Bonner is that the demon tells his name, or his nature and his works. The relevant New Testament parallel is Mark 5.9, 'What is your name?' 'My name is Legion.' Bauernfeind points out that the 'I am' formula is often found with the 'My name is' type – both expressing an implied threat to the opponent.[87] So in *PGM* IV.1017ff. we read an appeal to the god to manifest himself, backed up with 'My name is Balnchoooch. I am he that sprang forth from heaven, my name is Balsames.' The request for the name of the demon or deity is often found, e.g. *PGM* I.162f.[88]

The demon must be made to speak, but he must not be allowed to say too much. The advantage gained by knowing the demon's name is lost if, before you have a chance to use it on him, he begins to use yours on you. Hence the commands to silence which, whatever their theological role in Mark's gospel, were in the earlier stage of the transmission part of the magical conflict. The command to be silent is found in similar contexts in the papyri. In POslo. 1 (*PGM* XXXVI.46f.) in a charm to restrain the wrath of enemies, a silencing formula is to be pronounced three times. Rohde has pointed out[89] that the verb φιμόω which is used in the passage is almost equivalent in Greek magic to καταδεῖν and κατάδεσμος. The idea is to reduce an enemy by magical means to a state of impotence. Eitrem says,

These instances make an effective background for the use of the verb in the N.T., e.g. where Jesus threatens the impure spirit, Mark 1.25 . . . in the same way Jesus threatens the sea, Mark 4.39 . . .[90]

Mark 1.34 is an interesting case. Jesus will not allow the demons to speak because they know him. Bonner suggests that Jesus 'did not wish his nature and mission to be revealed prematurely.'[91] It seems possible, however, that the idea here is that Jesus knows the demons and recognizes them. They, for their part, return the knowledge and the recognition, which is less of his mission than of his name as 'Holy One of God' and 'Son of God Most High'. The superiority of Jesus' power is seen in his perfect knowledge, which expels many demons without having to inquire as to the name of each one, and also in the fact that he is able to silence them but they are not able to silence him. The theological ambiguity of the words 'they knew him' is created by the point of view of the evangelist and not by the nature of the exorcism itself. In the papyri the magician constantly emphasizes how much about the god or demon he knows. So in *PGM* VIII.6ff., the magician knows everything about Hermes, including 'Your heavenly name'. He recites a string of names to prove it, and concludes, 'Those are the names in the four corners of heaven. I also know your shapes, in the east you have the shape of an ibis, . . . in the north the shape of a serpent', etc. The pupil-magician in the 'Book of Moses' (*PGM* XIII.755f.) is to guard the name which has been revealed to him, for without the name nothing will work properly. 'Keep secret, child, the nine-letter name "aee-eei-ouo".' A similar solemn warning to protect the mystic knowledge of the name is found in *PGM* XII.321f. One of the most serious warnings about the danger if one's secret name is known is the story of how Isis stole the name of Ra. Ra said proudly, 'My father and mother told me my name; I have hidden it since my birth; and so no magician has any hold over me!' But Isis persuaded him to tell her what it was, and so she became mistress of the gods.[92] We need not wonder then that those who first told the stories of Jesus' exorcisms noticed and recorded the triumph of the devils at their possession of the sacred mystery of the name of Jesus, and they would understand why it was that he would not let them speak, 'because they knew him'.

Evidence for the magical context and magical interpretation of the exorcisms of Jesus appears in the fact that at a very early stage the name of Jesus was included in the repertoire of the professional magicians. The most famous case is found in the Great Paris Magical Papyrus (*PGM* IV.3019f.) in the 'Pibeches' exorcism, where the exorcist says, 'I adjure you by the God of the Hebrews, Jesus, iaba, iae, Abraoth'. Deissmann did not believe the passage was very old,[93] but Knox[94] presents a number of fairly strong arguments to show that it is an old addition to the original text of the spell. Knox points out that the distinction between Judaism and Christianity would surely be common knowledge even in the underworld of Hellenistic superstition by the end of the first century, and would be particularly familiar to a magician who would be collecting new names and for whom it would be essential that the deity should be correctly described. The later the text, the more difficult it would have been to describe Jesus as the God of the Hebrews. Knox concludes, 'I find it hard to believe that so casual an allusion as this would have been possible much after 100 AD.'[95] Knox and Eitrem agree that the name of Jesus has been added to an existing pagan Jewish exorcism; Eitrem suggests that the first of the mystical names which follows 'of the Hebrews' was originally $\iota o \upsilon$, so the series ran $\iota o \upsilon$ $\iota a \beta a$. $I[\eta \sigma] o \upsilon$ is an obvious adaptation to make the name more up to date. Knox believes the background to be basically Jewish liturgy, but Eitrem believes it to be an example of pagan syncretism, possibly from Alexandria. The main point for our present purpose is the early acceptance of the name.[96]

This is not an isolated case. In the same papyrus, in lines 1228f., there is an 'excellent method of casting out demons'. The word is to be spoken over the head of the possessed man from behind and olive branches are to be laid in front of him. The word is in Coptic and reads, 'Hail, God of Abraham, Hail, God of Isaac, Hail, God of Jacob, Jesus Chrestos, Holy Ghost, Son of the Father, who are under the seven and in the seven.' It goes on to speak of 'this impure spirit, this Satan' who is in the patient. This text is perhaps a century older than the papyrus itself and therefore indicates the use of the name of Jesus *c.*200–250, or not much later.[97] The name of Jesus was in use in Jewish circles *c.* AD 120 as a charm against snake bites,[98] a practice for which the longer ending of Mark, in 16.18, may also provide early witness.[99] More remarkable is the possible appearance of the name of Jesus twice in a leaden cursing tablet from Megara near Athens. The name of

Hecate also appears. The tablet is supposed to give the enemy sickness and fever and it is dated first or second century.[100]

But there is no need to look beyond the New Testament to find evidence of the name of Jesus being used by non-Christian exorcists. The story in Mark 9.38f. of the alien exorcist who 'followed not with us' and yet cast out demons in the name of Christ is clearly an example of a professional magical use. The remarkable feature of the story is that Jesus is described as being tolerant of such use of his name: 'Do not forbid him.' That the later church was unable to sustain this spirit of tolerance is seen from Matt. 7.22, where Jesus is said to disown completely those who have done the very deeds Mark 9.38f. allowed. The story of the Jewish exorcists in Acts 19.13ff. strikes a warning note similar to that of Matthew. It is interesting to see that the name of Paul as well as the name of Jesus was thought to be familiar to the spirits. One would expect to find cases of Paul's name in magical formulae, especially in view of the fact that his escape from snake bite in Acts 28.1-6 is not attributed to the name of Jesus. The pagans think Paul himself is divine. The point of the story in ch. 19 however is that it is very dangerous to use the Christian names of exorcism unless you do it according to the Christian ritual[101] and with the Christian δύναμις. All this material indicates the manner in which the synoptic healing stories and especially the exorcisms were received and interpreted in their early environment.[102]

V

MARK

1. *A problem of interpretation*

Details of some of the healing stories in Mark indicate a magical context just as details of the exorcisms seem to. The healing of the deaf mute in Mark 7.32ff. is perhaps the clearest case. Jesus takes the man aside privately, puts his fingers into his ears, spits, touches his tongue, looks up to heaven, sighs, utters a word of command, and the man is instantly healed.

There are three possible ways of interpreting these actions. First, they may be taken as symbols of Christ's mercy, of his power, of his grace in awakening faith. This was the normal view in the nineteenth century,[1] and finds its classical expression in the work of T. M. Lindsay.[2] Gould accepts this view,[3] as does H. B. Swete,[4] to name but two of the great commentators of the turn of the century. The symbolic interpretation has been revived by A. M. Hunter who quotes Lindsay fully and with approval.

> The man was deaf and could not be spoken to. Jesus speaks in signs: (1) takes him aside from the multitude – *alone with Jesus*; (2) puts his fingers in his ears – *these are to be opened*; (3) touched his tongue with his saliva – *Christ's tongue is to heal his*.[5]

A weakness of this view is that it assumes Jesus required faith from his patients. But in this miracle there is no sign of faith, unless it be faith which prompts the sufferer's friends to escort him to Jesus. If so, then the effort to raise the faith of the patient himself would be supererogatory. In fact faith is not mentioned at all, before, during or after the healing. The exponents of the symbolic interpretation have difficulty in accounting for the word of command, 'Be opened.' Gould seems to think that it is the word which actually accomplishes the miracle, but if the man's faith had at this point been raised to the necessary pitch the need for further commands is still obscure. Since the man is deaf, the command can hardly be a communication. Vincent Taylor suggests that 'either he was not completely deaf or was able to read the lips of Jesus.'[6] If the man could all the time hear what people said to him, the miracle itself is in danger, and it is doubtful whether the lip-reading suggestion has very much to commend it.

A more serious problem is that it is difficult to avoid the impression that these actions are more than a preparation for healing; they seem to be rather part of the healing itself; they are the healing method. This is seen particularly clearly in the story of the blind man in Mark 8.22–26, when the question, 'Can you see?', clearly supposes that the cure has been effective. When the answer is only partly in the affirmative, the treatment (for so it must be) is applied for a second time. And oddly enough, this is one of the few miracles where there is no word of command. So Jesus speaks to a deaf man but does not speak to a man who is merely blind! This is a strange way of adapting the signs to the capacity of the patient.

The second interpretation of the actions is to regard them as part of the healing ritual but in a medical sense. Jesus heals the man by a combination of shrewd psychology and physiotherapy. E. R. Micklem is one of the most enthusiastic defenders of this view.[7] Micklem's main contention is that the treatment is to be understood in the light of the physiotherapeutic treatment of hysterical stammerers. He quotes cases of soldiers who developed a stammer or even became deaf and dumb under the stress of warfare. The most interesting case, and the one referred to with approval by Vincent Taylor, who is also an exponent of this view,[8] is documented in a work by Dr Wilson Gill.

> The treatment . . . is by direct persuasion, but it is often advisable to perform simultaneously gentle manipulations with the fingers over the glottis, giving verbal encouragement and persuasion all the time. The cure is almost invariably complete in anything from half a minute to one hour . . . If fatigued or unfit, the medical officer will find it better to delay treatment until a more suitable occasion arises, as temporary failure tends to make one less confident in the treatment.[9]

But the treatment offered by Jesus is not at all like this. He does not gently manipulate the glottis, he does not give continuous verbal encouragement, he utters only the word of command.[10] We must also ask whether it is historically credible and theologically permissible to credit Jesus with anticipations of modern physiotherapy, how his actions, for whatever reason they may have been performed, would have been understood in the Hellenistic world in which the story circulated, and indeed how the immediate participants envisaged by the account would have interpreted what Jesus did. For even if Jesus understood physiotherapy and hypnotic suggestion the ordinary people of the ancient world did not. It is common for modern observers to misunderstand the actions of people from oral cultures, attributing to them a scientific motivation and a medical insight which is in fact quite foreign to them. Many examples could be quoted, but this one illustrates the point.

The natives of Eddystone island in the Solomons employ manipulations which so closely resemble those of our own massage that if simply observed, and not made the subject of special enquiry, they would undoubtedly be regarded as the equivalent of this remedy as practised by ourselves. Enquiry showed however, that the object of the manipulations of the Eddystone leech in one case was to act upon an imaginary octopus which was supposed to have taken up its abode in the body of the patient, while in other cases the object was to extract from the body an immaterial object or principle which was held to be the cause of fever or other forms of disease.[11]

Incidentally it is one of the remarkable features of the cures of Jesus that he never gave directions or instructions about natural remedies. The one apparent exception, where in Mark 5.43 the parents of the little girl are told to give her something to eat, is in fact a feature of the style of such stories, the eating being a proof of the reality of the cure. Whatever the actual physical value of the advice given by Jesus to sufferers, it is never ostensibly rational, in striking contrast to the cures of Asclepius and Apollonius of Tyana, who sometimes prescribed exercise, bathing or diet.[12]

The third possible interpretation of these strange actions is that they are magical. This interpretation is found very rarely in commentaries which appeared before 1920[13] but is mentioned often in more recent works.[14]

2. Spittle

Spittle is used in three of the miracles. In John 9.6 paste made from the spittle of Jesus and clay is smeared on a man's eyes; in Mark 8.23 and 7.33 spitting is used in cases of blindness and dumbness. πτύω does not occur elsewhere in the New Testament but ἐμπτύω is found six times in connection with the sufferings of Jesus, always as a symbol of contempt. These references to contemptuous spitting have probably been influenced by the Old Testament, particularly Isa. 50.6, but there has been no Old Testament influence upon the New Testament use of healing spittle. Even the solitary case of this type of belief in Lev. 15.8 is not healing spittle but defiling spittle.[15] We must therefore seek to understand the significance of healing spittle from non-biblical contexts.

All races of antiquity attached magical significance to spittle. The Pyramid Texts (late third millennium BC) speak of Atum spitting out Shu, the air, in the act of creation.[16] The power of a man is in his saliva and it may be used against him. Budge quotes an Egyptian hieratic papyrus text containing a charm against snake bite. 'Now the divine one (i.e. Ra) had grown old; he dribbled at the mouth; his spittle fell upon the earth . . . and Isis kneaded it with earth in her hand, and formed thereof a sacred serpent . . .'[17] Isis attacks Ra with this serpent. The spittle of a powerful person may be used to perform all sorts of wonders. The Pyramid Texts describing the battle between Horus and Set tell us that Horus lost an eye, but when Set was defeated Thoth healed the eye by spitting upon it.[18]

The fact that spittle was used in folk-medicine has misled many commentators[19] into suggesting that the presence of this detail in the Marcan text is due to medical belief rather than to magical practices. But with the use of spittle we are in that shadowy world where medicine fades into magic and no sharp distinction can be made.

Nearly all the commentaries refer to the famous incident where Vespasian heals a blind man with his spittle[20] as an instance of the alleged belief in the medical value of spittle. But this is to misinterpret the event. If the spittle was valued for its medical properties one healthy man's spittle would be as good as another's. But the blind man pleads for the spittle of the Emperor; he will accept no inferior substitute. Vespasian receives the request with incredulity. This does not suggest that spittle was a normal method of healing. When Vespasian finally agrees to the request, his action is followed not by a gradual improvement in the condition of the patient but by his miraculous healing. One could not ask for a clearer case of magical miracle based on use of a physical substance.

The Epidaurus inscriptions describe miraculous cures wrought by the lick of sacred snakes and dogs within the temples of Asclepius or at least cases where patients dreamed that they were cured in this way and awoke to find it true. E. J. and L. Edelstein show that Asclepius advised such treatments as were common to medical practice at the time: 'In popular medicine, being licked by animals was always considered helpful.'[21] Such things 're-echo the medical belief or imagination of the people'. But do they in fact echo the medical belief or the superstitious and magical belief of the people? As far as the common people were concerned these distinctions had little significance. These people did not go when ill and get themselves licked by ordinary animals. Or, if they did, nothing happened, and they came to the sacred temple of the divine healer, there to dream of the special lick of the symbolic beasts, a saliva which produced an immediate and miraculous result.

Galen's description of the value of spittle is sometimes thought to illustrate the same medical point, but examination quickly shows that it is less medical than magical in its effects. Galen, in describing the role of saliva in aiding the digestive process, says:

You may observe the extent of the alteration which occurs to food in the mouth if you will chew some corn and then apply it to an unripe boil: you will see it rapidly transmuting . . . the boil, though it cannot do anything of the kind if you mix it with water. And do not let this surprise you; this phlegm [saliva] in the mouth is also a cure for skin diseases; it even rapidly destroys scorpions; while, as regards the animals which emit venom, some it kills at once, and others after an interval; to all of them in any case it does great damage.[22]

The magical powers of saliva were effective in the psychological realm as well as in the physical. In Petronius' *Satyricon* 131, there is a description of an old woman who casts a love spell in the following way:

Then the old woman took a twist of threads of different colours out of her dress and tied it round my neck. Then she mixed some dust with spittle and took it on her middle finger and made a mark on my forehead despite my protests.

The physicians of the ancient world may have considered spittle to be a medicine, just as they considered astrology to be a science, but we should not use the word 'medicine' if we wish to give modern readers a correct impression of their view. The use of spittle was not recommended because of its rational therapeutic value but because of its efficacy as healing magic.

Examination of the later history of Christian spittle miracles, clearly under the influence of the gospel accounts, indicates the same magical framework and thus illustrates the impact of such gospel stories on the contemporary mind. Anianus, the second Patriarch of Alexandria, the successor of St Mark, was converted in the following manner. He was a sandal maker when Mark visited him to have his shoes repaired.

> And when he took the sandal to sew it, he thrust his awl into it, and it passed right through it and pierced his finger; and he said in the Greek tongue, Îstâôs (Eis Theos) which being interpreted is, 'One God'. When Saint Mark the evangelist heard him mention the Name of God, he took up some dust from the ground and spat spittle upon it, and laid it upon the finger of Anianus and healed it immediately.[23]

Anianus' conversion follows. Here the spittle is clearly not a means of raising faith or expectation but is the actual means of the miraculous healing.

On day six of month nine the martyrdom of Abbâ Macarius, the Alexandrian priestly ascetic, was celebrated in the Ethiopian church. Whilst in the desert Macarius was led by a wolf to her cave and there found that her cubs were blind. 'And he took the cubs in his hand, and cried out, and spat into their eyes, and made the sign of the Life-giving Cross over them, and the cubs were healed immediately.'[24]

Of course in this case there can be no question of faith. It is no more mentioned than it is in the synoptic cases. And it is interesting to note that the healer cries out. Was this from the effort? Is it like the sigh of Jesus? Or is it to warn and frighten the spirits?

3. *Demonic illness*

We have observed that magical techniques are often associated with exorcism. Is the healing of the Marcan deaf-mute a case of exorcism? Was this man possessed by an evil spirit?

The man is described as being deaf, κωφός, and having an

impediment in his speech, μογιλάλος. The latter could imply that the man was partially dumb and this has occasioned a great deal of discussion as to the exact nature of the complaint. At first sight there seems little which might suggest spirit possession. The fact that the man was touched by Jesus might indicate that he was sick but not possessed, since it has been claimed that Jesus did not lay hands on the possessed but always touched the sick. The paralytic in Mark 2.1–12, blind Bartimaeus (Mark 10.46–52) and the man with the withered hand (Mark 3.5) are, however, cases where the sick are not touched, so there can be no hard and fast rule about this. Perhaps the usual reason why the possessed, who were strong in body, were not touched was that they were often too violent to be approached. In Luke 9.41f. Jesus commands the epileptic boy to be brought to him apparently intending to touch him but 'Before the boy could reach him, the devil dashed him to the ground and threw him into convulsions. Jesus rebuked the unclean spirit . . .'. In Q Jesus heals the centurion's servant without touching him but, on the other hand, the Q saying about casting out devils by the finger of God suggests that it was Jesus' practice to touch the possessed wherever this was practicable. The crippled woman of Luke 13.10ff. is a clear case of sickness due to possession, and hands *are* laid upon the patient. Evidently neither the distinction between possession and mere sickness, nor that between laying and not laying on of hands, can be used to determine the nature of any given case.

In favour of the possibility that this deafness or inability to speak might have been demonic are the references in Luke 11.14; Matt. 12.22; 9.32, which describe blind or dumb possession. In Mark the dumb demon of 9.17–27 is an example of this tendency to attribute these afflictions to demons.

Less obvious, but perhaps not completely irrelevant, is the interesting case of deafness reported in Luke 1.20–22. Zacharias is said to be κωφός, which initially means dumb, for the angel tells him that he will not be able to speak. When Zacharias tries to communicate to the crowd he has to use signs. But v. 62 shows that he is also deaf, for his relatives have to make signs to him. If he were merely dumb, they could have spoken to him, of course, even if he had been unable to reply. But the deafness is not a slip on the part of Luke.[26] His intention is to show that the whole man had been sealed by the angelic curse. The similarity with Dan. 10.7–

10 has often been noticed, and Luke may well have had the experience of Daniel in mind. But Zacharias is not merely suffering from numinous shock; he is under a divine interdiction. His case is not altogether dissimilar from that of Elymas in Acts 13.11, whose sight is shut off because of his stubborn unbelief, or that of Simon (Acts 8.20–24) who is placed under a kind of incipient curse. The description of the loosening, or opening, as it is called, of Zacharias is quite similar to the opening of the deaf mute, as described in Luke 1.64 and Mark 7.35. Both are best regarded as examples of sacred deafness and dumbness caused by supernatural powers whether good or bad.

The idea of possession is further supported by the famous variant of μογιλάλος, namely, the spelling with the double gamma – μογγιλάλος. I do not wish to argue that this reading should be accepted, although I think that so far as its meaning goes it is not so inappropriate as some have suggested. I merely wish to ask what could have made a reasonably varied collection of scribes, in MSS of Caesarean, Syrian and Alexandrine types, decide against a fairly common word meaning 'speaking with difficulty' in favour of an unusual word meaning 'speaking hoarsely'. Could the answer be that in the East at any rate this was regarded as a possession story? Change of voice is a feature of possession. T. K. Oesterreich says:

At the moment when the countenance alters, a more or less changed voice issues from the mouth of the person in the fit. The intonation also corresponds to the character of the new individuality manifesting itself in the organism and is conditioned by it. In particular the top register of the voice is displaced; the feminine voice is transformed into a bass one, for in all the cases of possession which it has hitherto been my lot to know the new individuality was a man.[27]

Oesterreich[28] quotes a case reported in 1853 by F. von Baader, 'Dr U. asked her in my presence the meaning of such a laugh, to which she replied in a hoarse and deep tenor voice, with furious gestures and burning glance . . .'.

That this was an accepted feature of possession stories may be seen from the case of the possessed lad in Philostratus' *Life of Apollonius of Tyana*, III.38, where the boy is described as speaking with a deep voice and looking with strange eyes.

This variant offers a tiny glimpse into the history of this ancient pericope, a history which had already begun before Mark recorded it and which continued in the MS tradition, after it had passed through his hands.

This reinterpretation was encouraged by the original μογιλάλος (assuming it to have been original), whatever its exact meaning may have been. For if it means 'speaking with difficulty', then this also was believed to be a feature of the voice of the possessed, possession indeed providing the link between μογι- and μογγιλάλος. Accounts of such things often describe the incoherence of speech which accompanied the possession. Oesterreich (p. 20) describes a case in which a voice was heard 'which might readily have been taken for a strange one, not so much from the timbre as from the expression and articulation'. And if the man was almost entirely dumb, then his case is again covered by the cases of dumbness we have discussed. In short there is nothing in the description of this man which would lead the ancient reader to suppose that the man was not possessed by a demon,[29] and there are some reasons for thinking that ancient readers would have regarded this as being the cause of the affliction. Jesus was therefore thought of as exorcizing a demon and using this particular technique in order to do so.

We have already noticed Deissmann's suggestion that the 'bond of the tongue' is a phrase taken from the technical vocabulary of magic. It is interesting to observe that in the leaden cursing tablets, where the expression 'to bind' is so common, parts of the body are usually listed very exactly and in detail. The miracle in Mark 7.32ff. is similarly remarkable for its precision in naming parts of the body. The loosing of Zacharias' tongue is the only other New Testament miracle which mentions the tongue, and Luke's account of the miraculous healing of the severed ear in Gethsemane (Luke 22.51) is the only other one to mention the ear. The finger is mentioned in no other miracle story. Deissmann's conclusion is: 'The evangelist wishes to relate not only that a dumb man was made to speak, but that a demonic chain was broken, and that one of the works of Satan was destroyed.'[30]

This observation has not received from English scholarship the attention it deserves. Micklem[31] quotes Deissmann at length and then dismisses the material without discussion with the remark that 'Looking up to heaven he sighed' 'is a valuable reminder of how human and non-magical the actual scene was'.[32] Micklem seems to mean that if Jesus showed human emotion there could be no question of magic. This is certainly a false assumption. Intense emotion was a feature of magical operations, so much so that στενάζω actually becomes a technical term, as we shall see. A similar kind of unconsidered rejection appears in Rawlinson's commentary (p. 102). Although he mentions Deissmann's suggestion, Rawlinson says that the expression 'is of course to be understood metaphorically'. Vincent Taylor mentions Deissmann very briefly and adds, 'There is, however, nothing to suggest a case of daemon possession, . . . and it is best to regard the phrase as a figurative description of the cure.'[33] But, as we have seen, it is overstating the case to say that nothing suggests demonic possession. Cranfield says that Jesus sighs because 'the disablement is thought of as the result of demonic activity as is indicated by Εφφαθα and δεσμός' and that *Ephphatha* 'is the command that shatters the fetters by which Satan has held his victim bound'.[34] Cranfield does not mention Deissmann by name, but this seems to be the first concession in an English commentary to the suggestion made fifty years before.

4. *Details of the healing rite*

Whilst healing this man, Jesus put his fingers into the man's ears. A number of references to the finger in the gospel describe the everyday use of the literal finger,[35] but in other biblical contexts the finger appears as the symbol of God's power.[36] In this latter use it may have connections with magic and exorcism,[37] and there are many parallels in the magical literature. The origin of the idea is to be found in Egypt; the finger amulet is a popular one, the fingers being those of Horus, by which he helped his father Osiris into heaven.[38] The idea passed into the Hellenistic world and was used in ritual magic. An ostracon spell, binding Hor, the son of Mary, and preventing him from speaking against the operator, adjures him by the finger of God.[39] The finger of God is used in this spell to prevent a man speaking, just as in the Marcan case it is used to open a man's speech.

The fingers were regarded as possessing sympathy with the various planets, and a certain type of coral was called 'the finger of Adonis' because of its sympathetic rapport with the Syrian god. Beliefs like these lie behind the widespread use of fingernails in magic – one is using the powerful extremities of a person against himself.[40]

The case in Mark 7.35 seems to be typical of magical exorcism. It is a case of casting out devils by the finger of God. It is noteworthy that Jesus thrusts his fingers into the man's ears,[41] and this can be understood in the light of exorcism. The evil spirit must make its exit through a particular part of the body, through an extremity, or an orifice. The reason for the screaming which accompanies the exit of demons is that the demon is considered to be leaving through the mouth.

> The ejected spirit left the patient's body in various ways: either it came out through the excretions of the body . . . or it passed out in wind. Sometimes however such natural channels of exit were not used, but the magician called upon the affected parts of the body to 'open their mouths' and disgorge what was within them, which seems to imply the belief that the magician could make a fortuitous opening in the body for the purpose of ridding it of its possessing influence.[42]

The man was often regarded often as being sealed off by the spirit and an opening must be made. This sealing off could be effected by a good spirit, and spittle as well as boring could be effective for both sealing or unsealing. In the *Book of the Saints of the Ethiopian Church* the twelfth day of the fourth month celebrates Abbâ Samuel of Wâldĕbbâ. The description of him contains this sentence: 'And as Abbâ Samuel was praying our Lord Jesus Christ came to him, and sealed his whole body and each limb thereof with His spittle, and he became filled with power.'

This elucidates the connection between spitting and opening the ears. Both are connected with the process of opening. The textual tradition bears witness to this association and again illustrates the familiarity of the ancient world with the technique used here. D a b c ff i q et al all have πτύσας before ἔβαλεν, so making both actions apply to the ears, and W, fam 13 et al, although reversing the order of the two words, agree that the spitting and boring both had to do with the ears. 0131 says that 'Jesus spat on his fingers and placed them in the ears of the deaf man and touched his tongue.' In none of these MSS is Jesus thought of as moistening the lips to encourage speech. He is regarded as carrying out the manual rite of exorcism in preparation for the brief oral rite which follows.

The break between the two parts of the ritual is marked by a sigh. Examples of this are found in the magical papyri. The Great Paris Papyrus contains a charm which ends with the rubric: 'After reciting this, throw incense on the fire, groan loudly, and descend, going backwards.'[44]

In *PGM* VII.768ff., instructions are given as to how parts of an incantation are to be said: 'The second, smacking of the lips or clucking, the third sighing, the fourth hissing'. In *PGM* XIII.946, the magician is to take as big a breath as he can and then, groaning, to let it out with a hissing sound.[45]

But may not the sighing indicate a mood of Jesus? This is unlikely. In general the accounts of the miracles are remarkable for the lack of interest shown in the emotions of Jesus and his patients.[46] Oddly enough, the use of the strongly emotional ἐμβριμάομαι in connection with miracles[47] is also illuminated by magical usage.[48] We cannot tell if the story of the deaf mute contained some such word, because the original ending of the story has been obscured by an editorial addition in which Jesus sternly charges them not to say anything. It looks as if in the healing stories, just as in the exorcisms proper, the original technical details of the ritual have been made to serve the interests of the later theological editor. An interesting comment is made by Menzies.

He sighs deeply, which might be taken to denote the act, to be imitated by the patient, of forcing up a blast of air from the lungs into the ear-tubes and the mouth, as if to clear away any obstruction which may exist there. . . . the sigh soon came to be taken as a sigh of emotion, though of what emotion, no one of course can say.[49]

Although he was not in a position to interpret his observation in the light of magic, Menzies had astutely seen that imitation is the vital thing about the action. Commentators usually refer to Rom. 8.26, the inexpressible groans, and it is certainly true that if this man had an impediment in his speech or was speaking in an unnatural or incoherent manner this expression would describe rather well what his efforts would sound like. But it is not the patient but Jesus who makes the sound. It seems likely that this is a case of sympathetic magic, the sighing being in imitation not only of the restoration of speech, but as Menzies' description suggests, of forcing out the in-dwelling demon.[50]

Next we have the word of power itself, 'Ephphatha', Mark adding 'which means "Be opened"'. Foreign words are a very familiar feature of magic spells and the papyri are full of examples. What counted as foreign names and strange sounds naturally depended on the situation of the magician. In the Coptic magical papyri Greek appears as the strange and forbiddingly authentic sound, while in the Greek magical world Jewish names and words had special prestige. The general practice was to summon a god or demon by the tongue he was believed to understand or which stood in some relationship of sympathy to that god.[51] So it is only to be expected that Jesus, a Jewish wonder-worker operating on Palestinian demons with the power of the great Hebrew God, should utter his commands in a Jewish language. Aramaic is used rather than Hebrew, perhaps since Aramaic, being the spoken tongue, would tend to creep into the stories as they were repeatedly told. The magicians would be little concerned about distinctions between the two languages; both had the flavour of authentic Palestinian power.

But in Mark's narrative the barbaric word is translated. Might that not expose the secret and destroy its magic power? The opposite may well be the case. For the magician usually needed to know the meaning of what he was controlling.[52] The foreign expressions are sometimes translated into Greek for the professional use of the healers and exorcists. So in the 'Door-opener' in *PGM* XXXVI.315, the Coptic words of power are introduced by 'This is the word' and followed by the Greek equivalent 'be opened be opened'. The translation of the powerful word therefore must not be thought inconsistent with its magical provenance.

A final indication that the actions associated with the cure of the deaf mute are indeed ritual and not merely symbolic or emotional may be seen in the influence which this particular story has had on the development of later Christian miracles. The type of influence suggests that the story was interpreted as therapeutic magic. The following story is told of St Peter Martyr (St Peter of Gallia Cisalpina) when he was preaching in Milan.

One day . . . some devout people brought to him a man who had been dumb for ten years. The holy man put his finger in the dumb man's mouth, touched the tongue, and cried, 'Be opened!' whereupon the man spake plainly.[53]

The foreign word is lacking in this account, but it is present – and translated into French this time – in the following story.

In the legend of Clotilde we learn how the blind and deaf were cured by Remi[54] who wet his fingers with saliva and applied them to the eyes and ears of the afflicted persons, pronouncing the word *Hephta* (ouvrez-vous).[55]

St Peter II, the archbishop of Tarentaise (1103–1174), was approached by a woman who implored him to heal her blind son.

The saint bade the lad come forward; then, wetting his fingers with spittle, he rubbed them across the sightless eyes, making on them the sign of the cross. The kings and princes watched anxiously the result. All of a sudden the boy exclaimed, 'Hurrah! hurrah! I see my mother, I see the trees, I see men and women, I see everything.'[56]

The continued use of Ephphatha in the baptism ritual of the church (which was also exorcism) can hardly be accounted for except by the supposition that the word was believed in itself to possess remarkable power.

Many other examples of the impact of the magical tradition on St Mark could be considered and some will be dealt with in the synoptic comparisons which follow. The material offered above must serve to illustrate the relationship between the Christian traditions and magic expressed in Dibelius' apt phrase, 'Mysterious magic surrounds the figure of the wonder-worker.'[57]

VI

LUKE: THE TRADITION
PENETRATED BY MAGIC

Luke is the only New Testament writer who specifically refers to the church's attack on magic. This is no accident, nor is it due to mere historical curiosity on the part of Luke. The magical episodes are an aspect of Luke's world-view. They follow from his view of angels, of demons, of spiritual reality in general, from his view of the cosmic conflict and its weapons of δύναμις and ἐξουσία. This is the framework of a magical universe.[1] In the writings of a first century Christianized Hellenist with such a background, magic was bound to emerge because it was merely an appropriate tactic in a battle the strategy of which demands such tactics. Luke wrote about magic because he saw and believed.

We shall trace the Lucan view and, having established its nature and determined the extent to which it is similar to the magical world-view, we will then be in a position to ascertain the significance of the specifically magical episodes.

1. *Angels*

In both Matthew and Luke the role of angels is prominent. Luke 1.9–20 describes the angel of the Lord, his name, his message and his curse. The same angel appears on another errand (vv. 26–38) and gives a blessing. A nameless angelic announcer is accompanied in 2.9–13 by the Host of the Lord. In 22.43 an angel brings strength to the praying Christ and in 24.4 two angels announce the resurrection. These are the only interventions by angels in the narrative sections of Luke's gospel but angels are referred to in a number of other contexts.[2]

Matthew's references to angelic interventions are as follows. In 1.20; 2.13 and 19 (cf. vv. 12 and 22) an angel appears in a dream to

Joseph. Angels minister to the victorious Christ after his temptations (4.11, cf. Mark 1.13) and a magnificent angel rolls back the stone from the tomb and terrifies the guards (28.2ff.), Matthew and Luke therefore both record three angelic visitations during the period covered by their gospels. They agree that angels were associated with both the birth and the resurrection of Christ but, whereas Matthew also associates them with the temptations in the wilderness, Luke connects them with the later temptation in Gethsemane. Matthew however records about twice as many sayings of Jesus about angels.[3]

To the evidence in Luke's gospel we are able to add that of the Acts. Here we find a quite phenomenal outburst of angelic activity, mostly in the form of direct intervention. Angels rebuke disciples for lingering after the ascension (1.10f.); in 5.19 an angel releases the apostles from prison and in 8.26 an angel tells Philip to make a journey. Cornelius sees in a vision (10.3ff.) an angel who is referred to also in vv. 22 and 30, and 11.13. Peter is released from prison by an angel in 12.7–10, an angel kills Herod Antipas in 12.23, and an angel brings a message of comfort to the storm-tossed Paul in 27.23. The distinction between angels and the Spirit is not made sharply in Acts, so one cannot attach great weight to the number, but there are about seven occasions upon which the divine intervention is attributed to angels.[4]

Both Matthew and Luke appear to accept the ordinary Jewish belief in angels,[5] in which angels were particularly associated with the events described in the apocalyptic books.[6] All of the dominical sayings mentioning angels recorded by Matthew have an eschatological context, with the exception of 18.10 (angels of 'little ones') and 26.53 (the angels Christ could have summoned). Matthew's emphasis on angels indicates little special interest in them as an order of spiritual beings, but is simply part of his emphasis on eschatology. This applies particularly to the synoptic allusions to God, the Son of Man, and the Holy Angels, a familiar triad in Jewish non-canonical apocalyptic.[7] But the fact that Luke retains the angels as witnesses of the Last Judgment in Luke 12.8f., while Matthew substitutes the phrase 'before my father in heaven' (Matt. 10.32, cf. Mark 8.38), is simply due to Luke's faithfulness to the eschatology of the Palestinian Q material,[8] and not to any particular interest in this eschatological feature of the angelic ministry on the part of Luke.

Matthew and Luke not only accept the view of the role of angels in the non-canonical apocalyptic; they also agree with the ideas about the role and theological significance of the Angel of the Lord in the canonical Old Testament. The role of the Angel of the Lord is often less distinct than that of an individual messenger of God; his role is rather that of representing God so intimately that 'He is the personification of Yahweh's assistance to Israel'.[9] This shift of identification to and fro between the Angel of the Lord and the Lord himself is clearly seen in the story about Philip and the eunuch. It is the 'Angel of the Lord' who speaks to Philip in Acts 8.26 but in v. 29 it is 'the Spirit' and in v. 39 the 'Spirit of the Lord' snatches Philip away. Note also that in Acts 16.6 they are forbidden by the 'Holy Spirit' to preach in Asia, in v. 7 the 'Spirit of Jesus' restrains them and in v. 10 they conclude, having seen 'a man of Macedonia', that 'God' is calling them.

We have a continuum from 'man' through 'angel' and 'Spirit' and 'Jesus' to 'God'.[10] Jesus is 'man' (Acts 17.31; 2.22) and the angels are also 'men' (Luke 24.4; Acts 1.10; 10.30). The divine messenger in Acts 16.9 is probably not a representation of an inhabitant of Macedonia but rather the representative angel of the Macedonians. This is likely, not only in view of the association of this 'man' with 'Spirit', 'Jesus', 'God', and the links between these words and 'angel', but also in view of the dependence of Luke's angelology at many points upon Daniel,[11] the only Old Testament book which refers to angels as representing various regions and their inhabitants. It will at any rate be generally agreed that in Luke and in Matthew the angels play little independent role but are the representatives of God and Jesus. Matthew 28 is the nearest approach in the New Testament to an independent angelic initiative.

Although there is this broad similarity between the conceptions and the roles of angels in Matthew and Luke, there are also certain differences which may not be wholly without significance. In Matt. 1.20; 2.13 and 2.19, the angel appears 'in a dream'. (In 2.12, 22 communication between God and man takes place by means of the dream alone without any mention of angelic ministration.) The angels are not seen; they arouse no fear. There is no human reaction of surprise, and usually no angelic salutation. When Joseph is told by the angel not to be afraid, the object of his fear is his uncertainty about Mary, not the sight of the angel; he sees no

angel face to face, only in sleep. The angels who minister to the
weary Christ after his temptations are introduced slightly more
dramatically than in Mark 1.13 by the addition of 'behold' (Matt.
4.11) and their presence is made more actual by the addition of
προσῆλθον. Their function is that of ministering, which is possibly
taken from Mark 1.13. The description however remains general
and stereotyped. Quite different and indeed unique in Matthew is
the description of the angel at the resurrection. We read of his
descent from heaven, the earthquake which accompanies it, his
action in rolling away the stone and sitting on it. This is no dream
nor vision; the appearance and clothing of the angel are described,
as are the reactions of the guards and the women. The external
reality is also indicated by the fact that unlike the dream-angels this
angel admonishes his conscious audience (the guards being 'like
dead men') not to fear.

The interesting feature of Luke is that this vivid reality which is
so unusual in Matthew is normal in his writings. The form in
which the angel appears in the Lucan writings is often expressed
by ὤφθη. This word often describes the appearing in visionary
form of a supernatural being; it is thus used of angels in Luke 1.11;
22.43; Acts 7.30, 35; 16.9. One must not overemphasize any
intangible visionary aspect which the word may suggest, for the
same word is used of the risen Christ in Luke 24.34 in spite of the
fact that Luke, more than any other New Testament writer,
stresses the physical and tangible nature of the risen body of the
Lord. This is not an isolated case; in Acts 9.17; 13.31 and 26.16a
the 'appearances' (if such a word can apply to the flesh and bones
Lord) are similarly described. In Luke 9.31 the appearance of
Moses and Elijah on the mountain is described by the use of the
same word and reasons will be given below to show that the
transfiguration in Luke is not regarded as a vision but as a literal
manifestation of spiritual realities. In Acts 2.3 the tongues of fire
distributed upon the apostles 'appear' to them, and this is clearly
not intended by Luke to describe an experience of a subjective
nature. The God of glory is said to 'appear' to Abraham in Acts
7.2, and in 7.26 Moses 'appears' to the quarrelling Egyptians.

The following further vivid details of angelic appearances in
Luke–Acts may be noted. In Luke 1.11 the exact place where the
angel is standing is described and in Acts 11.13 the angel of
Cornelius appears 'in his house' whilst Peter's angel appears in the

prison cell (Acts 12.7). The place from which the angel has come is mentioned in Luke 1.26 ('from God') and again in 22.43 'from heaven'. The time of the visitation is referred to in Luke 1.11: 'it was the hour of the incense offering'; 1.26: 'in the sixth month'; Acts 10.3: 'about three in the afternoon'. The approach of the angel is often mentioned,[12] and the reactions of the human beings are described. The range of activities performed by the angels is remarkably wide. They may convey news that prayer has been heard and answered (Luke 1.13: Acts 10.4), they may pronounce a curse (Luke 1.20) or even kill (Acts 12.23); they may be sent with a message which the recipient has not expected (Luke 1.30f.; 2.11), they may sing (Luke 2.13), they may bring strength (Luke 22.43), they may even open doors (Acts 5.19). In Acts 12.7 the angel actually taps Peter on the shoulder, waking him up. Then he gives Peter detailed dressing instructions and leads him through various corridors and guard posts to the street outside. The departure of an angel is often referred to just as clearly as his arrival.[13] In Luke 2.15 the angels return 'into heaven'.

We see then that in Luke the visits of the angels are regarded as literal events. The angels are sent, having arrived they 'enter', 'stand near' or 'appear', they perform their tasks and then they return to heaven. They are experienced by men more directly than in Matthew or indeed in any other part of the New Testament. Notice that Luke does not say that the angels appear κατ᾽ ὄναρ 'in a dream', but makes it clear on the contrary that the recipients of the appearances are fully awake. They may be busy about their duties (Luke 1.11; 2.8; 24.1f.) or praying (Luke 22.43f.; Acts 10.30). Only once does an angel appear to a sleeping man (Acts 12.6) and here the first thing the angel does is to wake him. Twice Luke uses ὀπτασία (Luke 1.22 and 24.23), but in both cases it describes what the people understand Zacharias and the women to have seen rather than a description of the actual appearance. In Acts 26.19 Paul describes the Damascus road experience as being an ὀπτασία; cf. also the use of the word in Luke 24.23. More frequent in Luke–Acts is the description ὅραμα 'vision'. Thus the Macedonian figure is a vision (Acts 16.9f.) and so is the sheet lowered from heaven (Acts 10.17, 19; 11.5). The Lord may speak through a vision (Acts 18.9; 9.10) and God himself appears as a vision in the burning bush (Acts 7.31). But only once is an angel described as appearing in a vision; that is in Acts 10.3 and it is significant that

Luke emphasizes the external vividness of the perception by adding 'clearly': 'He saw in a vision clearly'. Of the angel who
releases Peter from prison we are specifically told, in an expression
unusual even in Luke for its bluntness, that Peter had 'no idea that
the angel's intervention was real; he thought it was just a vision'
(Acts 12.9) but of the rest of the angelic appearances Luke never
uses ὄναρ, ὀπτασία or ὅραμα. The angels are real.

Luke's angels have a militant role to play. It is significant that
Luke 1.11–19 is modelled on Dan. 9.21–23, and that in Daniel for
the first time in Jewish literature we find an angelology as one side
of two cosmic warring forces. Luke's angels are not passive
spectators but actual combatants in the struggle. One who opposes
the angelic word which is of course the divine word is bound
with a solemn binding curse (Luke 1.20) and, when the bond
is broken by the fulfilment of the word, Zacharias speaks of
salvation from enemies 'and from the hand of all who hate us'
(Luke 1.71). The function of the angel in 2.10f. is to proclaim the
birth of the Hero–Saviour, at which announcement the heavenly
host appear. These are certainly not merely a choir but an army
hailing their Chieftain and proclaiming the peace which his salvation is to produce.[14] The angel in Gethsemane is likewise engaged
in conflict, participating in the final battle between Christ and
Satan, strengthening Christ for his ordeal. The angels in Acts intervene when enemy forces have locked the apostles in prison, or
when an enemy king is exulting in victory and supposed divinity
(Acts 12.23), or when the apostle is surrounded by potentially
hostile soldiers and in danger from the elements (Acts 27.23).

The angels are opposed by another host.[15] Sometimes they are
described as a legion (Luke 8.30) and they may move around in
smaller groups ('seven other spirits', Luke 11.26). Once this other
army is called 'the host of heaven' (Acts 7.42) but usually it dwells
on earth or under it.[16] It also has its Hero-Saviour, 'the leader of
the demons' (Luke 11.15) whereas Jesus is the true 'Leader and
Saviour' (Acts 5.31). Satan has a kingdom (Luke 11.18) as has
God, and each kingdom has its own ἐξουσία (Acts 26.18); one
realm is darkness, the other light (Acts 26.18).[17]

It is interesting to notice the similarity between angelic activity
in the book of Tobit and in Luke–Acts. In Tob. 3.16f. and 12.12
the angel Raphael is sent in answer to the prayers of the righteous,
as other angels are in Luke 1.13 and Acts 10.4. In Tob. 5.4 the

angel takes the form of a man and is mistaken by Tobias for one. The angel accompanies the hero on his journey (cf. Acts 8.26ff.) making it a prosperous and safe journey as in Acts 27.22ff. Paul describes his cheering companion as an angel of God, and Tobit speaks (5.16) of the angel of God who shall keep the traveller company. In Tob. 12.15, the climax of the story, the angel solemnly declares his name and his privileged position in God's presence, just as he does in Luke 1.19. In Tob. 12.19 the angel declares that during the adventure they have been seeing a vision (ὅρασις). Luke uses this word only in Acts 2.17, quoting Joel, but the conception is in full agreement with the literal and external reality of the angel 'appearances' in Luke–Acts. In Tob. 12.19 the angel explains his refusal to eat and drink as being due to his angelic constitution and this may be in Luke's mind when he, alone of the evangelists, describes the risen Christ as *both* eating and drinking.[18] If this is so, Luke's intention is to stress that the risen Christ is no angel. The anti-Docetic motif stresses that he is no spirit either. This polemic against both angel and spirit could be significant in view of the fact that in Acts 23.9 πνεῦμα and ἄγγελος are used as identical terms. For the manner in which the angel's departure is expressly described (Tob. 12.21), compare the Lucan passages referred to above, and for the thankful realization following his departure ('Then they confessed the great and wonderful works of God, and how the angel of the Lord had appeared unto them', Tob. 12.22), cf. Peter's words in Acts 12.11; 'Now I am sure that the Lord has sent his angel and rescued me', and possibly also the joy of the shepherds in Luke 2.15 over 'this thing which the Lord has made known to us'.

The particularly interesting feature of the Tobit angelology is that Tobit is one of the few non-apocalyptic books in which angels play a significant role.[19] We have already observed that unlike Matthew's angels those of Luke are not primarily connected with eschatological events, but are like Tobit's angel removed from the apocalyptic to the mundane plane, and are moreover involved in struggles against demons as warriors. Raphael is both a warrior and an exorcist of surpassing skill, and Luke's angels continue these roles, although less prominently because of the presence of the Lord himself.

In Luke 20.34–36 we are given a remarkable glimpse into the angelic world. Luke adds the phrase 'the sons of this age marry and are given in marriage' thus heightening the contrast between the customs of the inhabitants of this world and of the world to come, the world already realized by the angels. Mark's wording is a simple contrast between the two states (. . . 'but are as the angels' Mark 12.25) but Luke's version contains a reason for the absence of marriage and (his addition) death as well, when he writes '. . . for they are equal unto the angels'. Luke is drawing implications from angelic nature; Mark is merely stating a difference. For ὡς ἄγγελοι (Mark 12.25; Matt. 22.30) Luke writes ἰσάγγελοι γὰρ εἰσιν thus saying not what they are *like* but what they are. Once again we notice Luke's dislike for parable and metaphor when describing heavenly realities. An interesting point which arises is whether Luke thought these departed humans were an actual order of beings.

We have already seen that miracles are associated both with magical writings and with eschatological writings. The same is now seen to be true of angels. The main Jewish tradition associates them with eschatological events, but important witnesses also testify to angels in the magical tradition. In Matthew angels and miracles are firmly in the eschatological setting; in Luke they are more clearly influenced by the magical tradition. They appear in Luke not only as symbols of the final divine intervention, marking the inrush of the Kingdom of God, but also as literal powers competing in the struggle with demonic power on the worldly and temporal level. The angelology of the Testament of Solomon represents the complete conquest of the eschatological setting, for there angels play no eschatological role at all but are entirely concerned with defeating the demons by magical means.[20] Between Daniel and Matthew, on the one hand, and Tobit and the Testament of Solomon, on the other, the writings of Luke occupy an uneasy intermediate position.

The picture we have drawn of the objective reality of the angelic world in Luke's thought is further elaborated by the fact that manifestations of this spiritual world take an objectively realistic shape. One of the clearest examples is the dove descending upon Jesus bodily (Luke 3.22), a Lucan detail which has never been adequately explained. Bernhard Weiss found here an illustration of a tendency he believed he could trace for events to become more and more concrete in the course of the transmission of the tradition, but it is doubtful if this can be sustained.[21] Rengstorf, on the other hand, does not regard the dove in bodily form as a legendary addition; 'Luke selects the expression . . . because he wishes to describe not what the Baptist saw but what, during his baptism, Jesus saw.'[22] This however is surely a mistake. It is Mark who says 'Jesus saw', but Luke does not say who saw the dove. Because his view is more objective, the sight of the dove cannot be restricted to one person rather than another and Luke is quite consistent in omitting to mention the viewer. The words must be allowed their full force and seen in the light of the quasi-physical nature of both πνεῦμα and δύναμις in Luke.

One of the greatest manifestations of the reality of the super-natural world in Luke, as in all the synoptics, is the transfiguration. It is Luke alone however who stresses the objective reality of the incident. Luke in 9.32, a detail peculiar to him, mentions the fact that the disciples were not asleep. They had been asleep, and when they awoke they saw his glory. They were not in a trance or a dream but fully awake and conscious. Luke omits to record that Jesus was transfigured *before them*. There are in fact no human witnesses of the actual transformation and of the conversation. It is practically over before the disciples awake. Many commentators take the awakening to mean that it is taking place at night but in fact it is intended to heighten the objectivity. It is no subjective vision since it takes place independently of witnesses.[23] Luke refers to Moses and Elijah but their presence should be simply translated, with the Jerusalem Bible, 'appearing in glory' not, as Moffatt translates, 'who appeared in a vision of glory'; for the English word 'vision' suggests something rather less objective than what Luke had in mind. Luke is the only evangelist to report the substance of the heavenly conversation, making it clear that the event is really about something, a genuine conference on a vital subject and not merely a static image of splendour. Luke moves Peter's fear from his offer to build three tabernacles to the moment of actually entering the cloud. The expression 'they entered the cloud' is also peculiar to Luke. So the cloud is not only symbolic; it creates fear by its physical impact around them. In Matthew the fear is attached to the hearing of the divine voice, it is worshipful awe; in Mark it is numinous dread; in Luke it is numinous dread inspired by the physical presence of the cloud in such circumstances. Finally, whereas in Matt. 17.9 they are told not to tell anyone of the vision, in Luke 9.36 'they told no one what they had seen', it being no vision. The total impact of the Lucan version is one of remarkable actuality, fully consistent with his treatment of the baptism and resurrection appearances of Jesus, the Pentecostal outpouring, and the nature of the spiritual world itself, of which these are but the visible manifestations.

2. Demons

With his vivid sense of the reality of the angelic world, Luke as one would expect combines an equally vivid demonology and in particular a realistic view of Satan. Just as the angels intervene on the side of God, so Satan intervenes against God. As with the angels, so the most dramatic Satanic interventions take place at the beginning of Christ's ministry, at its end, and during the spread of the young church. Satan (as in Matthew) three times tempts Christ in the wilderness and then 'leaves him for a season' which indicates that the periods of temptation are intermittent. There is no general, continuous testing but a series of specific Satanic visitations.[24] The final temptation begins from Luke 22.3 when Satan takes possession of the body of Judas (cf. John 13.2 where Satan merely changes Judas' mind). The closing scenes are set against a backdrop of cosmic powers (Luke 22.31, 43ff., 53). Apart from his pressure upon Christ at these two vital points Satan has a remarkable range of contacts with men in the Lucan writings. He takes possession of people and keeps them his prisoners for many years (13.16, Luke only). Having successfully penetrated the apostolic ranks by his possession of Judas (22.3, Luke only) then he casts his eye on Peter also (22.31, Luke only) and is only held at bay by the prayers of Christ. He is anxious to prevent the addition of converts to the kingdom and so he 'takes away the word which has been sown in them', 'for fear', as only Luke adds, 'they should believe and be converted' (Luke 8.12). The angels on the other hand rejoice over the conversion of a sinner (15.7, 10, Luke only). What happens to Satan is however known to the Messiah (10.18, Luke only) who has seen him fall from heaven. Frustrated in the case of Peter (Luke 22.54–62) whom the Lord prayed for and looked at (22.61, Luke only) and having killed Judas (Acts 1.18f.) he seeks an abode in Ananias and is successful in possessing him and making him lie to the Holy Spirit (Acts 5.3). There are no signs of his activity during the forty days of the Lord's appearances, but the ascension with its consequent removal of Christ at least bodily from Satan's earthly kingdom, the sphere of his activity (Luke 4.6; 10.18), seems to bring about an outburst of renewed activity against the young church. Like Judas and the possessed swine of Luke 8.33, Ananias, his mind filled with Satan, does not survive long, and Satan's next opponent is Paul who is given a commission to do exactly what Satan most feared (Luke 8.12), namely, to bring men from his kingdom into that of God (Acts 26.18). In connection with Satan's kingdom Luke teaches that it was not always his but it has been given to him, presumably by God (Luke 4.6b). Nevertheless he has power over it, it is in his hands, he can delegate the authority to those of his own choice. This kingdom is firmly united under Satan (Luke 11.18) and although Christ weakens that kingdom by his onslaught he does not divide it internally. Just as the kingdom of God has its hours of crisis when it rushes in with great force (Luke 11.20; 9.27; 12.32–40; Acts 2.1ff.) so Satan's kingdom has its moments of great authority and power (Luke 22.53). Men enslaved by him are blinded in the darkness of his realm (Acts 26.18).

In contrast, Matthew's treatment of the devil, like his treatment of angels, is relatively colourless. He has no interest in the devil's rights and power (cf. Matt. 4.8 with Luke 4.6), and does not elaborate on his aims and purposes (Matt. 13.19; cf. Luke 8.12). In Matt. 13.39, one of the few references to the devil in the material unique to Matthew's gospel, the devil is described as an enemy, seeking to confuse the church by introducing his followers into it. Apart from the Q Beelzebul controversy, the only other reference to Satan in Matthew is the metaphorical description of Peter under that name in Matt. 16.23. There is no Lucan parallel to this. In the Matthew passage Peter is not Satan, nor is he possessed by Satan; all that Jesus means is that in tempting him Peter is acting like a Satan. Luke's view of the reality of Satan is such that, disliking ambiguous metaphor, he omits the reference altogether, having in its place a literal description of a moment when Peter was in real danger of actually becoming Satan (Luke 22.31f.). The contrast between the two gospels can be seen very clearly in their different attitudes towards Peter's denial. In Matthew it is a pietistic account of sin and repentance (Matt. 26.75); in Luke it is a description of Satan's attempt to 'sift you like wheat' (Luke 22.31) – there is a significant juxtaposition in Luke 22.6of. of the cock-crow (the

signal in rabbinic belief for the departure of the evil spirits)[25] and
the unique Lucan tradition of the Lord's look. This is undoubtedly
the incident Jesus was predicting in Luke 22.31f. But in Matthew
there is no sense of diabolical pressure, as there is in the writings
of Luke, where the devil is almost constantly prowling, probing,
testing a weak link here, snatching a trophy there, being opposed
and often defeated but returning to resume his relentless attack.

In Luke's work Satan is the chief of a vast number of spiritual
beings. This host is conceived in a much more detailed and vivid
manner than in the other gospels, in spite of the fact that Matthew's
demonic vocabulary is actually more varied than that of Luke. The
situation is rather similar to the angelology where, as we saw,
although Matthew has more actual references, his angelology is
less vivid than that of Luke. The Lucan demons and their leader
are engaged in a contest with Jesus and the kingdom of God, a
contest of which Jesus is fully conscious from the first.

This is seen in the Lucan version of the temptation story.
According to Matthew it is not until the end of the series of
temptations that Jesus identifies the tempter, greeting him as
Satan. Matthew regards the identification, naming, and consequent
departure of Satan as the climax of the incident and it is followed
by the relief provided by the angels (Matt. 4.11). We may assume
that it is the offer of the kingdoms of this world and the blasphe-
mous invitation to worship which revealed to Jesus the true nature
of his adversary. While in Luke the devil departs because he has
come to the end of his temptations, in Matthew he departs because
he has been commanded to depart. What in Matthew is a defeat for
Satan is in Luke merely a strategic and well-timed withdrawal. In
Luke's account there is no recognition scene. In Matthew the
recognition precludes further temptation, but in Luke Jesus is
tempted again and again although he knows full well that the
source of the temptation is diabolic. Since in the Lucan account of
the temptation to worship, Satan (in the manner of supernatural
visitors) declares his role and function and states his powers even
more clearly than he does in Matthew, we must assume that at this
point, if not earlier, the Lucan Jesus knew his enemy. Since in
Luke's order there is another temptation to come, Satan can hardly
be told to leave. And if Luke's order is original, we may assume
that Luke was not troubled over the fact that Jesus listens to what
he knows is the voice of the devil. Assuming the originality of

Luke's order we may conclude that Matthew was troubled by this thought and that this was indeed one of the factors which prompted him to move the worship temptation into the final position, adding the command to depart to emphasize the point. If, however, Matthew's order is original, it is a still more remarkable fact that Luke prolongs the period of self-conscious opposition to the devil by having the devil announce himself earlier than his source demanded. On either hypothesis the fact remains. Jesus and Satan are locked in mortal struggle.[26] Here is no simple demonstration of messianic power with an immediate result once the Saviour decides to terminate the struggle, but a tense drama with the outcome still wide open. Although temporarily frustrated, Satan, as the reader of the gospel is made to realize, will soon resume the onslaught.

Before we examine the manner by which Jesus deals with this evil host of Satan, let us look at some of the details of the Lucan demonology. In view of the principle we have seen working out in the ancient world-view, that magic does not necessarily include demonology but that demonology seems to be always associated in some degree with magic, this is an important part of our inquiry as to the general world-view of Luke.

In Luke 8.1–3 we find a section unique to Luke which includes a description of 'a number of women who had been set free from evil spirits' and in particular of Mary 'from whom seven devils had come out'. Here we have another case of demons moving about in groups of seven (cf. Luke 11.26 = Matt. 12.45). Although the commentaries are almost unanimous in claiming that this indicates nothing but a very severe case of possession, this is not the best explanation of the passage. When the degree of evil of a spirit is being described our sources simply say, as here, 'spirits more wicked'. If the devils are particularly dangerous they are described as χαλεποὶ λίαν (only Matt. 8.28). In cases of severe possession we are told that the possession is 'bad' as in Matt. 15.22. Compare the description of the epileptic lad in Matt. 17.15, 'He is possessed and is ill'. Details then follow which provide evidence of severity of this particular case. The fact that special varieties of spirits were recognized, some of which were more severe and more difficult to deal with is indicated by Mark's comment: 'This sort will only come out after prayer and fasting' (Mark 9.29 only). The degrees of relative strength in the spirit world are also indicated by

Luke 11.21f., where Luke, but not Matthew, has a contrast between a strong spirit and an even stronger one. In other cases the severe nature of such a disturbance is described by using such a verb as ἐνοχλέω (Luke 6.18).

There were then many ways by which severe possession by dangerous spirits could be described, and it seems most likely that when Luke did not use these expressions but spoke instead of seven spirits he meant what he said. We have here a diagnosis which, although it may have begun with the observation of severe symptoms, has moved behind the symptoms to find their cause in a demonic ontology.[27]

Another interesting case where demonic possession is described so as to imply a clear, detailed and literal demonic world is found in Luke's version of the Gerasene madman. Luke delays the description of the man's condition (Mark 5.4f.; Luke 8.29b) so that it seems to become part of the diabolical diagnosis and not, as it is in Mark, merely human interest. Luke's explanation of Legion, the name of the devils, is a little more explicit. Mark reports 'because we are many' but Luke says 'because many demons had entered into him.' Luke is explicit about their location 'in the man' and is equally explicit about their true dwelling place – 'into the abyss' (v. 31) while Mark merely has 'out of the country' (5.10).

Water was a potent demon-destroying force. In Test.Sol. 5.11 the demon Asmodeus pleads, 'I pray thee, King Solomon, condemn me not to go into water.' In Test.Sol. 11.6 there is a passage added to the document under Christian influence. It describes the method by which the lion-shaped demon is controlled, namely by Emmanuel, and the demon says, 'He it is who has bound us and who will then come and plunge us from the steep under water.' This text shows that the fate of the Gerasene demons was regarded by the Christian editor as that of extinction by drowning, a fate feared by the lion-demon also.

More than any other evangelist, Luke sees ordinary life as penetrated by diabolical agencies. His version in 4.38f. of the fever of Peter's mother-in-law is a typical case. Luke transforms the scene into an exorcism.[28] In reporting the question from John the Baptist, only Luke adds the comment that Jesus then and there healed many who had evil spirits (Luke 7.21; cf. Matt. 11.5) although this addition is quite gratuitous, since the answer of Jesus, derived from Q, contains no reference to evil spirits. This editorial addition speaks volumes for Luke's conception of the ever present demonic world. Luke's description of the crippled woman in 13.10–17 is another example of the way Luke sees the wiles of demons even in the most obviously physical of ailments. This woman is not mentally disturbed in any way (contrast Mark's possessed who are not physically disabled) yet she is described as having been bound by Satan for many years.

Comparison of the Lucan version of the alien exorcist with the Marcan parallel reveals a typical Lucan attitude towards demons. According to Mark, Jesus said to the disciples,

> Do not stop him; no one who does a work of divine power in my name will be able in the same breath to speak evil of me . . . If anyone gives you a cup of water to drink because you are followers of the Messiah, that man assuredly will not go unrewarded (Mark 9.39ff.)

The reason for accepting the alien exorcist is that in view of the nature of his work he cannot blaspheme Christ. The comment about giving the cup of water is consistent with this. Mark's interest is devotional; the outsider is acceptable because he is potentially (in the case of the exorcist) or actually (in the case of the charitable stranger who gives the drink) reverential towards Christ. For Luke these pious reflections are inappropriate. Jesus' answer is blunt; 'Do not stop him, for he who is not against you is on your side' (Luke 9.50). There is but a single reason for not hindering the work of the alien exorcist – 'he is on your side'. In the intensity of the struggle against the demons, any ally is accepted with relief.²⁹ Whereas Mark is concerned for the exorcizing warrior to pay due reverence to the king, Luke is concerned only for him to fight the kingdom's enemies. This is no time for well-meaning religious feelings, no time for cautious piety. The Marcan Christ says (9.40), 'He who is not against *us* is on *our* side'. The change reflects the position in Luke of the apostolic church which had been given power over all the power of the enemy (Luke 9.1). The battle is henceforth between the heavenly community and the diabolical community. Since the struggle between the respective heads of the communities, although still proceeding, has already been decided in principle (Luke 4.1–10), it is now up to the church. The struggle against demonic power so vividly portrayed in Acts is thus shown by the associated gospel to have had its beginning during the ministry of Christ, and to be under the personal direction of the supreme victor himself.[30]

A further example of the literal manner in which Luke thought of demons and of the seriousness with which he took them may be seen in his remarks about the evil spirit seeking rest, who takes seven stronger spirits and re-invades his lost territory (Luke 11.24–26; Matt. 12.43–45). The difference between the two accounts is that in Matthew it is treated as a parable of the state of Christ's contemporaries, the generation which rejects him. Matthew allegorizes and devotionalizes what to Luke was a terrible spiritual reality. In Luke it remains what it originally was in Q and no doubt in the teaching of Jesus – an actual description of behaviour and reactions under certain conditions of varieties of evil spirits. Such knowledge is an essential part of the battle. The church must know its enemy.

Luke also describes a number of particular types of demon. It is often difficult to tell if an ancient author intends to indicate a recognized category of demon or whether he is merely listing the diagnostic characteristics, but in the case of the girl in Acts 16.16–18 the former is certainly the case. The girl has a Pythonic spirit, that is, one specializing in oracles and ventriloquism.[31] In Acts 5.3 and Luke 22.3 the possessing spirit is specifically named as Satan. Luke's description of Simon's wife's mother (Luke 4.38) appears to be a diagnosis of the particular spirit which affects her, not merely, or not at all, a medical observation. So she was 'in the grip of a high fever'. Categories of fever spirits were numerous in the ancient world.[32] Test.Sol. 7.6 describes one whose particular role, once he had been controlled by the archangel Azael, was to master the convulsions of fever. In Test.Sol. 18.20, Katrax the sixteenth of the Thirty-six World Rulers, says, 'I inflict upon them fever, irremediable and harmful,' and then confesses to Solomon the method of exorcism which will make the demon retreat at once. The nineteenth (18.23) of the same series, Mardero, also causes fever: 'I send on men incurable fever' and then describes the phylactery which will cause him to retreat. The twenty-fifth, Anatreth, sends 'burnings and fevers into the entrails'. These are not tasks which these spirits perform by choice, as if they happened from a number of possibilities to select fever as their particular sphere, but their names, their functions and what frustrates them are all prescribed for them by inscrutable destiny. Luke's spirit is similarly a fever-spirit, fleeing at Messiah's rebuke.

We have seen that Luke's description of the seven spirits is to be understood literally and it should be noted that, this being so, we have here another class of special demons in sevenfold shape. Certain demons were distributed into a number of spiritual sections but remained united in fundamental nature and in activity. For example, the Thirty-six World Rulers in Test.Sol. 18 each have their distinct task, but they all have the same appearance (human with animal or bird-like faces), share the same nature and they speak with 'one accord with one voice'. In Test.Sol. 12.2 there is a demon like a τρίβολος i.e., a three-spiked weapon. He has three heads and says his activity is in 'three lines', i.e., three kinds of activity. He is in fact a sort of trinity in unity. Enepsigos (15.2–6) is a female demon and although not permanently in triple form she can appear in any of three different forms. In 8.1 is described a similarly distributed yet unified spirit form. Solomon orders 'another demon' to come before him 'and there came seven spirits, females, bound and woven together'. So these seven spirits constitute one demon. Notice by the way that the seventh one makes you 'worse off than you were'. This is relevant to the strange expression in Luke 11.26; Matt. 12.45, where the expelled spirit 'goes and takes seven other spirits more evil than itself and entering in they dwell there'. The united spirits act not as many but as one. This multiform type of demon was understood by Luke better than by Matthew, for Matthew includes the words μεθ' ἑαυτοῦ (Matt. 12.45) 'then he goes and takes with himself seven other spirits'. Matthew means that he is then accompanied by the seven other spirits. Luke omits μεθ' ἑαυτοῦ and his use of παραλαμβάνω is to be interpreted in the light of καταλαμβάνω in Mark 9.18 and λαμβάνω in Luke 9.39. The correct translation is not 'he brings along seven other spirits to help him' but 'he receives or arrests another seven-spirits'. Luke's idea is not that of a little assorted crowd of spirits but rather that the desperate spirit manages to fuse himself with or to get hold of a united group. They were more evil but not necessarily more powerful. Their evil nature is not uncomfortable or ill-at-ease in the swept and clean room in the way the nature of a slightly less evil spirit might have been. So the sevenfold unity becomes an eightfold unity in order to accomplish a specific task. This ability to transform into a more menacing combination is the particular trick of this type of spirit which the pericope is intended to expose; this is why in Luke's version it should be read as retaining its solemn literalness.[33]

The Gerasene incident describes a water-hating, desert-loving demon. This characteristic appears more clearly in Luke than in the other gospels, Luke alone saying (8.29) that the Legion would take the man 'off to the solitary places'. But while to Legion the water is the place of punishment, the evil spirit described in Matt. 12.43ff. and Luke 11.24ff. is not at home in the desert region at all, but finds the exposed waterless regions uncongenial. He wanders through waterless places seeking rest but finds none and wishes to return into the house. Satan himself likes uninhabited places, as the references in all three gospels to the temptation of Christ show. It is Luke alone however who, having recorded the possession by the devil of Judas, describes how his death fulfilled the verse 'let his homestead fall desolate; let there be no one to inhabit it' (Acts 1.20). The death of Judas left Satan in a congenial place, whereas the death of the swine left Legion in a most uncongenial place, a lake. Once again we note that these are not fluctuating whims of the devils concerned but are part of their constitution, part of that which they reveal under compulsion as being their nature.[34] So Asmodeus let out a great groan when compelled to carry a water jar and tread clay with his feet[35] (Test.Sol. 5.11). Beelzebul has a demonic child who haunts the Red Sea (Test.Sol. 6.3) and has been trapped there against his will (Test.Sol. 25.7). But in Test.Sol. 16.5 Kunopegon, the horse with fish's tail, is a sea demon by nature and says, 'In two or three days the spirit that converses with thee will fail because I shall have no water', whereupon Solomon keeps him in a bottle of sea water.

A further example of specialized demons is provided by the dumb devils. In Matt. 9.32 and Luke 11.14 the difference between Matthew and Luke is strikingly clear. In Matthew it is the man who is dumb. The spirit possessing him is merely the cause of his dumbness. But in Luke the demon causes dumbness because it is a dumb spirit. In Mark 9.25 exactly the same situation prevails – the spirit is dumb. Matthew however is perfectly consistent since the parallel Matt. 12.22 also attributes the blindness and dumbness to the man, rather than to the spirit. Matthew is describing a type of sickness, Mark and Luke a type of demon.[36]

All these examples show that both Mark and Luke recognize

the classes and characteristics of demons, and that sometimes Luke adds a detail or a class whereas usually Matthew subtracts.

3. *Magical power*

Luke and Acts thus portray a spiritual world divided into two realms each with its classes and divisions. Each hierarchy has its type of relationship with the world of men and each has its appropriate and distinct aims. Each opposing army also has its force, its might, its strength, which emanates from it in varying degrees of intensity. The dramatic story which Luke–Acts unfolds is largely the description of this clash of rival powers. The words used are δύναμις and ἐξουσία. Both these words have a particular meaning in the Lucan writings. In the thought of Luke, the most remarkable feature is the concentration upon δύναμις not as miracle itself but as miracle-working power. It is regarded by Luke as a substance, a *mana*-like charge of divine potency, spiritual in so far as it emanates from the world of spirits, but as actual, as vital as the beings who possess it. Luke does not stress that Jesus possessed the impressive authority of the prophets,[37] nor that he had moral power, nor does he use the expression in the sense that Jesus had great power (as we say) to perform feats, as if it were an ability or a skill. 'Power' is not a metaphor but is that reality which carries the actual potency of the spirit world into our world.

The power is not possessed by Jesus alone; John the Baptist also has it (Luke 1.17). The identification of John with Elijah is not made elsewhere in Luke. This is a trace of a pre-synoptic tradition coming ultimately from baptist circles, and it is possible that Luke 7.18f. also originated in controversy between the disciples of Jesus and those of John on the question of their respective miracles. In Luke 7.26 John is admitted to be 'more than a prophet' and in 1.17 the miracle-working power of Elijah is applied to him. The contrast is not, as it is in John's gospel (John 10.41) between a miracle-less John and a miracle-working Christ; both are 'powerful' figures. Both are equipped with supernatural δύναμις. But whereas the power of John has affinities with that of Elijah, that of Jesus is of even higher origin. The early history of the struggle between the followers of the Baptist and those of Jesus is similar no doubt to the struggle between the Simonites and the Christians, and the clash between the church and magic in general, i.e., a superior power swallowed up and negated an inferior one.

The power comes upon Jesus particularly after his successful struggle with Satan. It is not Christ but Mary who in Luke 1.35 is overshadowed by the power in order to conceive Christ; there is little suggestion that the power became, as it were, a part of Christ's permanent personal nature. Luke 2.40 says that he was strong in spirit, full of wisdom,[38] and that the grace of God was upon him. Luke 2.52 repeats roughly similar ideas but not until 3.22, when the dove has descended bodily upon him, do we read that Jesus is full of the Holy Spirit (4.1) and not until his conquest of Satan is he 'in the power of the Spirit' (4.14). In view of the fact that the mature Christ experienced fluctuations in the activity of his power, it is not to be wondered at that there is a gradual increase of power this way.

The power is particularly effective in exorcism and is often associated there with ἐξουσία as in Luke 4.36: 'What word is this! In authority and power he commands the unclean spirits, and they come out.' Mark's wording is significantly different: 'What is this? A new teaching with authority? He even commands the unclean spirits and they obey him' (Mark 1.27). In Luke they are not amazed at his teaching but at his word. Mark does not tell us by what means Jesus casts the spirits out, but Luke says plainly that it was this authority and this power acting in his λόγός, i.e., in his spoken word, his breath or πνεῦμα.[39]

The power is elsewhere described as being the 'power of the Lord', the Lord here probably being God, the Highest, referred to in Luke 1.35. It was localized and was noticeably present on some occasions rather than on others. In 5.17 Luke describes Jesus teaching in the presence of Pharisees and lawyers and in the presence of the power. The power is not only effective against demons; it has wider use – 'it was present to heal them.' The best text however reads αὐτόν and this may mean: 'The power of the Lord was in him to heal.' This is not as odd as it sounds; in Luke 8.46 Jesus says that he feels power going out of him. If the power can thus come out, it can apparently at other times go in with unusual force.

A good deal more can be learned about the power from Luke's account of the woman with the haemorrhage in 8.43–48. Here we learn that the power set up a sort of field around Jesus, the same sort of field suggested by 5.17 where Jesus is the centre of healing power, which affected his clothing right down to the hem of his outer garment. The power works immediately and impersonally; it responds to the contact of any believing person without the knowledge or approval of the power-bearer himself. In Mark 5.31 no answer is given to the disciples' incredulous question about Jesus being touched, but in Luke Christ's secret knowledge is used to explain to the disciples what had happened: 'Someone touched me; for I know a power has left me.' The conception of power is used to satisfy the surprised questioners. It is only touching for a deliberate purpose which can bring about this depletion of power, and this is why the woman is said to have 'explained why she touched him' (8.47). The problem of distinguishing between the many touches from the surrounding crowd and the touch of the woman is thus satisfactorily solved. It is this confidence in the power which constitutes the faith for which the woman is praised, and which Jesus said had saved her. It will be noted that this idea is also accepted by Mark but this is the only story in which Mark refers to it. The idea is more prominent in Luke because the power occupies a place in his theory of the relationships between representatives of the spiritual world and mankind and this explains the greater degree of precision which the idea has in the Lucan writings.

The power can be passed from one person to another. It is not a moral quality nor a learned skill but an acquisition, a property which can be conveyed either with the will of the donor, as in Luke 9.1, or without it, as in 8.46. The woman did not apparently receive sufficient power to enable her to become a healer. For that the will of the donor must be exerted as it is in 9.1, where Luke alone adds 'power' to the 'authority' of Mark 6.7 and Matt. 10.1.

Luke's gospel closes with a promise of more power which is to come from the same quarter as the original power of Jesus – 'power from the heights' (24.49). We are not told what the purpose of this power is, but in view of 9.1, where the power is given in order to exorcize and to heal, we may assume that 24.49 is the same sort of idea. That which they had previously received from the earthly Jesus, who acted as an intermediary, they are now to receive directly from the source of power itself. This is why the success of the church in Acts is more dramatic than the limited and partial success of the disciples during the ministry of Jesus.

In Acts 1.8 the power is again connected with the Spirit (cf. Acts 10.38). As a result of the power the apostles will be able to witness to the Christ through their mighty deeds. The power however never becomes the property of the person in his own right, but flows always as a living force from the most high God. Thus, questioned in Acts 3.12 about their miracle-working ability, Peter denies that it is his own power. He is but the channel or the vessel. This conception of the power as derivative is also found in the descriptions of Jesus' power, but it is emphasized more in the Acts when describing the power of apostles.

The power which comes from the Highest through Jesus is not the only power. Hence the possibility arose of interpreting the miracles of Jesus in various ways, and the question asked of Peter in Acts 4.7, 'By what power or by what name have you done these things?' The mighty works of the apostles are open to the same dubious implication. The crucial point of enquiry into the miracles of Jesus, as of those of the early church, was not whether they had in fact happened but the nature and origin of the power used to perform them. By means such as these 'the apostles gave witness with great power', i.e., not simply with great impact but the aid of a mighty force (Acts 4.33). The connection between the apostolic power and miracle is made specific in the description of Stephen, 'who was full of grace and power' and 'began to work great miracles and signs' (Acts 6.8).

Just as one case of Luke's use of the word 'power' takes on an added significance when seen in the context of the total Lucan view, so Luke's whole conception of power needs to be interpreted against its appropriate background.

But what is that background? We have seen that in Luke's writings we have a highly distinctive use of power which presupposes certain realities and relationships. Where did these presuppositions come from? Certainly not from the Old Testament. There is hardly a trace in the LXX of the particular meaning given to the word in Mark and Luke.[40] 'Power' is not used to describe miracle-working power in any noticeable way at all, nor for miracle itself, for God's power was just as truly manifest in the great winds and thunder (Ps. 29) as in what we would call supernatural events. The New Testament use we are examining does not spring from the Hebrew conception of nature and history, but from the ancient universal idea of the magical miracle, which in turn rests upon a primitive conception of *mana*.[41]

This was effectively demonstrated by Friedrich Preisigke in 1922 in his little book *Die Gotteskraft der Frühristlichen Zeit*. This is such an important work that it deserves a brief exposition and commentary. Preisigke begins with a study of Luke 8.43ff. and makes the following observations:[42]

1. The woman seeks healing only. She has not the slightest interest in personal contact with Jesus.
2. She knows that this healing power is available quite independently of Christ's personality or of his will – it is enough, she knows, to touch his garment.
3. This is popular knowledge; the woman has no secret information. The evangelist himself shares this popular knowledge and attitude.
4. Christ also shares this popular knowledge of the impersonal nature of his power. Although he knows power has gone he does not know to whom it has gone.
5. Christ is thus not in control of the power. The power has its own controls.
6. Any determined touch makes the power overflow like electricity.
7. Christ is no more than the bearer, the vessel of this power. A vessel is necessary to the power as a surface is necessary to light. But only certain persons can carry such high tension, else why should the woman have come to Christ?
8. The power is in the garment as well as in the body; Christ has not willed to fill the garment with power; his will is not an issue. Touching unites the lifeless matter and the living body of Christ in one unity of power; the living woman is also united in the same unity.
9. Christ notices not the incident nor the touching but the diminution of power in his own body.
10. The touch must however be (i) deliberate, (ii) with faith.
11. The trust is not in Christ's mission, nor in him as salvation bringer in the Christian sense, for then the request would have been to the person of Christ, not to his garment. The faith is in the power. What the woman wants is the power, not the Christ; the water, not the fireman.

12. Christ does not find the woman's attitude or behaviour blameworthy; indeed he blesses her.

13. Since Christ does not will it and nevertheless only a touch of faith secures the response, the question arises as to whether the power itself has a self-consciousness. The power is probably looked upon as living and as the servant of the one who summons it with deliberate knowledge of its presence.

The view of power in the story is fragmentary and many unanswered questions remain. Preisigke lists three:

1. Will the power in Christ remain permanently diminished or will it be replenished, and if so, from what source?
2. The woman was temporarily brought into unity with the high tension but will she remain so? And for how long? Is the woman now as much a bearer as Christ himself?
3. How does the power heal the woman? What in other words is the connection between the overflow and the sickness? The answers to these questions are provided not by the story but by the conception of God's power in the heathen world.

Preisigke goes on to trace the Egyptian idea of the influence of Ra or Amon-Ra, the sun god.[43] Everything lives as a consequence of the flooding of Amon-Ra into everything. This flooding is made known to men as a power or a spirit, and as divine substance. But it cannot work without a vessel or container. This divine presence exists in different degrees in plants, animals and men, and in the highest degree of all in the king who is the living portrait of the god. There may also be lifeless images of the god similarly full of high tension – such as statues or the property of the king. The power is used up in the course of living and must be replenished from another bearer of the power and ultimately from the sun itself. The replenishing can only take place if there is no hostile power which might resist the inrush of the good power of God. If for some such reason the inrush of power is weakened it must be strengthened by exposure, usually in the form of touching, to a source of stronger power. The god is grateful to the one who by thus accepting the power confirms his place as a recipient within the sphere of that divine power.

The oustanding questions about Christ's power can now be answered. Christ is like the divine king; he will suffer no permanent depletion of his energy because he is directly sustained by the divine Father of all. But the woman will return to the tension of the normal mass of humanity when the power has accomplished the healing. Should the healing not be complete, she would have to touch again, or seek other methods of securing an overflow. As for the third question, the connection between sickness and power, every sickness is an advance of death. Life will be awakened when the force opposite to it is driven out. Contact with the power of life frees the woman from the power of death. In the case of a clash between two opposing powers battle will result. This is why sick folk often had to spend long periods in the temple of the god whose good power they were seeking. But in the case of this woman Christ's power was so great that it healed immediately.

In the case of the early Christian miracles the battle was not only against the evil power of sickness and death but against any power not coming directly from Christ. These rival powers were regarded as coming from genuine existing sources and the Christian power had therefore to attack the base of these other powers. In Acts 19.11 the idea is that Paul's clothes are charged with the same high tension, a higher tension than that of the sick-ness-power, and therefore the evil spirits (the life-denying threat) must escape its thrust.[44]

This theme is enriched in Preisigke's exposition[45] by many illustrations from pre-Christian, early Christian and medieval Christian periods. From the sixth century AD comes a fine example of a silken cloak laid for the night over the coffin of St Martin which in the morning was so highly charged with the saint's power that it successfully healed the king of Spain. The mantle is actually said to weigh more in the morning. In many of these examples there is a double discharge of power – from the saint into the life-less vessel (a robe, a spring of water, a relic) and from that into the supplicant. The power in the lifeless bearer is no less than that in the living source as long as contact by means of radiation or touch is maintained. The bodily products of the divine king are thus as effective as his own person, hence the virtue of the spittle of Vespasian who in Alexandria shares the virtues of the divine king. Jesus, understanding himself as such a divine king, would also regard himself as full of such power and would accept the implications.

The vessels of power may thus be grouped into living vessels:

the divine king, Christ, apostles, saints, martyrs, as against lifeless ones: bones, statues of gods, cultic objects, other objects like clothes. Normally a deliberate contact is required, but the healing power of Peter's shadow (Acts 5.15) looks like an exception and is a case of radiation rather than deliberate contact.[46]

Preisigke discusses the relationship between the original source of power and the vehicle. Although the latter (statue, robe, shadow, handkerchief) is equally full of power, the original suffers no diminution on this account. The original even transfers sensations to it together with the actual power. If you damage his image the god will feel pain. This is the source of the reverence paid to statues both of gods and men. This is also the source of the ancient connection between the name and thing named; the name represents the thing and shares its power. This contributes to an understanding of the preference for oil in early Christian baptism and exorcism. Oil remains longer on the skin and the power can therefore penetrate further. In the *Acts of Thomas* the exorcist prays that the power of the cross will come upon the oil. The prayer begins with an invocation to Jesus so that the power of Jesus will fill the breath of the exorcist who utters his name. The exorcist then breathes over the oil and the power enters the oil. As the oil is spread upon the candidate Christ enters him, for Christ and his power are identical. The exorcizing effect of the oil is based on the idea of the divine power driving out the evil power.[47]

This conception is not metaphorical or picturesque, but fully material and literal, however crude it may seem to us. *The Syrian Didaskalia* remarks that every man is full of spirit (= power), either holy spirit or evil spirit. At baptism the evil spirit is driven out and Holy Spirit takes its place. *Hermas (Mand.* 5.1.2.) says that, if you are blessed, the Holy Spirit remains in you as its vessel, but in face of a renewed attack from the evil spirit the Holy Spirit retreats, because it is 'tender and delicate'. *Mand.* 5.2.5 describes the situation, likening it to what happens when more liquid is poured into an already full vessel. The inrush of the evil power has the effect of expelling the Holy Spirit completely.[48]

Normally the skin provides the opening for the power but if an extraordinarily large influx is needed a larger opening will be used. So God breathed his spirit into man through the nose, and in John 20.22 the power leaves Christ through his mouth. In *Pistis Sophia* 141 we read: 'Christ blessed the disciples and breathed into their eyes'. Here the eyes form an entry for the power. If the blower is not himself a bearer of power he must say the name of someone who is as he breathes out, and he can then guide the power in the right direction. But water evaporates, and even oil will ultimately be wiped off, so the best way to retain power is to swallow something. From this arises the custom of swallowing an amulet or swallowing water with which a magical charm has been washed. Eating food is the best method of all, for the food if it has been in contact with a power source will carry the power actually into the body more or less permanently. In *Pistis Sophia* the spirit about to enter the boy Jesus appears to Mary in the shape of Jesus so that she thinks it is he. The power is capable of assuming the shape of anything it is going to fill. Mary ties the spirit to the bed but when Jesus comes in the spirit is released and goes into him so that as it disappears they become perfectly united. But even before the union the spirit is still perfectly tangible. There can therefore be little doubt that this ancient conception of power is to be taken literally.[49]

Preisigke has thus shown a convincing background for the Lucan concept of power in the ancient idea of magical *mana*. It may be that he has exaggerated the importance of Egyptian conceptions in the Hellenistic period, since the original idea (if it was Egyptian originally) had by then become common property, but in general his analysis is sound. Examination of the power concept in the specifically magical literature fully supports this finding. Let us, for example, take the idea of power in the Testament of Solomon. The word δύναμις occurs about nineteen times, never in the Marcan sense of miracle but often in the Lucan sense of an emanation from a spiritual being of his energy. There are a number of incidental cases where the word is used in some of the senses found in the LXX and the apocryphal literature, such as Test.Sol. 18.11 (the power of a muscle); 2.4; 11.6 (P); 25.7 (B) (the power of the hosts of God or the hosts of the devil); 12.1 (C) (the ability of Solomon); but there are also a number of passages which are harmonious with the ancient view of power as a magical force, and there are some passages which demand it. Demons have power (3.5), but their power is subject to the greater power of God (5.11) or of the angels (3.2, D), who undo all the devil's power (22.20, B). The power of the demons returns when they are set free from God's power (15.9), but is slack when they are under it (22.20, B).

The demons receive their power from their leader (7.1f., D) and pass it on to men (8.10). Christ receives his power from God (6.8), as does Solomon (3.5), and this power knows the demons (5.11). God's power frustrates them (13.6, C and 3.2, D), subjects them (3.5) and makes them disappear (6.8). Here we find the same picture as in Luke–Acts – two hierarchies of power, each attacking the other, each retreating before the other, each present in particular vessels (Solomon, Christ, angels, certain devils, Beelzebul, Samael) and the evil power yielding at last to the superior power of the most high God.

The same conception is found in the magical papyri and could be illustrated in great detail. In *PGM* XXXVI. 312, the magician is to take the umbilical cord of a newborn ram before it has touched the ground. The idea is that contact with the earth causes a loss of magical energy. In the bilingual papyrus edited by Bell and Nock, 'the power of Osiris' and 'the grace of the gods' are identified.[50] In the same line sacred olive oil is called 'the power of Osiris'. Speaking over the oil, the magician says, 'I am invested with the power of the great God, the name which none save me alone, who am master, may name.' Here the magician has managed to control the power of Osiris and now he can gain access to even more power by his mastery of the name. 'Power' and 'spirit' are often linked. In *PGM* XXXV.25, the magician prays that he may have 'power and spirit', the latter word being translated by Preisendanz as 'Zauberkraft'. The custom of conducting magic on the roof of a house rests upon the belief that this provided insulation for the power.[51]

4. *Magical authority*

Turning now to the related idea of authority we find the same distinct meaning in Luke–Acts as we have found for power. Power is the positive active power emanating from both sides in the spiritual battle. Luke 10.19 refers to the 'power of the enemy', and 'authority' is the control or freedom which makes it possible for a side to make effective use of its power. Hence Jesus does not give his disciples power against the power of the enemy, which would mean a prolonged struggle to see which power had authority; he gives them authority over the enemy's power, i.e., the power to restrict the effectiveness of the power of the other side.

Just as power without authority is not decisive, so authority without power is not active. So whereas Matthew and Mark have Jesus giving the disciples authority over unclean spirits (Matt. 10.1; Mark 3.15; 6.7) Luke has him giving them authority and power, the former giving them potential control, control by right of lordship, the latter enabling them to actualize this in particular victories. Authority is strategic, power is tactical. The same formula is constructed (again by Luke alone) in Luke 4.36 (cf. Mark 1.27) where to the authority of Mark power is added.[52]

Was the power of Jesus prophetic power? There is not a single case in LXX where the word $\delta\acute{v}\nu\alpha\mu\iota s$ is used in this Lucan way. In the expression 'the power of Elijah' (Luke 1.17) we are dealing not with an application to John of a prophetic power but the application to Elijah of the sort of power which John and to a greater degree Jesus had. In the light of the power conception in the Hellenistic world the activity of the old Hebrew prophets was re-assessed. They also were now seen to have been bearers and vessels of the high tension power. Jesus, like Moses, becomes a prophet 'mighty in deed and word before God' (Luke 24.19; Acts 7.22), but the power with which he and the prophets operate is not some special kind of 'prophetic power' but the same power used by Christ and the apostles as well as by the prophets. Here we have not the prophetic power of the ancient Hebrews, but the power from the Heights familiar to the Hellenistic world.[53]

VII

MATTHEW: THE TRADITION
PURIFIED OF MAGIC

1. *Signs and portents*

In Matthew's gospel we find two developments. In the first place, signs and portents occupy a more significant role than in the other gospel traditions. In the second place, the Matthean material to some extent, but not systematically, is purged of details which might give rise to a magical interpretation. The interest in signs and portents is to be accounted for by Matthew's general acceptance of astrology; his ambiguous reaction to magical healing is due to his rejection of it as lacking in christological significance. There was no difficulty in reconciling these two attitudes, for acceptance of astrology and contempt for popular thaumaturgical magic was a normal combination in the educated Hellenistic world of the early Empire, including Judaism.

Let us examine Matthew's treatment of portents and signs with a view to establishing his attitude to astrology, and as a preface to seeking the significance of Matthew's non-magical re-interpretation of the miracles of Jesus. The opening chapter describes the prodigy of the virgin's son and the account continues with the heavenly witness of the astrologers' star. The gospel closes in similar manner. To the darkness and the supernaturally rent veil Matthew adds the earthquake and the resurrection of the saints, whilst the account of Easter morning is embellished with a further violent earthquake and an angelic appearance. The ministry of Messiah is also enclosed within portentous dreams. No less than five dreams surround the divine birth and Messiah goes to his death in the ominous mystery of Pilate's wife's dream (27.19). The parousia of the Messiah is also to be accompanied by warning portents. The references to 'the signal for your coming' and 'the sign that heralds the Son of Man' (24.3,30) are unique to this gospel. So the birth, death and reappearance of Jesus Christ are all authenticated by signs.

All of these attestations are external to the Messiah himself. The three synoptic gospels agree that the miracles of Jesus are mighty works.[1] But the description of Jesus and his works as signs is almost as rare in the synoptics as it is common in John. Luke does regard Jesus himself as a sign and his miracles are also signs but this idea is almost entirely absent in Matthew. The first occurrence of σημεῖον in Luke is in 2.12, where the sign may be the dress and position of the baby, but it is more probable that the baby himself is to be the sign. If the former sense is intended however, the word merely means 'identifying mark' and the use would be similar to the sign of the kiss in Matt. 26.48. Much clearer is Luke 2.34: 'This child is destined to be a sign.' The most famous synoptic passage containing the word 'sign' is the demand by the Pharisees for a sign. This is present in both Mark and Q.[2] In the Marcan version of the incident, Jesus refuses absolutely to give a sign. In Matthew Jesus adds 'except the sign of Jonah'. This is elaborated in the Q passage, but there is a significant difference between Matthew and Luke about the nature of this sign. Luke adds 'for just as Jonah was a sign to the Ninevites, so will the Son of Man be to this generation' (Luke 11.30). The sign here is the witness of the preaching of Jesus himself (cf. v. 32, 'they repented at the preaching of Jonah'). The appearance of a great prophet announces a crisis in the near future; the prophet is himself a warning sign. Matthew however introduces the comparison between the swallowing of Jonah and the burial of Jesus. The sign is not Jesus himself nor his works but the supernatural resurrection from the dead. It is significant that the request of the Pharisees in Matt. 12.38, 'Master, we should like you to show us a sign,' is displaced by Luke so that it is asked not before the sign of Jonah saying (11.29) but before the Beelzebul controversy (11.16): 'Others, by way of a test, demanded of him a sign from heaven.' The Lucan position of the demand leads to the supposition that the exorcisms were signs. Not satisfied with these, the Pharisees seek a more dramatic heavenly sign and are told (Luke 11.29ff.) that this preaching and this exorcizing ministry is all the sign they will get. Matthew rejects this interpretation of the exorcisms as messianic signs. Exorcism was for him too ambiguous to serve in this vital capacity. That is why the demand for a sign comes in Matt. 12.38 as a new twist in the controversy. In Luke therefore two signs are offered: (i) the exorcisms and (ii) the call to repentance. In Matthew there is but one sign, the resurrection.³ There were many exorcists, but only one man had risen from the dead.

This conclusion makes it clear that when Matthew adds the enigmatic words 'except the sign of Jonah' to Mark 8.12 (Matt. 16.4) he means that the miracles are not given to them as signs. 'No sign shall be given them', except the resurrection. How is the resurrection given to them? By means of the supernatural visitation described in Matt. 28.2–4. This is why those verses contain the only account in the New Testament of pagans and unbelievers witnessing to the resurrection. The guards do not see the risen one; that is reserved as always for the eye of faith. But they do see the signs, and through them the sign is given to the elders and chief priests (vv. 11f.). The account of the guards is therefore much more than a piece of late Christian apology; it is the fulfilment of the sign of Jonah. The same consideration explains the eclipse and earthquake which accompany the death of Christ. When the greater Jonah is swallowed by death, both his descent and his ascent are marked by signs.

It should be noted that our observations on Luke 2.34; 11.16, 29ff. are supported by Luke 23.8. This is the only occasion in the synoptics when the miracles are specifically called signs⁴ (unless we accept the longer ending of Mark: Mark 16.17, 20) and is fully in the style of the Lucan thinking which has been described. In Acts 4.16, 22 the miracles of the early church are also referred to as signs.

Matthew's view, that the signs and portents by which the Messiah was guaranteed to the unbelieving world were apart from and external to the miraculous works of Christ himself, may be further illustrated by contrasting his view with Q and with John.

The material in Q is not primarily catechetical, exhortatory or ethical but christological and eschatological. The predominant note sounded is that of the crisis caused by the coming of Christ, a crisis which consists in the coming itself and the following demand for radical existential and ethical response from men. The crisis preaching of the Baptist centres on the imminent arrival of him who is to usher in the messianic age (Matt. 3.7–12 = Luke

3.7–9, 16f.); the sayings about the relationship between John and Jesus make the same point (Matt. 11.11–19 = Luke 7.28; 16.16); and the question of John from prison makes it particularly clear that the only sign which is offered to the enquirer is the witness of the deeds of Jesus himself (Matt. 11.2–6 = Luke 7.18–23). The point is equally clear in the Beelzebul controversy where Jesus, in denouncing unbelief and refusing to give a sign, points to the meaning of his healings which, he says, indicate the eschatological crisis created by his advent (especially Matt. 12.28 = Luke 11.20).[5]

The attitude of Luke towards Jesus as himself the self-authenticating sign is in general harmony with that of Q, although neither in Luke nor in Q are the implications worked out as fully as in John. Matthew however is at variance with Q, as is made clear in Matt. 12.39ff. Verse 40, the interpretation of the sign of Jonah in terms of the resurrection, disrupts the passage, for the original meaning of the sign (the preaching of Jesus) is retained in v. 41. Matthew indeed omits the crucial words, 'for just as Jonah was a sign to the Ninevites, so will the Son of Man be to this generation' (Luke 11.30), because these state explicitly what Matthew wishes to avoid, namely, that the sign is the Son of Man himself. But he does retain the verse about the men of Nineveh repenting at the preaching of Jonah, even bringing it into immediate juxtaposition with the rival interpretation about the whale which he has just offered, by reversing the order of the illustrations about the Queen of Sheba and the men of Nineveh (Matt. 12.41f. = Luke 11.31f.). In spite of the omission of Luke 11.30, therefore, the two inconsistent interpretations of the sign stand side by side.[6]

Matthew 12.28, 'But if it is by the spirit of God that I cast out devils, then be sure the kingdom of God has already come upon you', is also alien to Matthew's thinking about the significance of the miracles. The following points may be noticed as part of Matthew's attempt to deal with this saying:

(i) Unlike Luke, he refrains from drawing attention to the sign aspect of the exorcisms; he does not attach the demand for a sign to the actual Beelzebul controversy itself, but instead defers it to v. 38.

(ii) He qualifies the Marcan version of the saying about blasphemy against the Holy Spirit by adding the somewhat different Q version (Mark 3.28–30; Matt. 12.31f.; Luke 12.10). Matthew 12.31

is substantially from Mark 3.28f.: 'No sin, no slander, is beyond forgiveness for men, except slander spoken against the Spirit, and that will not be forgiven.' Instead of concluding by adding Mark's comment, 'he said this because they had declared that he was possessed by an evil spirit', Matthew continues with the Q version, 'anyone who speaks a word against the Son of Man will be forgiven; but if anyone speaks against the Holy Spirit, for him there is no forgiveness'. The difference between the two original versions, those of Mark and Q, is that, as Mark's editorial comment makes clear, the Marcan version identifies Jesus with the Holy Spirit, or at least indicates that his exorcisms are signs wrought by the Spirit. But the Q version distinguishes between Jesus and the Spirit. The implication in Matthew's account is, 'You have committed a great sin in thinking my works are done in co-operation with evil spirits. But you can still be forgiven. It would have been worse had you blasphemed against the Holy Spirit.'[7] This concept of the external nature of the Spirit, a Spirit which is not realized in the exorcisms, is in conflict with the original intention of the account of the Beelzebul controversy. Luke has understood this, which is why in his account the Q saying about the blasphemy against the Spirit is not included in the Beelzebul section at all (Luke 11.14–26) but deferred until the group of sayings in Luke 12. As a matter of fact this Q saying is at variance with the Q teaching as a whole, and Matthew seems to have used it here for precisely that reason, and because it was, from his point of view, less dubious than the version he found in Mark.

(iii) Luke 11.33–36 is probably preserved in its correct Q position and the verses have to do with the nature of the true sign, the shining of light into the lives of men. The thought is similar to that in John 3.19ff.[8] Why does Matthew place these sayings in the Sermon on the Mount (Matt. 5.15; 6.22f.) rather than in the original position? Is it, as Manson says, merely 'his belief, which is no doubt correct, that they were originally addressed to the disciples'?[9] It certainly would be in harmony with the other details we have noticed concerning Matthew's attitude to signs, if he moved the sayings from the signs section just because he preferred not to make the point that Jesus as a sign is given in his illuminating words to the unbelieving Jews. According to Matthew he is not given to them but only to the church (Matt. 13.11, 16f.). Thus in Matthew the words are moralized, their content of existentially

realized eschatology is removed and they are placed in the address
to the members of the kingdom.

A further example of Matthew's treatment of Q is the interpretation he gives to the thanksgiving of Jesus, 'thou hast hidden these
things from the learned and wise' (Matt. 11.25 = Luke 10.21). In
Luke the saying follows the triumphant return of disciples and the
'things' which have been revealed to the simple are the powers of
exorcism possessed by believers. In Matthew the prayer is preceded by the warnings of judgment upon the unresponsive villages. The 'things' are the results of the preaching of Jesus.
Emphasis is removed from the miracles as signs and placed upon
the character of Jesus's message.

Although, as we have seen, Matthew's view differs from that of
Q, and the Q passages are imperfectly assimilated, it is not until
we examine the fourth gospel that Matthew's position emerges
most clearly. In the fourth gospel we find two features in striking
contrast to Matthew. The miracles are constantly called signs, and,
secondly, there is a total absence of any other sort of sign. These
two factors are connected and they indicate that John has conceived of a different type of apology for the messiahship of Jesus
from that which is presented by Matthew.

The crucial point about the Johannine interpretation of the
miracles as signs is John's re-assessment of eschatology. More
thoroughly than any other gospel tradition, except perhaps Q,
John presents the person and work of the historical Jesus as the
intrinsic eschatological crisis. It is because of this that he no longer
needs to speak of signs as being external and future. Matthew has
the most futuristic eschatology and therefore his signs are future
and external. This is also why, of all the gospels, Matthew's
miracles least express eschatological fulfilment, and why he has so
many portents. As we shall see, Matthew's miracles are neither
eschatological power-filled signs nor works of mystical magic.
They have become devotional allegories.

The absence of external signs is the other striking contrast
between John and Matthew. It is often pointed out that the reason
the transfiguration is omitted is because, for John, the whole of
Christ's ministry reveals his glory. An additional reason is because
John wished to delete the central feature of the transfiguration, the
attestation offered by the heavenly voice. No external testimony is
necessary. This also accounts for John's peculiar treatment of the

baptism. John seems to talk all round the incident but never describes it. If we did not know the synoptic accounts, we would not realize that the dove mentioned in John 1.32 was seen at the time of the baptism. In place of the heavenly voice John has the voice of the Baptist. By this he intends his readers to understand that history itself, the personalities and happenings of history, are the witness to Messiah, and this history requires no extraneous testimony.[10] In the same way we can understand the omission of the rent veil and the darkness at the crucifixion. It has been thought odd, in view of John's liking for the light-darkness metaphor, that he omits to mention the darkness over all the land. This omission has even been used as an argument to show that John could not have been familiar with the synoptic accounts. The explanation however is to be found in the nature of the testimony to Christ offered in John's gospel as a whole. The death of Christ needs no eclipse, no earthquake. The water and the blood are observed and recorded; this is sufficient 'that you may believe'. Neither Matthew's dreams nor Luke's angels are summoned to witness to Messiah. Only at John 20.12 do angels appear in the action of this gospel and their role is reduced to a minimum. This is the only gospel account of the resurrection in which the angels are robbed of the privilege of the announcement. They merely ask the question, 'Why are you weeping?' (John 20.13). The Lord himself announces his resurrection. In John Jesus becomes the only mediator between God and man: voices, dreams, visions, angels, signs all disappear. All are absorbed within the glory of the one who is the sole channel of traffic between heaven and earth (John 1.51).

Matthew's attitude towards signs is clarified by the omission of Matt. 16.2a–3 on independent textual grounds. The rejected passage suggests that those with insight can see the quality of Jesus' works as easily as they can read the skies for the weather. The implication is that the ministry of Jesus provides a series of signs. This idea is, as we have seen, in harmony with both Q and Luke and John but the coherence of Matthew's view is restored by the omission of this passage: Matthew thus consistently teaches that 'the only sign that will be given is the sign of Jonah'.

2. *A favourable view of astrology: the magi*

It is against this background of signs that we must examine the most vital passage for an understanding of Matthew's attitude towards magic and astrology, the story of the magi.

The nature and role of the magi in Matt. 2 are ambiguous. Matthew's own attitude towards them is equally uncertain. Are the magi magicians in the evil sense of the word, and is the story then intended to describe their submission to the Messiah? Or are they to be regarded as wise men, good men, who add their witness to the witness provided by scripture?

The most vigorous defence of the former view is to be found in an article written by W. K. Lowther Clarke in 1936. Lowther Clarke claims that the ambiguity of Matthew may be clarified by reference to Acts and to the apostolic fathers. In Acts 8.11 and 13.6, 8 magi are magicians in the evil sense. The apostolic fathers always use the word μάγος in a bad sense.[11] The apologists use μάγος and its cognates about sixteen times and always in the bad sense.[12] The magi could be Jewish magicians from the dispersal in Babylon. Tobit and Dan. 5.11 are evidence for the existence of Jewish magic in Babylon. Lowther Clarke's most interesting suggestion is that the evil magicians by their gifts were offering symbolic submission. 'The two almost invariable accompaniments of the incantations are incense and myrrh' (p. 47). 'They . . . offered the instruments of their trade, incense and myrrh; also the gold which they had amassed as privileged possessors of knowledge greatly prized' (ibid.). Lowther Clarke concludes that the story is Matthew's equivalent to Acts 8.13, 19 and is symbolic of the triumph over the magicians.

We must first observe that while this sort of interpretation of the magi is found in some of the early church fathers, notably Ignatius, the early commentators are by no means unanimous. Indeed the possibility that Matthew was *approving* of magic and encouraging Christian patronage of the wise art whose exponents could even seek out the Christ was an embarrassment to a number of them.[13]

Secondly, it is true that Jewish magic was very important in the ancient magical world and that one of its strongholds was in Syria. But it is unlikely that Matthew has Jewish magicians in mind here. It is important to distinguish between astrology and wizardry. Matthew disliked the latter but was not averse to using the former. His purpose was not to confound the Jewish magicians but to include the witness of the stars amongst the signs. It is true that Jewish magic had long been established in Babylon, but no argument can be made on this basis, since Babylon was also an area famed for its Gentile astrology. In favour of a Gentile-astrological background rather than a Jewish-magical one are certain passages from the Old Testament. Most important is Isa. 60.1–7: 'Darkness shall cover the earth and gross darkness the peoples, but the Lord shall arise upon thee, and his glory shall be seen upon thee. And nations shall come to thy light and kings to the brightness of thy rising.' There can be little doubt that this passage was in the mind of Matthew, especially in view of the references to the gifts in v. 6, and that the kings who come are Gentiles, as the use of τὰ ἔθνη in the LXX indicates. Incidentally the fact that in Matthew the star is regarded as the personification of Christ himself (e.g. 'they rejoiced when they saw the star') is explained by Isaiah, where it is the Lord who arises upon them. 'His star' (Matt. 2.2) is the glory of the Lord (Isa. 60.1). The other important passage is the Balaam cycle in Num. 22–24. It has been thought odd that Matthew does not make specific reference to the Balaam story if it was so much in his mind. The answer may be provided by Krister Stendahl, who argues that it is wrong to read Matthew in the light of Luke and to assume that he is telling the simple birth story of the Messiah. It is in fact not a birth cycle at all which he gives us, but a sort of geographical apology, seeking to answer the question, 'How was it Jesus the Messiah came from Galilee?' Just as ch. 2 is concentrated on the place names, so ch. 1 is on personal names – 'why Jesus?' The cycle is thus divided not into genealogy and birth stories (of which there are none) but names and places. This explains why the Balaam incident is not explicitly mentioned. All the formulae quotations are based on their inclusion of relevant geographical terms in ch. 2, and the Balaam story did not contain any. We may guess that if the star prophecy (Num. 24.17) had referred to Judah, rather than to Israel and Jacob, Matthew might well have used it. The same explanation applies to the Isaiah passage, 60.1–7.[14]

Another Old Testament passage which may have influenced the story of the magi is the account in Exodus of the conflict between the magicians of Pharaoh and Moses.[15] The influence of Moses is however less likely than that of Balaam for the following reasons.

Firstly, the crucial aspect of the struggle of Moses with the magicians is that of conflict. The magicians are forced after a contest to submit. But in Matthew there is no conflict between the magi and Christ; the conflict is between Herod and Christ. This situation fits the Balaam story exactly, where Balak equals Herod, and Balaam and the magi are both guided from the first towards the truth, which they receive with willing admiration.

Secondly, it is true that in both stories the magicians are intended to subserve the purpose of the evil ruler but the difference is also important. In Exodus the magicians fail to serve Pharaoh because they have met a magic stronger than their own; in Matthew they only co-operate with the ruler out of ignorance of Herod's true intentions, and when these are discovered, they withdraw voluntarily. Pharaoh's magi stop because they cannot go on; Herod's because they will not. Here again the parallel is much closer to Balaam who chooses, under divine constraint, not to use his power against Israel. The emphasis in both Balaam and Matthew is on the witness to the truth given in spite of threats.

Thirdly, the Egyptian magicians are a different species from that represented by Balaam. The Egyptians are wizards, conjurors, enchanters. The word used here is *chartummim* which is translated in the LXX ἐπαοιδοί (Ex. 7.11, 22), and their activities are ταῖς φαρμακείαις. They are not described as μάγοι here. But in the Balaam story it is not a matter of doing tricks but of interpreting dreams and showing wisdom in general advice.[16] Hence the assumption of Symmachus that the Balaam group were highly esteemed μάγοι. The magicians in Exodus perform the sort of feat which in the New Testament would have been described as that of a γόης.

Balaam is an ecstatic prophet of a more or less respectable kind. He is a diviner, an astrologer, a man powerful in word rather than in particular feats of magic. The difference between the two types is discussed in A. D. Nock's essay on 'Paul and the Magus' in *The Beginnings of Christianity* V. It is clear from Nock's account that the magi in Matthew fall into the Balaam category rather than into the Egyptian wizard class of magi as evil professional consultants. Herodotus says that a magus had to be present at every sacrifice and sing a chant narrating the birth of the gods (I. 132). Is there not a connection here with the magi of Matthew, celebrating the holy birth? The Persian magi were skilled at interpreting dreams, which again fits the dream patterns of Matthew and explains Symmachus' translation of Gen. 41.8, 24. Nock shows that by Hellenistic times the original national function of the Persian magi had become less familiar and this gave rise to the bad sense of the word – the magi were now unfamiliar and alien. The ancient tribes of the magi were broken up and dispersed by the conquests of Alexander, and this led not only to the word having a more general application (since to be a magus no longer implied Persian blood) but many magi, robbed of their traditional means of support, turned to private practice, and this again led to the word having an evil implication. Such μάγοι were then called γόητες, but the latter was not a word which any magician would apply to himself. The self-styled name of the magicians was magi, for this description had a mysterious sacred history behind it.

Now it seems from this reasonably clear that had Matthew wished to show the rout of Egyptian-type magicians, evil persons of the sort we encounter in Acts, he would have made his account much less ambiguous. Would he not have called them γόητες? We may be tempted to interpret his ambiguity by the clarity of Acts, but Matthew could hardly expect his readers to do that. If his purpose was polemical, as Lowther Clarke supposes, why did he use the ambiguous word 'magi', setting it in a context of sacred knowledge and religious devotion?

Nock points out that Matthew and Luke in Acts differ in their use of magus.[17] Now from what has been said above it is clear why they differ. Matthew's magi are connected with astrology and with the ancient religious traditions of the Persian magi which were respected and revered. Those in Acts are connected with professional spell-making for personal profit, intended to help or harm individuals. We shall see that when Matthew comes up against this latter type of magic, he is as offended as Luke is hostile.[18]

Finally, Lowther Clarke has not proved his case about the gifts of the magi being magical apparatus and thus signifying the renunciation of their arts. It is certainly true that myrrh and frankincense were frequently used in magical recipes.[19] Jewish magic is also familiar with the use of myrrh. In the Babylonian Talmud (*Shabbath* 62b) myrrh is mentioned as being a potent love charm used by the women of Jerusalem to attract men's love. But the evidence falls short of proving that the magi in Matthew were offering the tools of their trade as an indication of the abandonment of their magical profession. For although myrrh was important in magic, it had many other uses in the ancient world. The formula for the composition of incense used in the temple at Jerusalem included frankincense (Ex. 30.34ff.), and we know that myrrh was later added to the formula.[20] The anointing oil described in Ex. 30.23ff. included myrrh. It also had associations with royalty (Ps. 45.8 and S. of Sol. 3.6). The important passage in Isa. 60.6 tells us that gold and frankincense were regarded as suitable gifts for kings to offer. We cannot draw an absolute distinction between the use of these perfumes in the ancient world in worship and in magic, since we always have the possibility, for example, that the incense was burned in the temple in order to exorcize it. But we have sufficient information to try to come to some conclusions.

Matthew may have described the gifts of the magi in the way he did for the following reasons:

(i) He wished to show the reverential worship offered by the sacred astrologers in obedient response to the heavenly sign. His familiarity with the use of myrrh and frankincense in both religious and secular adoration made this an obvious choice.

(ii) The religious associations would have been reinforced in his mind by his local knowledge of the importance of these products, assuming a Syrian origin for Matthew. Antioch was famous for its perfumes.[21]

(iii) Prominent in Matthew's mind were Isa. 60.1–6 and the Balaam story. These both mention gold (Num. 22.18 and 24.13). The gold is offered to the diviner Balaam; Matthew goes further; the diviners offer the chosen one gold. Isa. 60 does not mention myrrh but this need cause no difficulty. The two perfumes were associated very closely, not only geographically with regard to country of origin, but also regarding use. They were even botanically confused by some, as Theophrastus tells us.[22] So Matthew may have added myrrh simply because of this association. The later Christian imagination which made the magi kings and placed them on camels was drawing on the details of Isa. 60 in just the same way as the imagination of Matthew was drawing on the same source for the gifts.[23]

It may be concluded thus that Matthew is not talking about magi in the evil sense of the word but the good. While he does not make a case *against* astrology, there can be no doubt that the Matthew's magi are astrologers. But if the magi were professional astrologers and if Matthew does not attack them why does he include them? There is more to this than a desire to have representatives of the Gentile world. What this last suggestion overlooks is the positive meaning of the heavenly sign and its interpretation by the magi. Matthew is not concerned with the pros and cons of astrology (although he appears to have regarded it as quite respectable) but with the attestation of the divine child. The voice of prophecy is supplemented by the voice of the heavens; the word which must be fulfilled and the heavens which shall not pass away until the Son of Man is revealed continue to offer a double witness to Christ throughout the rest of the gospel.

3. *Resistance to magical exorcism*

We have shown that Matthew does not regard the miracles of Jesus as signs. One of the most important reasons for this is that in the richest tradition of such stories available to him, Mark's gospel, Matthew found that the miracle stories were clothed with magical traits which might not only be undesirable in themselves from the point of view of an educated man but drew the attention of the reader away from the messianic significance of Jesus in relationship to the Torah and the prophets.

Matthew's point of view is seen most clearly in his attitude towards exorcism. He refers to exorcism on several occasions, including healing summaries (8.16; 4.24), editorial constructions based on Q (9.32–34; 12.22f.) and Q passages (12.25–29; 12.43–45). Jesus' disciples share his ability as an exorcist (7.22; 10.1, 8) and the exorcisms of Jewish healers are referred to (12.27). On three occasions Matthew makes use of established stories dealing with possession. These are the Gadarene madmen (8.28–34), the epileptic boy (17.14–18) and the daughter of the Canaanite woman (15.21–28).

Considering that a fair amount of material is available in the gospel it is remarkable how little we learn about the actual methods of exorcism. Only in the story of the Gadarene swine do we have any indication of reaction from the spirits. Here they speak twice (8.29, 31) but there are important differences between the wording in Matthew and Mark. Elsewhere in Matthew the spirits do not scream or shout; there is utter silence. The only details we can gather about the method are that every act of exorcism must be by means of or in the name of some thing, person or power other than the exorcist himself. The disciples cast out devils by means of the name of Jesus (7.22); it is possible to perform these feats by means of a powerful familiar spirit (9.34; 12.24); Jesus challenges the Jewish exorcists to reveal by what or in whose name they do their work, and himself claims to work by the Spirit of God (12.28). This relationship between the exorcist and his power is usually expressed by ἐν with the dative.

It is remarkable that there is no clear case in Matthew where we are informed about the style or manner by which Jesus addressed the evil spirits. In 17.18 there is a possible case, but does Jesus 'speak sternly' to the spirit or to the boy? Probably the lad is addressed.

Not only is the manner of his speaking unrecorded but only once in Matthew do we find an actual word spoken by Jesus to any evil spirit, and even that is not a word of exorcistic power but simply an agreement to their request (8.32). In 8.16 Jesus is described as casting out the spirit 'with a word', but this indicates only the ease with which his healings were performed and not use of a special verbal technique.

When Jesus passes on his power to his disciples he does not tell them his secret or commit any form of words or actions to them. They are simply given authority (ἐξουσία) over the spirits. He does not give any further instructions because he does not know any; he passes on no technique because he uses none. No esoteric magical tradition is to be permitted. All that is said in most cases is that he healed the possessed or merely that the spirit 'came out'.

The most interesting detail is in the parable of the strong man in 12.29. Matthew follows Mark 3.27 closely here and this is the only reference in Matthew to the exorcists' classical feat of binding Satan. But the fact, not the method, is mentioned, and it is significant that Matthew prefers the Marcan rather than the Lucan (Q?) version (see below, pp. 130f.).

Finally, Matthew's reticence about technique is seen in 12.28 (= Luke 11.20) where the change from 'finger' to 'spirit' is to be explained in terms of the association with magical technique which the finger of God had. The only place in the gospel where Jesus seems to be on the point of disclosing his method is thus spiritualized.

Luke, in contrast, offers a rich variety of detail about exorcism. Luke places more emphasis upon Jesus' words to the demons. While Matthew uses ἐπιτιμάω but once in this connection and then in an ambiguous manner (Matt. 17.18), four times Luke tells us that Jesus rebuked spirits (4.35, 39, 41; 9.42). On one occasion Jesus orders a spirit, παρήγγελλεν (8.29), and twice he reduces spirits to silence (4.35, 41). Once he enquires the name of a spirit (8.30).

Several additional details are provided by Luke about the power or authority by which the exorcist does his work. The name of Jesus was effective whether used by the disciples of Jesus or anyone else (Luke 9.49; 10.17). It will be noticed that the rejected ones in Matt. 7.22 regarded themselves as disciples of Christ, whereas the exorcist in Luke 9.49 is clearly schismatic. Jesus describes his own authority as resting in his use of 'the finger of God' (11.20).

Luke tells us far more about the relationships between Jesus and the spirits. He records nine words spoken by Jesus to devils in direct speech and three or four in reported speech (Luke 4.35; 8.29a, 30). Matthew reports only one word spoken to a spirit (Matt. 8.32 ὑπάγετε). In Luke thirty-four words spoken by devils to Christ are reported and ten or eleven more are implied, a total of about forty-four words of direct and reported devil-talk. But in Matthew only twenty-three words of devils are recorded. Luke's devils scream with loud shouts (4.33; 8.28), shout and talk (4.41), implore (8.31, 32), give sudden shrieks (9.39) and are reduced to submission (10.17, 20) – to mention only their oral activity. In Matthew κράζω and παρακαλέω are each used once only of the evil spirits (8.29f.). Otherwise there is no reaction from the spirits at all in Matthew; no tearing or throwing people about; they simply leave in silence.

It is possible even from this brief and by no means exhaustive survey to see that in Luke the rudiments of an exorcist technique may be found. A would-be exorcist could gather a certain amount of information about how to cast out a spirit and about the reactions for which he must prepare should he do so. This accounts for the greater detail of Luke's version of the binding of the strong man (Luke 11.21f.). In Luke the metaphor is military rather than domestic; the stronger one is not a housebreaker but a warrior. Only here in the New Testament is καθοπλίζω used in a literal sense, and the same is true of πανοπλία. The latter word is found in Eph. 6.11, in the description of the battles against evil spirits, and this type of military language is more normal in the exorcizing situation than is the housebreaking metaphor. Phobos, a son of Mars, is described in *PGM* XIII.529, appearing fully armed. It is interesting to see that his name which follows is Βερβαλϊ Βαλβιθι which could be a corruption of Βεεζεβουλ. The idea of conflict is appropriate to the subject; it is a real conflict, not a walk-over as in Matthew, and the 'armour' consists of the behaviour and defensive techniques of the spirits which is stripped from them by the power of Jesus. This is why Matthew has preferred the Marcan version of the saying. This is also why the description of the ejected wandering spirit in Matt. 12.43–45 concludes: 'So shall it be with this evil generation.' In Matthew the paragraph thus becomes a parable, but in Luke it remains a real warning about the dangers which may follow an inadequate exorcism.

It is wholly in keeping with Matthew's attitude that the passage about the return of the disciples from their mission (Luke 10.17–20, probably Q) is omitted; it is too specific in describing the power which Christians had over demonic agencies.

Let us now examine the particular stories about possession which Matthew offers. The first is the incident of the Gadarene swine (Matt. 8.28–34 = Mark 5.1–20; Luke 8.26–39). Matthew introduces some remarkable alterations in the words of the madmen. Jesus is no longer addressed as 'Jesus, Son of the most high God', as in both Mark and Luke, but simply as 'Son of God'. In Mark the spirits try to compel Jesus or to exorcize him; in Luke this is softened to an entreaty (Luke 8.28). But in Matthew even the request has disappeared and is replaced by a question, 'Are you come before the time to torture us?' The exorcizing words of Jesus are omitted by Matthew altogether and the name-enquiring incident has likewise disappeared. There is no mention of Legion. The plurality of demons is maintained, but this is achieved by means of doubling the possessed rather than describing many possessors in a single man.

It is sometimes suggested that these alterations are simply intended to abbreviate the story by removing novelistic features.[24] This cannot be the case, however, because the omissions and abbreviations are too consistent. Matthew in fact leaves out all the features of the story which have to do with the technique of exorcism, i.e. with magic. Again, far from discriminating against the merely novelistic, Matthew actually adds one or two details;

he alone says that the presence of the possessed made it impossible for anyone to pass by that way and he also adds the description of the men as being χαλεποὶ λίαν (v. 28b).

The effect is that in Matthew the story practically ceases to be an exorcism. The devils are not compelled to go; they simply flee before Messiah. All element of struggle, of menace, of tension is gone. The spirits have not been exorcized by a wonder worker; they have perished for ever before the face of Messiah.[25]

The second story about demon possession offered by Matthew is the story of the possessed daughter of the Canaanite woman (Matt. 15.21–28; Mark 7.24–30; not in Luke). In Mark 7.26 the woman asks Jesus to cast the demon out of her daughter, but Matthew simply records the woman as saying, 'Help me'. Twice again in the story Mark refers to the demon (vv. 29 and 30), and on both occasions Matthew substitutes innocuous expressions. For Mark's 'The demon has departed from your daughter' he writes, 'Be it unto you as you wish', and for Mark's 'She found her daughter lying on a bed and the demon gone out of her' Matthew writes 'Her daughter was healed the same hour'.

The third story about demon possession is that of the epileptic boy (Matt. 17.14–21; Mark 9.14–29; Luke 9.37–43). The main point of the reinterpretation provided by Matthew is that interest is no longer in the question of whether or not Jesus can heal the boy, and if so how, but in the mere fact that Jesus does heal him and the implications of this for discipleship. The story in Mark points to the origin of miracle-working faith and the mystery of its power in the person of Jesus. In Matthew there is no interest in the power as such, but rather in the quality of discipleship which the Messiah expects. This shift in emphasis is achieved by omitting the part of the story which deals with the contrast between the master and the disciples (Mark 9.14–19), omitting the father's doubt and its implied challenge to Jesus' power (Mark 9.22b–24), and changing the final comment from 'There is no means of casting this sort out but prayer' (Mark 9.29), to 'Your faith is too weak' (Matt. 17.20). The comment in Mark is not about the nature of discipleship but merely recommends a particular approach towards a particular (τοῦτο τὸ γένος Mark 9.29) type of evil spirit. Mark is making a clinical observation.

Of particular interest is the fact that Matthew minimizes the place and activity of the evil spirit. Mark describes the boy as 'having a dumb spirit' (Mark 9.17b) but Matthew says 'He is an epileptic and has bad fits' (17.15). Mark stresses the personal nature of the possession and personal animosity of the spirit. 'It seizes him: it tears him'; 'it often casts him into fire and water'; it has a malignant desire to destroy him. When the boy is brought to Jesus the spirit (not the boy!) sees Jesus and convulses the boy (v. 20). But in Matthew there is nothing like this. The boy simply does fall into fire and water – it is merely a symptom of his condition. The only indication of personal possession which appears in Matthew's version at all is the note in v. 18 'and the devil left him'. Missing from Matthew is the dramatic climax when Jesus rebukes the spirit and utters the dreadful binding words of power (Mark 9.25f.). In Matthew we are simply told that Jesus rebuked it or him. If the latter is correct then Jesus does not speak to the spirit at all but only to the boy.

Matthew's treatment of the exorcisms is thus perfectly clear. He tends to modify them by substituting general expressions for Mark's vivid personalistic ones. Where Mark already has words of which Matthew approves, he carries on his policy by simply omitting most references to the demonic aspect. In its place he puts sayings about the mission of Jesus, so that the exorcisms become teaching illustrations.

4. Resistance to magical healing

(i) Seven Matthean miracles
We shall now consider several other miracles in Matthew's gospel in so far as these are relevant to his attitudes towards the magical.

(a) The healing of the leper (Matt. 8.1–4; Mark 1.40–45; Luke 5.12–15)

Matthew omits all reference to the emotion of Jesus. Neither σπλαγχνισθείς, ὀργισθείς nor ἐμβριμησάμενος occur. The reason for this is deeper than a mere disliking for publicizing Jesus' feelings. The gospels are of course reticent about the emotions of Jesus, but Matthew does not hesitate to say that Jesus marvels (8.10) and is full of grief and dismay (26.37). Indeed three times Matthew uses σπλαγχνίζομαι of Jesus (9.36; 14.14; 20.34) and ἐμβριμάομαι is used of Jesus in 9.30. So why does Matthew reject these words in the leper story? The omission of σπλαγχνισθείς could be accounted for if it was lacking in the original text of Mark, and if what Matthew read there was ὀργισθείς. Matthew would then have left it out because he could not understand its suitability. This, although a probable explanation in itself, does not account for the omission of ἐμβριμάομαι in Matt. 8.4a. The word certainly is most unusual and inappropriate but as we have noticed Matthew does not shrink from using it in 9.30. The explanation has to do with the ambiguity of ἐμβριμάομαι. It may mean 'snorting', 'storming at', or 'scolding' and this sort of meaning must be attached to the word in 9.30. A second meaning is more unusual. ἐμβριμάομαι can be used to describe the agitated raving of an ecstatic magician about to pronounce a spell.[26] Now this was an intense activity performed by the magician *before* the performance of the action. If the word had been used *after* the miracle had been wrought it might still strike the reader as being extravagantly forceful but it would not necessarily be as offensive or prone to misunderstanding as if it came prior to the action. The fact that Matthew has used the word after the action in 9.30 assures us that he would not have bothered to omit it if he had found it after the action in Mark 1.40–45. Is it possible then that in the text of Mark which Matthew used ἐμβριμάομαι was located not in v.43 (after the action) but in v.41 (before the action)?[27] It may have been removed to its present position, where it follows the action, in order to lessen the suspicion which the word might well have aroused when it was read in its original place prior to the action. Delaying the word robbed it of its suspect associations.

Matthew also heightens the value of the story for devotional meditation by placing it immediately after the Sermon on the Mount so that it is witnessed by the crowd who had heard the sermon (8.1). It thus becomes an illustration of the grace offered to sick men to enable them to meet the demand of the sermon. Worship and obedience are stressed as appropriate attitudes for the supplicant and the disobedience of the healed man is omitted.

(b) Peter's mother-in-law (Matt. 8.14f.; Mark 1.29ff.; Luke 4.38f.)

Matthew dislikes exorcist technique and this little incident illustrates his attitude in contrast to Luke who has Jesus rebuking the fever. Matthew however does not show Jesus as an exorcist but by concentrating attention on the figures of Jesus and the woman alone (the names of the disciples are left out, so is the request that Jesus should act, and when healed the woman serves Jesus only, not the whole company) makes the incident less thaumaturgical and more devotional.

(c) *The summary and formula quotation* (Matt. 8.16f.; Mark 1.32ff.; Luke 4.40f.)

Held is correct in pointing out that this is a christological summary, rather than (as in Mark) merely a further incident in a crowded day, but he does not sufficiently stress the contrast Matthew is making between the Hellenistic God-man of Mark and his own concept of the prophetic Servant-Messiah. Held says for example that the summary 'becomes a statement about the power of Jesus by his mere word',[28] but the fact is that the previous healings, of which 8.16f. is the summary, do not show the power of Jesus by his mere word. In the first miracle (the leper) Jesus both touches and speaks, in the second he speaks but does not touch, and in the third he touches but does not speak! This variety may be intended to make technique of whatever kind as insignificant as possible. When Matthew says that Jesus 'drove out the spirits by a word and healed all who were sick' he is describing the ease and simplicity of Jesus' healings, not drawing attention to any method, whether use of words of any kind or of manual manipulation. The idea is that normal healing methods fade into insignificance in the merciful works of him who is no thaumaturge but the very Messiah of God. Contrast Luke's description: 'He laid his hands on them one by one and cured them. Devils also came out of many of them, shouting, "You are the Son of God".' Here the emphasis, whilst still christological, is upon the miracles themselves as mighty works. This is impossible in Matthew. The miracles are neither mighty works in themselves, nor signs of anything, but only become significant in the light of prophecy.

(d) *The stilling of the storm* (Matt. 8.23–27; Mark 4.35–41; Luke 8.22–25)

This incident is also placed in a setting of discipleship so as to take emphasis away from the wonder itself. We notice that the word of power (Mark 4.39) is lacking. Matthew uses φιμόω in 22.12 where the man without the wedding garment 'has nothing to say', but he leaves it out when it could be connected with magical technique. This explains his omission of both its Marcan occurrences (Mark 1.25 and 4.39). Luke retains it in the former case. It is obvious that φιμόω, like ἐμβριμάομαι, is a word with both a normal and a magical use. These words are treated with great caution by Matthew, only being used in contexts where it is perfectly clear there can be no question of magical technique.

(e) The paralytic (Matt. 9.2–8; Mark 2.1–12; Luke 5.17–26)

The most noticeable feature is the absence of the roof-raising incident in Matthew. This is probably merely in order to concentrate attention on the main point of the story, the question about authority to forgive, but Bultmann[29] quotes with approval H. Jahnow, who suggests that the roof incident is a demonic deception motif which has been forgotten or transformed in the Christian tradition and finally dropped out altogether. This would at least be consistent with what we have observed of Matthew's behaviour elsewhere, but the suggestion must still be regarded as highly speculative.

(f) The daughter of Jairus and the woman with the haemorrhage (Matt. 9.18–26; Mark 5.21–43; Luke 8.40–56)

Matthew's treatment of this is a good example of his sensitivity towards the problem of cause and effect in the miracles of Jesus. It is notorious that in Mark the woman is healed automatically without the knowledge or consent of Jesus. She is healed by a power which Jesus emits. Matthew changes the order of the healing so that the woman is not healed by the touching of the cloak and there is no power, no miracle-working aura surrounding Jesus which the superstitious can tap. The impersonal atmosphere of compulsion in Mark's account, where the woman manages to control the power for herself, is transformed into a personal faith relationship. In Mark the woman expects magic and gets it. Jesus struggles to control her and it ('Who touched me?'). In Matthew she expects magic but instead is met by the healing grace of the messianic Servant.

Matthew tells us much less about Jairus' daughter than does Mark. In Mark the picture is of Jesus and his patient; he is practically a consultant; we are told the child's father's name, the child's age, what Jesus said to her, how she walked around when she had got up and so on. Matthew shows no interest in this type of 'case history'. This is not because he does not want to draw attention to the miracle – on the contrary the miracle is heightened, for the girl is already dead before Jesus hears about it (Matt. 9.18). The reason is Matthew's distaste for technical details of miracles as such. The famous and controversial word of power 'Talitha *cumi*' is simply omitted. Jesus speaks to the mourners but when performing the miracle he is silent.

The episode in Matt. 14.35f. is fully consistent with Matthew's version of the story about the little girl, for Jesus is *asked* if his garment may be touched. It is Mark whose account, which is similar, is at odds with his version of Jairus' daughter. Contrast Mark 6.56 with Mark 5.27ff. We would expect Mark to say something rather like Acts 5.15, where the shadow of Peter automatically heals all those upon whom it falls. But we do not expect Matthew to say anything like that, and examination reveals that in fact he does not.

(g) *Walking on the water* (Matt. 14.22–34; Mark 6.45–52)

It may be thought odd that Matthew should retain this story with its many Hellenistic parallels and its magical atmosphere. It is clear however that, as in the other storm story (Matt. 8.23–27), the interest in the story is in discipleship. The first story includes examples of discipleship (Matt. 8.19–22) of which the stilling of the storm has become a symbol, and in a similar way the walking on the water is preceded by the feeding of the five thousand (note the added emphasis on the responsibilities of the disciples, Matt. 14.19b; cf. Mark 6.41b) and includes a didactic account of Peter walking on the water. This incident should be read with Acts 28.1–6 in mind as a foil. The story of Paul's miraculous escape from prison and the sea, with its naked admiration of Paul as the semi-divine hero (no reproof follows the islanders' comment 'he is a god') is a striking contrast with the Matthean failure of discipleship and the demand for faith and the climactic admiration of the Son of God.

(ii) *Three Matthean omissions*

Three miracles recorded by Mark are omitted by Matthew.

(a) *The demoniac in the synagogue at Capernaum* (Mark 1.21–28)

The omission of this story is not difficult to understand in the light of Matthew's reticence about exorcism. There is no specially valuable point of Christian teaching which Matthew would have obtained from this story, which he had not already derived from other less objectionable stories. The story of the Canaanite woman could be utilized for the sake of the sayings about Jesus' mission and the epileptic boy because of the teaching on faith, but both stories were severely purged before use. What would be left of the Capernaum incident once it was purged? Nothing would be left but the mighty power of the word of Jesus, which Matthew has included in any case in his general summary (Mark 1.27b; Matt. 8.16). Matthew appears to have wanted but one story of exorcism as such. The story of the Gadarene madmen was selected to serve for this purpose because even when the specific exorcist technique was eliminated there was still enough of a story left to make it possible to tell it. This is not true of the Capernaum story.[30]

(*b*) and (*c*) *The deaf mute and the blind man of Bethsaida* (Mark 7.32ff.; 8.22ff.)

Contrary to the first impression, these two spittle miracles are not omitted in Matthew but are broken up, dispersed and edited so as to make them acceptable.

The method of Matthew in retaining certain items in these two stories is exactly similar to his retention of certain details in the story of Mark 1.21–28. Other aspects of this story are included in Matthew's version of the Gadarene maniac. This observation also helps to explain Matthew's famous doubling of patients in both those examples. The story in Matt. 8.28–32 is the story of both the madman of Mark 5 and the demoniac of Mark 1. The story of the two blind men in Matt. 20.30–34 is the story both of Bartimaeus and the man of Bethsaida. The repetition of the account in Matt. 9.27–31 seems to be due to Matthew's desire for ten mighty works in chapters eight and nine, and the fact that both the spittle miracles of Mark were associated in Matthew's mind is shown by the fact that his edited versions of them are grouped together in Matt. 9.27–31, 32–34, and occupy the final place in the ten. They are kept till last presumably because the editing of them presented particularly difficult problems.

Why does Matthew behave like this? Wellhausen[31] suggested long ago that Matthew was 'put off by the magical procedure'. 'But then', says Held, 'the question immediately arises why he has not done the same here as in the case of the healing of the woman with the haemorrhage, which he stripped of all its magical traits?' The answer is that this is just what Matthew has done. The simple fact is that in the spittle miracles there is far more magic. It is not simply a matter, as with the woman with a flow of blood, of reversing the order of touching and being healed and having faith. The spittle miracles consist very largely in a list of detailed magical therapeutic actions, and omission of them leaves but a skeleton, barely recognizable. Held's own explanation is that Matthew omitted the stories because he could not find in them any point of departure for his re-interpretation, either in terms of faith (which is not mentioned in the original story) or Christology (Jesus is a mere Hellenistic wonder-worker) or of discipleship (not mentioned either). This is perfectly true, but we must go on to add that the reason for this was that they were too thoroughly impregnated with magical ideas. What Matthew finally did was to include the faith element by fusing 'the two blind men'. Hence both the stress on faith in Matt. 9.28f. and the christological element were included by rewriting the cry of the spectators in terms of Israel and the Servant-Messiah (Matt. 9.33b; 12.23b; cf. 8.16f. and 12.17ff.).

Our examination of the miracles in Matthew has indicated the following aspects of Matthew's treatment.

Matthew generally omits or rewrites the 'word of power' which is associated with the Marcan miracles. No word of power is reported at Matt. 8.26, 29ff.; 9.25; 17.18; 20.34. A word of power or at least a saying exists in all the Marcan parallels. It is especially noteworthy that all of the Aramaic words are omitted in spite of the fact that Matthew's gospel, if addressed to Jews in Syria, would have been a more natural place for these words than Mark's gospel. Matthew even omits the famous 'Abba' from 26.39, but retains the Aramaic words from the cross (27.46).

Sometimes the words of power are rewritten so as to remove suspicion that they were magical power formulae. The command 'begone' in Matt. 8.32 is not a word of power but a granting of the request of the already vanquished demons. The saying to the woman with the flow of blood is shortened so that the pronouncement of faith is left. Matthew omits 'Be healed from your infirmity' (Mark 5.34). It is noteworthy that Matthew tends to retain the healing words when the story has a teaching content, i.e. when it is a pronouncement story rather than a miracle story. See Matt. 9.6, 'Stand up, take up your bed and go home'; Matt. 8.3, 'Indeed

I will, be clean again' (assuming the meaning of the story is governed by its position immediately after the Sermon on the Mount); Matt. 12.13, 'Stretch out your arm'; Matt. 14.29, 'Come' (the word to Peter about to walk on the waves). But when the story is in its Marcan form a wonder, a mere mighty work, the word of power is omitted. The reason for this is not only that these words of power sometimes contain specifically dubious items like the foreign words or such words as φιμόω, but because the concept of the word of power as a healing technique was associated with Hellenistic magic. Jewish rabbinic healing on the other hand was usually by means of prayer alone. Sometimes a command might be given or oil administered. Rabbinic prayer miracles were perhaps more acceptable to Matthew.

In view of Matthew's reticence about technique, his references to the touch of Jesus are really quite remarkable. The element of touching with the hand or hands, placing the hands upon, taking by the hand, and being touched is retained by Matthew at 8.3 (Mark 1.41, the leper); 8.15 (Mark 1.31, Simon's wife's mother); 9.18 (Mark 5.23, the request of Jairus); 9.21 (Mark 5.28, the intention of the woman with the flow of blood); 9.25 (Mark 5.41, Jairus' daughter); 14.36 (Mark 6.56, general touching by the crowd) and 19.13ff. (Mark 10.13,16, the blessing of the children). Four times he omits the touch when Mark mentions it. In Matt. 12.15 the reference to the general desire to touch him (Mark 3.10; Luke 6.19) is omitted presumably because Matthew felt it to be uncomfortably like the automatic touching which he had so carefully removed from the story of the sick woman. Mark 6.56 is retained in Matt. 14.36 because Mark says that the sick *asked* that they might touch him; nothing automatic is implied. The second Matthean omission of the touch is in the story found in Mark 7.32ff., which is omitted for reasons we have discussed. The third case is in the longer ending of Mark (16.18), which was of course unknown to Matthew, and finally Matt. 13.58 omits the reference to the laying on of hands in Mark 6.5 because this is part of a phrase the whole of which suggests that Jesus would have done more if he could, an implication rejected by Matthew. Twice he adds the touch where Mark lacks it, in the healing of the blind men (Matt. 9.29 and 20.34). Matthew's desire here is possibly to retain as much as he can of the story in Mark 8.22ff. It may be said that the detail of the touch is the only activity of Jesus in the Mark

8.22ff. pericope which Matthew does retain. It is interesting to see that Luke adds the touch to several stories quite gratuitously. It is added in Luke 4.40 (sunset healings); 7.14 (the incident at Nain); 8.47b (the woman's confession); 13.13 (the crippled woman); and 22.51 (the servant's ear). Luke omits the touch only twice, on both occasions apparently by accident. Jairus does not ask Jesus to touch his daughter but later Jesus in fact does take her by the hand (Luke 8.41) and although he records the desire of the mothers that their children should be touched, he does not actually say that Jesus did so (Luke 18.16).

It is clear that although Matthew did not seek to add the touch he has no objection to the idea of touching except when an impersonal automatic magical idea is implied, as it is in Mark 3.10 and 5.28ff. The reason for this is almost certainly that the action of touching was familiar to Matthew in the Old Testament and the rabbinic tradition of healings, and was therefore not associated in his mind with the pagan Hellenistic techniques implied by Mark.[32]

Matthew has a suspicion of exorcism. We have seen how although the messianic authority over the evil spirits is maintained, almost all details of technique are omitted. This is because exorcism was one of the main functions of the magician. The magic consisted in the method; Matthew retains the fact without the method, trying in this way to purify the subject.[33] The extent of his sensitivity towards exorcism can be judged by the fact that Mark 1.21, Luke 4.31ff. and Acts 13.6ff. equate exorcism with teaching, but Matthew separates the two. For him the new teaching and the authority of Jesus are shown not by the submission of demons but by his own words. Compare Matt. 7.28f. and Mark 1.21. Teaching and action are split again at Matt. 21.23 where the question about authority is referred to the teaching of Jesus, not the cleansing of the temple. It is possible that, in thus distinguishing between teaching and acting, Matthew's Christ is rather unlike the figure of the great Rabbi, who did both. If this is so, then Matthew seems to have felt that the sacrifice of a detail of the Jewish ideal was a reasonable price to pay to avoid misunderstanding by his readers of the nature of the wonders of Christ.

CONCLUSION

The results of our investigation must not be exaggerated. We do not find Jesus portrayed in the gospels as waving a wand, mumbling an elaborate incantation or carrying out the kind of magical ritual familiar in the papyri. We do find however certain aspects of the gospels which are at home in the magical world-view of the first century of our era, and a number of details relevant to the central concern of magic, namely the health, happiness, life and death of individuals threatened by hostile powers. We find that the miracles of Jesus and particularly his exorcisms and healings were interpreted as being magical at an early date, that in the light of contemporary presuppositions it was inevitable that they should have been so interpreted, and that the gospels themselves witness to early stages of this interpretation.

It is to be expected that any presentation of a religious message at any place or time would be modified by the presuppositions of the people to whom the message is addressed. This modification may take place unconsciously, as in the West today, when most Christians do not realize how Westernized is the Christianity to which they are accustomed, or consciously, as when the church in Europe seeks to adapt its message to those who live in industrial centres.

Mark's gospel presents the acts of Jesus so that they would meet the needs, interests and expectations of people exposed to the dangers of ordinary life in the first century, dangers from which a wonder-worker, a divine magician might deliver them. This adaptation was made unconsciously; it was already in process before the earliest gospel was written.

By the time the earliest gospel was written the tradition of the acts of Jesus had already become saturated with the outlook of Hellenistic magic. The Jewish Son of Man was already radiant with the mysterious magical power of the Hellenistic wonder-working Saviour. This process was aided by two factors. The first was that Jesus himself was not remembered as performing all his cures in the manner which the later, more reflective strata of the tradition presents him as doing, by a mere command. Sickness and disease did not always simply flee before the glance of the Messiah. As well as using faith, prayer, knowledge of the Torah and holiness of life, the means by which God was believed to work miracles through the rabbis, Jesus was thought to have used folk remedies. Sometimes his cures took time and trouble. It was not unknown – or so primitive elements in more than one gospel would have us believe – for him to recommend the potency of a particular holy pool or spring, for him to use popular remedies such as spittle, and for him to ask his patients if they were aware of any improvement. Above all, the two earliest of all the sets of collected materials, Q and Mark, make it clear that Jesus entered without reserve into the central conflict of the magician's art, the struggle with evil powers directly confronted in the persons of the possessed. What methods he used, whether magical or otherwise, made no difference to the immense impact made by the fact upon the early Christian communities. For them it was enough that Jesus was known to have healed the sick by various mysterious methods and to have cast out spirits. This was the starting point justified by the tradition itself from which the same tradition was to become so fully penetrated by the magical ideal.

The second impetus for this interpretation in the light of magical beliefs came from the early Hellenistic or mixed Jewish-Gentile communities set in the pagan empire. The gospel tradition was inevitable adapted to meet the needs of those who, as the Epistle to the Hebrews puts it, 'were all their life-time in bondage through the fear of death to the devil'. Just as the Christ figure of the Apocalypse is triumphantly adapted to meet the terrors of those suffering beneath the Roman persecution, just as the cosmic Christ of the Colossian letter satisfies the needs of those caught up in the worship of the aeons, so the Saviour described by Mark's gospel was a deliverer for those whose lives were lived in fear of evil spirits, the constant threat of the powers of darkness to the body and mind, and to the limitations of human skill and strength.

It is due to those two pressures – the need of the exposed Christian communities and the invitation offered by the exorcism and folk healing already present in the stories of Jesus – that the Messiah in Mark has become a divine man, a wonder-working Son of God.

But although magical beliefs have so deeply influenced Mark, this is also the gospel in which these beliefs are most naïve, least self-conscious. There is no awareness of the danger of pollution, of the threat of counter-attack from pagan sources – the sort of attack against which by the middle and latter part of the next century Justin and Origen were fighting. There is as yet no reaction against magic. Mark represents the first stage in any preaching of the gospel – the stage of presentation in terms suitable to the needs and expectations of the hearers. The next stage, of correction, of self-consciousness, of qualification and polemic against distortion is found in the later gospels.

In Luke we find a world-view arranged along magical lines, the battle between Jesus and his foes being presented in terms harmonious with the sort of significance attached in magic to the battle between spiritual forces. Christianity, face to face with magic as described in Acts, overcomes it by a greater power of the same kind, the source of which is traced back to the one who, indwelt bodily by the energy of the spirit world, passed his authority over the demons on to the church which confessed his mighty name.

In Matthew we find a deeper awareness of the danger of this view. Not all those who say the name shall enter the kingdom, and there are exorcists who use the name but are unknown to the Lord. The miracles are removed from the sphere of miraculous magic and replaced in the setting of the Old Testament, where in accordance with prophecy they become witnesses to the moral authority of the Servant-Messiah. If space allowed it could be shown that magic interpreted by Luke and expunged by Matthew is baptized in the Apocalypse of John, where the relationship between Christianity and magic becomes creative, and magical images and customs are taken over wholesale without compromise to the essentially eschatological nature of the church's faith.

Was Jesus a magician? We have made little attempt to press back behind the records to the original beliefs and attitudes of Jesus. We can perhaps venture to suggest however that Jesus did not think of himself as a magician, any more than he thought of himself as pre-existent Logos or as metaphysical Son of God. But to the early Christian the myth of the magus was helpful in various ways; it drew attention to certain aspects of the salvation of Christ in a manner which no other myth was able to do. It is because the myth of the magus has been dead for so long, much earlier in its decease than the effective death of the myths of Logos and Son of of God, that we find it especially difficult to appreciate today.

But perhaps the most abiding impression left by the New Testament treatment of Jesus as the Master-Magician is the restraint of that treatment. The value of the myth is recognized, at least by Mark and Luke, but even in Luke, Jesus is described as warning his church not to rejoice because the spirits were subject to them, but because their names were written in heaven. The potential of the magus-myth for Christology was not very great. He was greater than Solomon, who when invited to ask of the Lord God whatever he wished made a request; whereas Jesus, in a prayer which expresses the heart of religion, asked not for his own will but God's to be done. The records of magic contain nothing like the self-sacrifice of the Gethsemane Christ.

NOTES

I. Introduction

1. For references see the article 'Jesus' in *The Jewish Encyclopaedia* VII, 1904, p. 171.
2. Bab. *Sanhedrin* VI, 43a.
3. Dalman, *Jesus Christ in the Talmud*, pp. 10, 33; Blau, *Altjüdische Zauberwesen*, p. 57, esp. n. 4; Klausner, *Jesus of Nazareth*, pp. 117–54.
4. Irenaeus, *Adversus Haereses* I.14.
5. Hippolytus, *Refutatio* VII.20.
6. Ibid., 15.
7. Burkitt, *Church and Gnosis*, pp. 39, 82f.; Eitrem, *Pap. Osloenses* I, pp. 35, 55; Bonner, *Magical Amulets*, p. 203.
8. *Pseudo-Clem. Hom.* VII.9, *NT Apoc.* II, p. 562. (See *NT Apoc.* for all the citations in this paragraph.)
9. Harnack, *Mission and Expansion of Christianity* I², p. 233; see also Barb, 'The Survival of the Magical Arts' in Mŏmigliano, *Conflict between Paganism and Christianity*, pp. 100ff.
10. Bieler, Θεῖος ἀνήρ II, pp. 36ff., discusses Origen and magic.
11. Ad-Damîrî's *Hayât al-Hayawân* I, p. 703.
12. Thorndike, *History of Magic* I, p. 383.

II. The Recovery of Hellenistic Magic

1. Abt, *Die Apologie des Apuleius*, 1908, is still the most important discussion.
2. Tavenner, *Studies in Magic from Latin Literature*, 1916.
3. E.g. Lowe, *Magic in Greek and Latin Literature*, 1929.
4. Preisendanz, *Papyrusfunde und Papyrusforschung*, pp. 91–5.
5. See the articles by Maurice and Martroye in *Rev. hist. de droit français et étranger* IV.6, 1927, and IV.9, 1930.
6. Both possibilities are suggested by Preisendanz (*Leyh Festgabe*, p. 234).
7. These are now available as *PGM* XII and XIII.

8. In *Göttingische Gelehrte Anzeigen* 2, 1831, pp. 545–60.

9. Kenyon, *Greek Papyri in the British Museum*, p. 65.

10. *PGM*, vol. I, p. 180.

11. Lenormant published a catalogue of the collection.

12. PLond.10070 and PLeid.J383, published together by Griffith and Thompson as *The Demotic Magical Papyrus of London and Leiden*, 1904–9 (*PGM* XIV).

13. PLond.10588, published by Bell, Nock and Thompson in *Proc. Br. Acad.* 17, 1931, pp. 235–87 (*PGM* LXI, vol. III, pp. 1–4).

14. Hunt, 'An Incantation in the Ashmolean Museum', *JEA* 15, 1929, pp. 155–7.

15. There are at least three copies in England, in the library of University College, London, at the Warburg Institute in London, and in the Ashmolean at Oxford.

16. Published by Hunt in *Studies presented to F.Ll. Griffith*, pp. 233–40; David, *The Warren Papyri*, no. 21, plates VI and VII.

17. Schubart, *Pap. . . . Erlangen* no. 15, pp. 22f.

18. Both published by Vogliano, *Annali . . . di Milano*, pp. 226–9.

19. Knudtzon, *Lunder Papyrussammlung* no. 12, pp. 69–74.

20. Preisendanz, *Leyh Festgabe*, p. 236.

21. Collingwood, *Archaeologia* 78, 1928, pp. 157–9; Oxé, *Germanica* 15, 1931, pp. 16–19.

22. Wünsch published two collections, in 1873 and 1898, and a further small selection in 1912 (see Bibliography).

23. Delatte, *Anecd. Athen.* I, p. 97, lines 3ff. The similarity was noticed by Cormack, *HTR* 44, 1951, p. 29.

24. Examples and discussion in Nock, *JEA* 15, 1929, pp. 221, and Youtie and Bonner, *Trans. Amer. Philol. Assoc.* 67, 1937, pp. 43ff.

25. E.g. Chifflet, editor of *Abraxas*, 1657, and de Montfaucon, *L'antiquité expliquée*, 1719ff. Bonner, *Magical Amulets*, lists in his bibliography about a dozen works published before 1850.

26. Bonner, *Studies in Magical Amulets, chiefly Egyptian*, 1950.

27. Irenaeus, *Adv. Haereses* I. 24.7; Hippolytus, *Refut.* VII.14.

28. 365 is the sum of the numerical value of the letters in the word Άβραξας.

29. King, *The Gnostics and their Remains*, pp. 241f.

30. Burkitt, *Church and Gnosis*, pp. 35–40, and Doresse, *Secret Books of the Egyptian Gnostics*, pp. 103ff., describe some of the magical features of Gnosticism.

31. Bonner, *Amulets*, pp. 22–44.

32. An interesting although ambiguous example is discussed by Barb in *Conflict between Paganism and Christianity*, pp. 100ff.

33. Appreciation of the value of ostraca is a nineteenth-century development. Deissmann, *Light from the Ancient East*, p. 51 n. 4, refers to ostraca being thrown away as useless rubbish as late as 1819. The foundation works of modern ostraca study are Wilcken, *Griechische Ostraka* 1899, and Crum, *Coptic Ostraka*, 1902. Deissmann, op. cit., pp. 50–60, offers a brief review of ostraca studies and their significance for biblical scholarship.

34. Text in Crum, op. cit., no. 522, p. 4. *PGM* Ostrakon 1, vol. II, p. 209.

Translation in Deissmann, op. cit., p. 306, where it is also illustrated, fig. 56.

35. Tait and Préaux, *Greek Ostraca in the Bodleian* . . . , nos. 2159, 2161 and 2162.

36. *PGM* XXXVI. 189.

37. *PGM* XLVI. 5.

38. Apuleius, *Apology* 45.

39. Delatte, *Bull. Corr. Hellenique* 37, 1913, p. 278.

40. Wünsch, 'Antikes Zaubergerat . . .', and Hopfner, *Offenbarungs-zauber* II, §§ 306ff., pp. 144ff. Various other magic nails and rings are described by Preisendanz, *Archiv für Papyrusforschung* 11, 1935, pp. 162f.

41. Clermont-Ganneau, *PEFQS* 1901, esp. p. 58. Bibliography for these and other figurines in Preisendanz, op. cit., p. 163.

42. For other early editions of magical papyri see the introductions to *PGM* vol. I and Hopfner, op. cit., vol. I.

43. Full details of Dieterich's many other contributions to the study of magic appear in the list of his published works in his posthumously published *Kleine Schriften*, pp. XLff.

44. Festugière, *Le révélation d'Hermès Trismégeste* I: *L'astrologie et les sciences occultes*, 1944, esp. pp. 283ff. Festugière's greatest direct contribution to the study of magic is however his Excursus, 'La valeur religieuse des papyrus magiques', in *L'idéal religieux des grecs et l'évangile*, 1932, pp. 281-328.

45. Schürer, *Gesch. des jüd. Volkes* III, 1898², pp. 294ff. (not in ET); see also the bibliography on pp. 300-304, which became a standard source. Conybeare, 'Christian Demonology', *JQR* 8-9, 1896-7, is one of the earliest British studies.

46. *Bible Studies*, 1901, is an ET of both series. The lectures were translated in 1907 as *New Light on the NT*.

47. First translated as *Light from the Ancient East* in 1910; quoted here as Deissmann, *LAE*, from the revised ET of 1927, based on the 4th German ed.

48. Deissmann, *LAE*, pp. 304ff.; cf. *New Light*, pp. 84ff.

49. *LAE*, p. 260 and n. 3.

50. Ibid., p. 261 n. 7. See *Bible Studies*, p. 281 n. 2, for an earlier comment on NT demonology and exorcism.

51. *Bible Studies*, p. 323 n. 5.

52. *New Light*, p. 69; cf. *LAE*, p. 254, and *Bible Studies*, p. 323, for similar comments on the burning of the books.

53. Deissmann's review of Heitmüller in *TLZ*, 1904, is still interesting reading. Heitmuller's methods meet with approval and his conclusions are thought important for sacramental theology.

54. Von Wetter, *'Der Sohn Gottes'*, 1916, pp. 73-82.

55. Other early studies which use exegetical material based on the magical discoveries included Bousset, *Kyrios Christos*, 1913, and Weinreich, *Antike Heilungswunder*, 1909. By now the commentaries were also including such material, e.g. J. Weiss, *Die Schriften des NT* I, 1907, pp. 81, 163, 284, 620 etc., and works by Wellhausen and Harnack. An interesting example of over-enthusiasm is Dell, 'Mt. 16.17-19', *ZNW* 15, 1914, pp. 1-14.

56. Bultmann, *History of the Synoptic Tradition*, p. 224 n. 3.

57. Dibelius, *From Tradition to Gospel*, pp. 79-84. The miracle technique is

not specifically called magical but on p. 83 it is described as 'technical therapeutic'. It is technical in the sense that it incorporated magical techniques. This is clear from p. 85 where parallels to the synoptic healings are offered from the magical papyri.

58. Ibid., pp. 94f. Dibelius overlooks the fact that magic is not mere technique but is revelation based on theophany. The distinction between magic and theophany is thus much too simple.

59. Taylor, *Mark*, p. 171.

60. Ibid., p. 276.

61. Ibid., p. 355. Vincent Taylor does not seem to have accepted the force of the parallels which he quotes. For instance, on p. 352, 'the details of the story, the insertion of the fingers into the man's ears, the use of saliva, . . . the sighing . . . suggest that it is taken from life,' but on p. 354 we read that 'such actions are common to the technique of Greek and Jewish healers'. Now we know that these practitioners used some bizarre methods. Was Jesus one of them? It would seem so. The distinction between 'love for the bizarre' and 'sober exegesis' is not then justified in this case.

III. The Main Features of Hellenistic Magic

1. The opening verses of each gospel are found in a papyrus of the fourth/fifth century (*PGM* 19); Matt. 4.23f. is found in a sixth-century papyrus (*PGM* 4), and the Lord's Prayer in another sixth-century papyrus (*PGM* 9). (Preisendanz uses roman numbers for pagan papyri, arabic numbers for Christian ones.)

2. Kenyon, *Greek Papyri in the British Museum*, pp. 83–115; *PGM* VII.

3. Published by Vogliano in *Annali . . . di Milano*, 1948, pp. 226–8.

4. Cf. also pp. 17f. above.

5. *PGM* V. 3ff.

6. Lane, *Manners and Customs of the Modern Egyptians* 1846, vol. II, pp. 90–99; III, pp. 240–6. My attention was drawn to Lane by C. W. Goodwin's edition of PLond.46, where the work is cited.

7. Op. cit., II, pp. 93–98. See the diagram (p. 94) of the magic square with the patch of ink in the middle.

8. Bouché-Leclercq, *L'astrologie grecque* I, pp. 185ff. and 339f.; Abt, *Apologie des Apuleius*, pp. 232ff.

9. The design in the column has been reproduced by the scribe hardly at all. That this is not due to deterioration of the papyrus can be seen by comparison with the rest of that very column – the ink is clear and black. See Eitrem, *Pap. Osloenses* I, p. 11 (text), pp. 82–4 (notes) and plate VIII.

10. Details in Wessely's edition, p. 36.

11. This conclusion is unaffected by the two places where Jesus is mentioned.

12. See Dieterich's discussion, *Mithrasliturgie*, pp. 43–46.

13. Festugière, *Hermès Trismégiste* I, p. 303 n. 1.

14. Griffith and Thompson, *Demotic Magical Papyrus* I, pp. 10–13.

15. Hunt, *Proc. Br. Acad.* 15, 1929, pp. 127–34.

16. *PGM* XXXa; Grenfell et al., *Fayum Towns*, p. 292.

17. POxy. 1148; *PGM* XXXIb.

18. Festugière, *L'idéal religieux*, p. 282n.

19. Preisendanz (*Leyh Festgabe*, p. 231) concludes that the original forms of many sections of our papyri must go back to the second or third centuries BC and must have had their origin in iatromagical works of which the Bolos-Democritus fragments are also survivals. Nock, *JEA* 15, 1929, p. 227, concludes that 'by the first century of our era, Graeco-Egyptian magic had taken shape'.

20. Budge, *Egyptian Magic*, pp. 3f.

21. Ibid., p. 28.

22. *PGM* IV. 239ff.

23. Budge, *The Book of the Dead*, translation, p. 87.

24. *PGM* V. 146ff.

25. Budge, *Egyptian Magic*, p. 28.

26. Ibid., p. 43.

27. POslo.1 (*PGM* XXXVI). 315–20.

28. For the Egyptian contribution to magic, see Bonner, *Magical Amulets*, pp. 22–26, and Nock, *JEA* 15, 1929, p. 228.

29. Arnobius, *Adversus Gentes* I.5.

30. Lucian, *Menippus* 6, refers to the Zoroastrian magicians as being equivalent to the Chaldeans.

31. Pliny, *Nat.Hist.* XXX.4. The major study of the influence of Zoroaster is that of Bidez-Cumont, *Les mages hellénisés* I–II, 1938.

32. On questions of Egyptian demonology, see Budge, *Egyptian Magic*, p. 206; Budge, *From Fetish to God*, pp. 139f. and 207–11; Boylan, *Thoth, the Hermes of Egypt*, p. 129, and for exorcism in Ptolemaic Egypt, Cumont, *L'Egypte des astrologues*, pp. 167–171.

33. Bidez-Cumont, op. cit., I, pp. 147, 169f. and 188f.

34. Pliny, *Nat.Hist.* XXX.8.

35. On the study of sympathy note that its origin was also attributed to Hermes-Thoth, and that a literature rather similar to that of the Zoroaster-Ostanes group gathered around this name in the second century BC. See Hopfner, *Offenbarungszauber* I, §385, but especially Festugière, *Hermès Trismégiste* I, pp. 76ff. On the growth of the philosophy of sympathy, Festugière suggests (ibid., pp. 90f. n. 1) that the idea of sympathetic bonds between particular things is perhaps older than universal sympathy. The Stoa, especially Posidonius, played an important role in the formation of the larger theory, as did Neoplatonism, especially Plotinus, Iamblichus and Proclus.

36. Cramer, *Astrology in Roman Law and Politics*, 1954, p. 3.

37. On the origins and growth of astrology see Cramer, op. cit.; Cumont, *Astrology and Religion among the Romans*, 1912, and *L'Egypte des astrologues*; R. C. Thompson, *The Reports of . . . the Astrologers of Nineveh . . .*, 1900; Bouché-Leclercq, *L'astrologie grecque*. On the Persian contribution to magic, see Hopfner, op. cit., II, §§ 18f., and Bonner, *Magical Amulets*, pp. 32–39.

38. Pliny, *Nat. Hist.* XXX.11.

39. Justin, *Dialogue with Trypho* 85.3 (ANCL pp. 205f.).

40. Origen, *Contra Celsum* I.26.

41. *Antiquities* VIII.45–49.

42. The power of magic to cure sickness is recognized in the Babylonian Talmud, *Shabbath* 33a. It discusses the problems raised by healing through amulets (ibid. 61b) and refers to magical remedies (ibid. 66b–67a). In *Bab. Sukkah* Rabbi Johanan ben Zakkai is approved of because of his familiarity with the language of demons. Magic is approved in *Kiddushin* 39b but condemned in *Sanhedrin* 67b. (For a summary of the Talmudic attitude to magic see the note on *Kiddushin* 39b, Soncino ed., p. 196 n. 3.)

43. Eusebius, *Praep. Evang.* IX.27, 432ab, quoting Alexander Polyhistor.

44. Apuleius, *Apology* 90; Strabo, XVI.2.36–39.

45. *Demotic Magical Papyrus*, col. V, lines 13f. (Griffith and Thompson, I, p. 47).

46. Ibid., verso col. XII (p. 185).

47. Edited by Gaster in 1896. The introduction, pp. 3–26, is particularly valuable.

48. Jude is reproducing a tradition already known from the Assumption of Moses. Cf. Clement of Alexandria, *Comments on the Epistle of Jude*, and Origen, *De Principiis* III.2.1 (ANCL I, p. 222).

49. The problem of this passage is discussed by Dieterich, *Abraxas*, Reitzenstein, *Poimandres*, and Gaster, op. cit., p. 19.

50. Montfaucon, *L'antiquité* II.2, plate 156; Bonner, *Magical Amulets*, no. 13, pp. 171 and 255 and plate I.

51. Charles, *Apoc. and Pseudepig.* I, p. 546, misunderstands this passage.

52. *Antiquities* VIII.45.

53. F. C. Conybeare, *JQR* 11, 1898, p. 12, suggests that the original Jewish traditions may be contemporary with Josephus and that the Christian additions are from the end of the first or early second century AD. The internal evidence adduced by McCown is convincing for an early third-century date. The magic is much too undeveloped for the fourth century and the demonology is similar to that of Celsus and Origen.

54. Bonner discusses this type, op. cit., pp. 208ff.

55. On the origins of Semitic magic, see R. C. Thompson, *Semitic Magic*, 1908, and for the OT developments, T. Witton Davies, *Magic . . . among the Hebrews*, 1898, and Blau, *Altjüd. Zauberwesen*. Jewish magic during the Roman empire is discussed by Simon, *Verus Israel*, pp. 394–431.

56. Jayne, *The Healing Gods of Ancient Civilizations*, p. 332, and Nilsson, *Opusc. Sel.*III, pp. 139f.

57. Nilsson, ibid., p. 139, reports the results of a count of the names of Greek gods mentioned in *PGM* vols. I–II. Hermes is mentioned 33 times, Selene 18, Hecate 12 and Apollo 8.

58. Eitrem, 'Kronos und der Magie', *Mélanges Bidez* II, pp. 351–60.

59. Origen however, in *First Principles* I. 8. 2–4, denies that the position of the angels and demons is a consequence of their created essence. It is rather, he claims, the result of their moral choice.

60. Langton, *Ministries of the Angelic Powers*.

61. II Enoch 3.1ff. (stars); 11.1–5 (sun); 16.7f. (moon); III Enoch 17.6f. (angels, moving stars, and planets).

62. Simon, op. cit., p. 404.

63. Origen, *Contra Celsum* I.25. Apollonius of Tyana had a ring inscribed with the names of the planets and the days of the week: Philostratus, *Vit. Apoll.* IV.41.

64. Arnobius, *Adversus Gentes* I.43 (ANCL, p.34).

65. Hopfner, op. cit., I, §§ 1–134.

66. Eusebius, *Praep. Evang.* IV.5, 141cd.

67. *PGM* IV. 1968ff. and 2541 are typical examples.

68. Bonner, op. cit., p.95.

69. Ibid., no.57, p.263, and no.111, p.271.

70. Test.Sol. 20.12–17.

71. Iamblichus quoted by Proclus in the latter's *Commentary on the First Alcibiades of Plato* 84 (ed. Westerink, 1954, p.37).

72. There are numerous examples of these signs of departure. Eleazar's demon (Josephus, *Antiquities* VIII.48) upset a bowl of water. Apollonius had a case in which a statue was overturned: Philostratus, *Vit.Apoll.* IV.20.

73. Hopfner, op. cit., I, §§ 201–203.

74. Ibid., § 206.

75. Origen, *Contra Celsum* III.28; VII.5; Tertullian, *De Idol.* 7, and many others.

76. *Vita Apoll.* VI.27.

77. Aelian, *Hist. Animalium* XI.32.

78. On ancient demonology, a much studied subject, see especially the article 'Daimon' by Andres in Pauly-Wissowa, pp.293ff. Bousset's article in *Archiv für Religionswissenschaft* 18, 1915, is still valuable; and see W. M. Alexander, *Demonic Possession in the NT*, 1902, although Alexander's application to the New Testament is not adequate. Psellus, *De Operatione Daemonum*, is an invaluable source of demonological lore. (Collisson's translation of 1843 is quaint but adequate.) It may be thought that the late date of this Byzantine 'Dialogue' would preclude its use for the Hellenistic period, but this is by no means the case. Svoboda, *La Démonologie de Michel Psellos*, 1927, has shown how much older material has been used by the great Byzantine scholar.

79. Iamblichus, *De Mysteriis* II.11.

80. Ibid. III.27.

81. *PGM* VII. 56off.

82. Plotinus, *Ennead* IV.4.26.

83. Festugière, fragment XXIII, *Corp. Herm.* IV, pp.1ff.

84. *Praep. Evang.* IV.1, 131c–132a.

85. This is one of many examples offered by Hopfner, op. cit., I, § 400.

86. Reitzenstein, *Poimandres*, pp.256ff. The origin of number mysticism is greatly simplified in the brief account I have given. See Dornseiff, *Das Alphabet in Mystik und Magie*, 1922.

87. POslo. 1 (*PGM* XXXVI. 190f.).

88. Ibid., 214–219.

89. Ibid., 335–9.

90. *PGM* 13 (vol. II, pp.200f.) is a good example.

91. *PGM* XXXVI. 220ff.

92. Riesenfeld, 'Remarques sur les hymnes magiques', *Eranos* 44, 1946, pp.153–60.

IV. Miracle and Magic

1. Grant, *Miracle and Natural Law*, pp. 135ff.
2. Brandon, *Creation Legends*, pp. 37f. Brandon rightly emphasizes that in both Egyptian and Hebrew myths, the magical form has become a vehicle for theology.
3. Frankfort, *The Intellectual Adventure of Ancient Man*, p. 297.
4. The ancient Hebrews, believing in the direct causation of all phenomena by God, lacked a conception of natural law. It is thus possible to agree both with Koehler, *Hebrew Man*, p. 134, who remarks that the Hebrew experience was one of 'continuous miracle', and also with J. P. Ross (in Moule, *Miracles*, p. 45) that the conception of miracle was unknown to the Hebrew since there was no contrast between miracle and natural law. Both agree that the wonderful was part of the Hebrew world-view. This constancy of the world of wonders was part of its magical quality and an aspect of the primitive link between magic and miracle. See Frankfort, op. cit., pp. 297 and 302.
5. The magical associations of the utterances of the prophets have received more attention than the magical associations of their miracles. But both share in the magical quality. See Frankfort, op. cit., pp. 298ff., Loisy, *Origins of the NT*, pp. 15ff., and Föhrer, 'Prophetie und Magie', *ZAW* 78, 1966, pp. 25ff.
6. Note the interesting rejection of the magical association of the brazen serpent found in Wisd. 16.7: 'He that turned towards it was not saved by that which he saw, but by thee, the Saviour of all.'
7. Although greater attention has been given to the question of Jewish versus pagan influences on the miracles of Jesus, an equally important but overlooked study is the question of the relative importance of magic and apocalyptic in the creation of the miracle tradition. Miracles of both types were found in both Judaism and paganism. For eschatology and its associated miracles in paganism, especially in pre-Christian times, see Knox, *St Paul and the Church of the Gentiles*, pp. 1–26.
8. Grant, op. cit., p. 172.
9. Josephus, *Antiquities* II.274. God exhorts Moses to 'use miracles to convince all men that thou art sent by me'. Other cases in MacRae, 'Miracle in the *Antiquities* of Josephus', in Moule, *Miracles*, pp. 134ff.
10. Grant, op. cit., p. 172.
11. Moore, *Judaism* II, p. 349. Moore is speaking of Tannaite sources and so this does not entirely escape Grant's objection about the late date of the non-apocalyptic miracles. Moore's point about Messiah is however valid.
12. Moore, ibid. I, pp. 377 and 426; vol. II, pp. 235ff.
13. Ehnmark, *Anthropomorphism and Miracle*, pp. 3f.
14. Athene becomes invisible by wearing Hades' helmet and both Hermes and Athene use magical sandals (Ehnmark, op. cit., p. 6).
15. Ehnmark, op. cit., p. 31; Weinreich, *Antike Heilungswunder*, pp. 13f. One naturally asks to what extent these elements of the Homeric epics are poetry, or myth, or anthropomorphic imagery. To investigate this very question is the main object of Ehnmark's work; it is considered very care-

fully, and while the subtlety of his analysis cannot be described here, it is enough for our purposes to notice that the connection between magic and miracle is firmly asserted.

16. Other cases in Herodotus VII.129, 189 and 191.

17. McDonald, 'Herodotus on the Miraculous' in Moule, *Miracles*, p. 89.

18. Nilsson, *Geschichte der griechischen Religion* II², p. 520.

19. See the texts collected by Westermann and Keller (see Bibliography).

20. Reitzenstein, *Hellenistiche Wundererzählungen*, p. 3; Weinreich, op. cit., p. 173 n. 3.

21. Lucian, *Philopseudes* 17. The cross did not receive its potency because of association with the death of Jesus, but anything connected with violent death was believed to be a potent force. Demons were afraid of iron, hence these bits of iron from crosses.

22. It appears in Augustine, *De Cura pro Mortuis Gerenda* XII.15.Cf. Reitzenstein, op. cit., pp. 4–6; Rohde, *Psyche*, pp. 562f. n. 87.

23. *Philopseudes* 29–31.

24. Ibid., 38, 40.

25. Clement of Alexandria, *Stromateis* VI.3 (ANCL II, pp. 319ff.).

26. Thorndike, *History of Magic*, pp. 41–334.

27. *Clementine Recognitions* 3.57 (ANCL pp. 269f.).

28. Loc. cit. Had Niceta read the account of the magical snakes in Philo's *Life of Moses* I.91–94, he would have been still more puzzled.

29. E.g. Matt. 7.22; II Thess. 2.9; I John 4.1; Rev. 13.13ff. See Fridrichsen, *La problème du miracle dans le Christianisme primitif*, 1925.

30. Lampe, 'Miracles and Early Christian Apologetic' in Moule, *Miracles*, esp. pp. 211 and 213.

31. Grundmann, *TDNT* II, p. 302. Jesus works his miracles by his own powerful word 'which has nothing to do with magic'. See also Grundmann, *Begriff der Kraft in der NT Gedankenwelt*, pp. 65–68. Remarks like this are frequent in the commentaries.

32. As an illustration, we read in Dan. 3.24f. that when the three Hebrews were thrown into the furnace, they walked about in it and were unharmed. Nothing happens to bring this about. The cause, we may presume, is the divine presence with them. So the Lord may cause the sun to stand still or the waters to part, but we are not told how he caused it.

33. Jensen, *Myth and Cult among Primitive People*, for example, attacks it severely. See also Marett, *Threshold of Religion*, pp. 52–4.

34. Marett, op. cit., p. 71.

35. Ehnmark, op. cit., p. 7.

36. Ibid., pp. 20–28.

37. Ibid., p. 22.

38. Cook, *Zeus* II. 11, p. 1042.

39. Ibid., I, p. 14 n. 1.

40. Malinowski, *Argonauts of the Western Pacific*, p. 404.

41. Malinowski, *Magic, Science and Religion*, p. 57.

42. Grant, *Miracle and Natural Law*, p. 184; Sweet, 'The Theory of Miracles in the Wisdom of Solomon', in Moule, *Miracles*, pp. 115–17.

43. Grant, op. cit., pp. 186f.

44. Wiles, 'Miracles in the Early Church', in Moule, *Miracles*, especially p.230, where it is pointed out that, against Marcion, Christ's use of physical means was heightened to identify him with the Creator but, against others, the physical means were not mentioned, in order to avoid the charge of magic.

45. See Wiles, ibid., pp.226ff.

46. Ehnmark, op. cit., p.40; Cook, *Zeus* I, p.13.

47. The demythologization debate is relevant to the question of the magical miracle. For magic is the method by which the myth, which tells of the past, is brought into action in the present. Miracle, springing from a mythological view of the relation between God and the world, is thus associated with magic in yet a further way. Cf. Malinowski, *Magic*, pp.63f., and *Argonauts*, p.303.

48. Marett, op. cit., pp.118f. Compare Simon's desire in Acts 8.18f.

49. Without anticipating later discussion too much, it is worth observing that both kinds appear in the New Testament, and there is difference of opinion about whether the second is legitimate, or whether all power should be passed on personally. Cf. the story of the alien exorcist versus the story of the Ephesian exorcists (Mark 9.38f. and Acts 19.13ff.). Arnobius, *Adversus Gentes* I.48, comparing the healings of Christ with those of the heathen gods, says that the latter healed mainly by advising on special drugs, so the healing power is in the drug, but Christ's power was in him personally, since he could heal by a word.

50. MacRae in *Miracles*, p.139.

51. *Commentary on John* II.34 (on 1.7). See also Tertullian, *Adv. Marcion.* III.3.

52. Both examples are in Moore, *Judaism* I, pp.377f.

53. Lactantius, *Divine Institutes* IV.15 (ANCL pp.245f.). See also *Clementine Recognitions* III.58–60, Origen, *Contra Celsum* II.48, and Irenaeus, *Adv. Haer.* IV.29, for some of the many early discussions of the problem.

54. No.IV in a collection of 'Magical Formulae for Mother and Child', 15th century BC, in Lexa, *La magie dans l'Egypte* II, p.29.

55. Budge, *Egyptian Magic*, pp.207–12, for a partial translation into English; Lexa, op. cit., II, pp.118–21, for a complete translation into French; original text in Rougé, *Oeuvres diversées* III, facing p.144.

56. Considering the fact that demon possession was rare in ancient Egypt until Ptolemaic times, and that it was common in Mesopotamia, we could almost count the Bekhten incident as Mesopotamian, told so as to make the point that the Egyptian rulers were superior.

57. Thompson, *Devils and Evil Spirits of Babylon* I, pp.xlvii and l.

58. *Eumenides* 264–6; cf. also lines 304f.; Rohde, *Psyche*, p.213 n.162 and p.562 n.86.

59. Dodds, *The Greeks and the Irrational*, pp.78f., 98 n.103; Rohde, op. cit., p.255 and Appendix VIII, pp.595f.

60. Cumont, *L'Egypte des astrologues*, pp.167–71.

61. *The Greek Anthology* XI. 427; Cumont, op. cit., p.171 n.1.

62. *Ant.* VI. 166–8.

63. *Ant.* VIII. 46–48.

64. Rohde, op. cit., Appendix XII, pp.603–5.

65. The relevant passages are set out in Barrett, *The Holy Spirit and the Gospel Tradition*, p.58.

66. Testament of Zebulun 9.8: 'And healing and compassion shall be in his wings. He shall redeem all the captivity of the sons of men from Beliar; and every spirit of deceit shall be trodden down.' But this solitary passage is almost certainly a Christian addition! Barrett, op. cit., p.58 n.1.

67. Barrett, op. cit., p.57.

68. The Syrian from Palestine, the ring of Eutrates and the house-exorcism of Arignotus the Pythagorean (*Philopseudes* 16, 17, 31); see pp.50f.

69. Probably written late in the second century, perhaps even as late as AD 200 or 210. The *Life of Apollonius* was written soon after AD 217.

70. See Reitzenstein, *Wundererzählungen*, p.54. Campbell Bonner rejects the Egyptian origin, remarking that there are a number of ancient miracles involving restoration of shattered objects (*HTR* 36, 1943, pp.48f.). On the relationship between the two stories cf. Léon Vouaux, 1922, *Les Actes de Pierre*, p.299 n.8. Vouaux thinks the ultimate origin of the story is Christian, but Bonner (op. cit., p.48) thinks the origin may have been either pagan or Christian. Further evidence of the traditional nature of the demon stories these authors tell is found in the fact that the story of the exorcism of the haunted house in Corinth in Lucian, *Philops*. 30–31 (*c*. AD 160–170) is found in Pliny's *Letters* (VII. 27, to Sura), a correspondence coming from the period AD 97–109. The story has been transferred to Athens, and attributed to 'Athenodorus the Philosopher' of whom there were two, Athenodorus Canaanites, 74 BC–AD 7, and Athenodorus Cordylion, who was already an old man in 47 BC. See n.22 above.

71. The rabbinic parallels are set out in Strack-Billerbeck, *Kommentar zum NT IV*, pp.527ff.

72. No.III in a small collection of Apophthegmata Patrum in Lexa, op. cit., II, p.208.

73. V, ibid., pp.208f.

74. VIII B, ibid., p.210.

75. Cf. the utilitarian nature of the comment in Mark 9.29: 'This sort only comes out in response to prayer and fasting.'

76. Bultmann, *History of the Synoptic Tradition*, pp.223f. and 231f. (mainly however on the literary parallels from pagan and Jewish sources); Dibelius, *From Tradition to Gospel*, pp.85ff.; Bonner, *HTR* 36, pp.41ff.; Barrett, op. cit., pp.55ff.; Eitrem, *Demonology of the NT*; Bauernfeind, *Die Worte der Damonen in Markusevangelium*. But the significance of the parallels has never been brought out in the full context of ancient magic.

77. See also *PGM* IV. 2252f. and Bauernfeind, op. cit., pp.14ff.

78. *PGM* III. 570; IV. 870ff.

79. *PGM* IV. 1500, 2984ff.; V. 103ff.; Bauernfeind, op. cit., pp.19–23.

80. This particular case is however probably due to the influence of Mark itself since the passage in Test.Sol.11 continues by describing the legions under the demon. Marcan influence is probably also at work in Test.Sol. 6.8 and the variant (P) at 18.20: 'I adjure you by the throne of God most high.'

81. Diogenes Laertius, *Vie de Pythagore* 31 (see Delatte's comments, p.226); Festugière, *L'idéal religieux*, p.85 n.1; Reitzenstein, *Poimandres*, p.80 n.3.

82. Bell et al., *Proc. Br. Acad.* 17, 1931, p. 255. There are probably hundreds of cases where the 'I adjure you' formula is used in the magical papyri.

83. Cf. *PGM* V. 155–70.

84. Grundmann, *TDNT* III, pp. 898 and 900f.

85. Bonner, *HTR* 36, pp. 41ff.

86. Bonner (ibid., p. 43) refers to the *dumb* demons of the gospels, especially Mark 9.25, showing that the dumbness itself is an obstacle to exorcism, but he says nothing about the demonic confessions, e.g. Mark 3.11, which indicate victory for the exorcist.

87. Bauernfeind, op. cit., p. 27.

88. Bonner's third point, that the demon must leave a visible sign of his departure, we have already illustrated from several cases. The Gadarene swine come into this category. Bonner points out (p. 49) that the last convulsions of the possessed (Mark 1.26; 9.26) although we may attribute them to mental illness, would at the time be seen as the last struggle of the departing demon.

89. Rohde, *Psyche*, p. 604.

90. Eitrem, *Pap. Osloenses*, p. 77. Moulton, *Vocabulary of the Greek Testament*, under φιμόω refers to Eitrem with approval.

91. Bonner, op. cit., p. 41 n. 9.

92. Lexa, *La magie dans l'Egypte* II, pp. 45ff. The incident is found in one of the Turin papyri from the twelfth century BC.

93. Deissmann, *Light from the Ancient East*, p. 260 n. 4.

94. Knox, *HTR* 31, 1938, p. 193.

95. Ibid. Of course it is possible that the text intends the exorcism to be in the name of the God of the Hebrews, and in the name of Jesus and so on. But it is more likely that Jesus is understood as the name of the Hebrew deity.

96. Eitrem, *Demonology of the NT*, pp. 15–34. The exorcism goes on to speak of the fire burning in the temple at Jerusalem and this may, as Knox thinks (*St Paul and the Church of Jerusalem*, p. 208), indicate a date before AD 70, but I am more inclined to agree with Eitrem, op. cit., p. 15, that it is probably only a demon-frightening cliché.

97. F. Legge in an article in 1897 (see Bibliography) argued that since the text confuses the second and third persons of the Trinity, it cannot be much later than Tertullian, since by the time *Contra Praxeas* appeared that particular heresy was finished. This is probably expecting too much theological expertise from a pagan magician. The linguistic arguments advanced by Griffith in *Zeitschrift für Ägypt. Sprache* 39, 1901, pp. 78ff., are more convincing. Note also that the errors in the Coptic, which is transcribed into Greek in the papyrus, suggest the magician was writing a formula which he *said* in Coptic but did not understand.

98. Fiebig, *Jüdische Wundergeschichten*, no. 10, pp. 35f.

99. The promise goes back ultimately to Luke 10.19. The story in Acts 28.3–6 would perhaps inspire some confidence in the power of such charms.

100. Text in R. Wünsch, *Antike Fluchtafeln*, no. 1, pp. 4ff. The crucial line is line 13, where Γῆ Ἑκάτη appears, flanked either side by a space for six letters, only the last three of which are legible -οῦς. Wünsch reconstructs [=Ιησ]οῦς and Eitrem, *Demonology*, p. 16, along with most commentators, agrees that he is probably correct.

101. Festugière refers (*L'idéal*, p. 287 n. 3) to the expression ἐπικαλοῦμαι κατὰ τὸ πιστόν, 'I call in a manner conforming to received custom, in an authentic way', which occurs in liturgical texts with magical parallels and may not be entirely without relevance to the sons of Sceva, who failed to observe this important aspect of their craft.

102. Naturally, the claim that exorcism was nearly always associated with magic does not go unchallenged. W. L. Knox (*HTR* 31, 1938, p. 203) says that the appearance of exorcism of a liturgical nature in the magical papyri 'seems to represent a final stage of decline in the world; exorcism in itself cannot justly be regarded as a branch of magic, except on the assumption that the ancient world ought to have possessed a scientific knowledge of psychology.' But surely one might as well argue that astrology cannot be regarded as a *false* science, unless you assume the ancient world ought to have had a scientific knowledge of astronomy. One must find some reasonably objective criteria for these things. Damascius, in *Vita Isidori* 56, relates that Theosebius exorcized a demon from his wife, but that *otherwise* he was 'quite ignorant of magic and did not meddle with theurgy' (quoted by Eitrem, *Demonology*, p. 8 n. 1). This aptly summarizes the ancient point of view, confirmed by more recent study. Exorcism is a branch of magic.

V. Mark

1. Trench, *Notes on the Miracles*, 1847, pp. 377f.; Alford, *The Four Gospels*, 1849, ad loc.

2. T. M. Lindsay, *Mark*, 1883, p. 144.

3. Gould, *Mark* (ICC), 1896, pp. 138f.

4. Swete is uncertain about the purpose of the manipulations, and thinks they suggest 'the presence of unusual difficulties' (*Mark*, p. 151); he conjectures that the man, being a Decapolitan and deaf, 'needed all the support that visible signs could afford' (p. 152). This great commentary is one of the first to grapple seriously with the difficulties of the passage. Of the spittle (8.23) he concludes, 'The Lord condescends to use a popular remedy as a symbol of the healing power which resided in His own humanity' (p. 163).

5. Hunter, *Mark*, p. 82.

6. Taylor, *Mark*, p. 355.

7. Micklem, *Miracles and the New Psychology*, 1922, esp. pp. 114–120.

8. Taylor, op. cit., p. 354.

9. Gill, in *Neurological Studies*, no. 3, p. 158, quoted by Micklem, op. cit., p. 119.

10. The λέγει in 7.34 is merely a feature of Mark's style. The previous verbs are all aorist.

11. Rivers, *Medicine, Magic and Religion*, pp. 99f.

12. Further examples of medical practices which appear to be performed because of rational medicine but turn out to be magical may be found in Kemp, *Healing Ritual*, and Dawson, *Magician and Leech*. On the interpretations of the actions which we have been discussing, note Charles Plummer's warning against imposing our own subtle sacramental views upon the minds

of less sophisticated people. Discussing the clash between the claims of the church and the magic of the Druids in medieval Ireland (a situation not entirely without parallel in the history of the primitive church), he remarks that 'objects and formularies connected with the new religion came to be regarded as having not a spiritual and sacramental value but a magical and material force' (*Vitae Sanctorum Hiberniae*, p. clxxviii).

13. H. A. W. Meyer (*Mark and Luke*, p. 116) insisted that the reason Jesus took the man aside was to make the use of spittle and the touch efficacious. 'The *spittle* (like the oil in 6.13) is to be regarded as the *vehicle* of the miraculous power.' Meyer does not say why privacy was necessary for this to work, but it sounds rather like magic. Swete, op. cit., p. 152, does not mention magic, but says, 'Saliva was regarded as remedial, but the custom of applying it with incantations seems to have led the Rabbis to denounce its use.'

14. Bartlet (Century Bible, ad loc.), is puzzled and cautious; Lowrie, *Jesus according to St Mark*, 1929, p. 288, accepts the use of saliva as being magical; Branscomb, MNTC, 1937, ad loc., agrees but attributes the detail to later tradition; Taylor, p. 354, rejects the magical association, as does Cranfield, Camb. Greek Test. Comm., 1959, without adequate discussion. One of the frankest recognitions of the magical association is that of Beare, *The Earliest Records of Jesus*, p. 135.

15. This is the only OT trace of what has long been recognized as a widespread superstition about the use of saliva, that it contains the life-force of the individual.

16. Brandon, *Creation Legends of the Ancient Near East*, p. 22.

17. Budge, *Egyptian Magic*, p. 137.

18. Breasted, *Development of Religion and Thought in Ancient Egypt*, p. 31, where the use of spittle by Jesus is traced back to Egyptian origins.

19. E.g. Micklem, op. cit., p. 101.

20. Tacitus, *Histories* IV. 81; Suetonius, *Vespasian* 7.

21. Edelstein, *Asclepius* II, pp. 167.

22. Galen, *On the Natural Faculties* III. 7.

23. Budge, *Saints of the Ethiopian Church* I, pp. 264f.

24. Ibid., III, p. 857.

25. Branscomb, MNTC, ad loc.

26. As Creed, *Luke*, ad loc., suggests.

27. Oesterreich, *Possession, Demoniacal and Other*, pp. 19f.

28. Ibid., pp. 20f.

29. It may be thought that the lack of violence in this case indicates that possession cannot have been involved. This however is by no means certain. Not all cases of possession in the gospels are violent, although the most spectacular ones naturally are. Luke seems to regard the fever of Simon's mother-in-law as due to possession – Jesus drives away the fever by rebuking it, but there is no violence. There is some evidence that Jesus was regarded as possessed by the soul of John the Baptist, yet Jesus' behaviour was not characterized by uncontrolled violence. And the girl with the spirit of prophecy (Acts 16.16–18) although a nuisance was apparently quite easy to control. There were of course many varieties of possession and many types of spirits. Oesterreich (p. 25) says, 'However frequent motor hyper-excitement

may be in the possessed . . . it does not arise in every case; some are entirely without it, and show no tendency to violent activity. In particular it may be absent when the patient believes himself to be possessed not by a demon but by the soul of a deceased person.'

30. Deissmann, *New Light on the NT*, p. 88.

31. Micklem, *Miracles*, pp. 114ff. This is the earliest reference to the point Deissmann makes which I have been able to trace in an English commentary.

32. Op. cit., p. 116.

33. Taylor, p. 355.

34. Cranfield, op. cit., p. 252.

35. Matt. 23.4; Luke 16.24; John 8.6; 20.27.

36. Ps. 8.3.

37. Luke 11.20; Ex. 8.19.

38. Budge, *Egyptian Magic*, p. 55.

39. See above, p. 13.

40. Hopfner, *Offenbarungszauber* I, §§ 573, 623–4 and 672.

41. That is if the full force of εἶς is retained. Swete suggests that the idea is that the ears are bored.

42. Dawson, *Magician and Leech*, p. 62.

43. Budge, *Saints of the Ethiopian Church* II, p. 366.

44. *PGM* IV. 2494.

45. Bonner, *HTR* 20, 1927, pp. 171–4, gathers these references together and discusses them with the NT parallels.

46. If we omit the corrupt variant in Mark 1.43, Luke 7.13 is the only miracle performed from compassion. The compassion in Mark 6.34 is aroused by ignorance and met by teaching; it has little direct connection with the miracle of feeding. Jesus is angry in Mark 3.5. The fear of the woman with the flow of blood in Mark 5.33 and the tears of the father in Mark 9.24 are cases of patients' emotion.

47. Mark 1.43 and John 11.33.

48. Bonner, *HTR* 20, 1927, pp. 174ff.

49. Menzies, *The Earliest Gospel*, p. 159.

50. On στενάζω, the material gathered by Bonner was not of course available to Dibelius when the first edition of his study of the gospel tradition appeared in 1919, but the second edition (1933) includes a note acknowledging Bonner (ET, p. 185). Dibelius accepts the relevance of the magical parallels. Montefiore, *Synoptic Gospels*, agreed that the sighing may be part of the method of the cure. But the weighty opinion of Eitrem is 'Jesus . . . "sighs" in fervent attachment and devoted dependence on his Father's will. It is a simple "silent prayer" . . . just as natural in cult as in magic' (*Demonology of the NT*, p. 55).

51. Examples in Bultmann, *History of the Synoptic Tradition*, pp. 222f., and Hopfner, op. cit., I, § 706.

52. Practice varied considerably. Generally speaking names were retained in the original (Hopfner I, § 724) and instructions, commands and prayers translated. In Test. Sol. 13.6 (P) however an angel name is interpreted.

53. Brewer, *Dictionary of Miracles*, p. 123.

54. St Remigius, *c.* 438–*c.* 533.

55. Loomis, *White Magic*, pp. 103f.
56. Brewer, op. cit., p. 295.
57. Dibelius, *From Tradition to Gospel*, p. 80.

VI. Luke: The Tradition Penetrated by Magic

1. 'Here, on this field of "spirits", demons and souls . . . , and in the domain of power and powers . . . , Christians and heathens somehow understood each other. . . . This fact immensely favoured Christian propaganda and the development of Christian cult and Christian sacraments' (Eitrem, *Demonology*, p. 68). This is a point of great significance in understanding the whole stance of Luke–Acts towards the pagan world.

2. Luke 9.26, cf. Mark 8.38 and Matt. 16.27; Luke 12.9, cf. Matt. 10.32f.; Luke 15.10 and 7; 16.22; 20.36, cf. Matt. 22.30.

3. The remaining references to angels in Matt. are 13.39–41, 49; 16.27; 18.10; 22.30; 24.31, 36; 25.31, 41; 26.53.

4. See also Acts 6.15; 7.30, 35, 38, 53; 12.15; 23.8f.

5. On Jewish angelology see Frey, *Rev. sc. phil. et theol.* 5, 1911, pp. 75ff.; Langton, *Angel Teaching of the NT*; Kuhn, *JBL* 67, 1948, pp. 217ff.; and Kittel, *TDNT* I, pp. 80ff.

6. Kuhn, op. cit., pp. 231f.

7. Bernadin, *JBL* 57, 1938, p. 279.

8. Ibid., p. 276.

9. Von Rad, *TDNT* I, p. 771.

10. Luke uses the word ἄγγελος with a wide range of meanings. For example, Luke 7.24 and 9.51 are, with James 2.25, 'the only cases in which men sent by other men are called ἄγγελοι in the NT' (Kittel, *TDNT* I, p. 83). The quotation from Malachi in Matt. 11.10 et par, is not an example of independent choice of vocabulary.

11. E.g., the only canonical writings which mention Gabriel are Daniel and Luke. See below p. 92.

12. E.g. Luke 1.28; 2.9; Acts 1.10; 10.3; 12.7; 27.23.

13. Luke 1.38; 2.15; Acts 10.7; 12.10.

14. Easton, *Luke*, p. 24, says however, 'The "heavenly host" as a designation for the angels is a set Old Testament phrase, used here without the slightest reference to war.' But this comment is made without any examination of Luke's attitude towards spiritual reality and conflict as a whole.

15. K. Lake, 'The Holy Spirit', in Foakes-Jackson (ed.), *Beginnings* V, p. 102.

16. Jesus had seen Satan cast out of heaven (Luke 10.18); all the inhabited earth is within Satan's power of patronage (Luke 4.7); the abyss is the place to which the demons finally go (Luke 8.31); until then they wander in waterless regions of the earth (Luke 11.24).

17. Cf. Gerhard von Rad (*TDNT* I, p. 80), speaking of demons in the OT, who 'do not have the slightest religious significance. At this point, in contrast with Babylonian and Egyptian religion, in which everyday life was a tormenting struggle with demons, we are confronted with a distinctive element in OT

belief, namely, that Yahweh is the only creative causality in nature and history. In principle, therefore, belief in demons is strangled.' We can, I think, see this 'distinctive element' worked out in Matthew, where demonology is reduced to a minimum and there is really no struggle at all. But in Mark, and more so in Luke, there is a fairly active demonology, and in Luke there is a tense struggle. In the latter part of the same article (p. 84), Kittel claims that there is no interest in an independent angelic activity in the gospels, Matt. 28 being the nearest approach. Usually they are merely servants of God and Jesus. On angels in Acts, Kittel speaks of 'the extent to which the angel has ceased to play any autonomous part' (p. 85). Now, it depends on what is meant by 'independent activity' or autonomy. Certainly angels, like apostles, do nothing without orders. But one would not claim that apostles have no independent activity, although Acts 8.26; 12.1–3 and many others might support such a claim. On the other hand stories such as those in Acts 5.19; 12.7ff.; 12.23 show that the activity of angels, although in subservience to the Lord, is significant in its own right.

18. Lake and Cadbury in Foakes-Jackson (ed.), *Beginnings* IV, p. 121. Note also that John the Baptist was believed to be possessed because he neither ate nor drank (Matt. 11.18 and Luke 7.33f.).

19. Other examples of non-apocalyptic angel activity appear in II Macc. 3.24–34; 11.8; Song of the Three Children vv. 23ff.; III Macc. 6.18 and Bel and the Dragon vv. 33–39. Tobit remains by far the most sustained and detailed non-apocalyptic angelic incident. It is important to notice that it appears in an atmosphere of magic. Works such as I Maccabees, without interest in either eschatology or magic, are free of any doctrine of angels. Langton (op. cit., p. 87) points out that the care shown by the angel for Tobias is the first actual case of an angel guarding an individual, and we may notice in addition that Acts 12.15 is the only specific NT reference to this sort of thing.

20. Note that in Test. Sol., in spite of frequent references to angels, only Gabriel and Raphael appear as actual actors. Cf. Luke–Acts, where although angels brood over the scene, only Gabriel is actually named. The angel names in Test. Sol. do not so much refer to personalities as to charms. There is no angelic hierarchy (the appearance of the word ἀρχάγγελος is the only indication) and the angelology is not developed in the sense of being more complex. It is simply taken over absolutely by magic. McCown (*The Testament of Solomon*, p. 50) remarks on the absence of any apocalyptic hope. The writer 'sees no happier future for the world than in the continued use of his wretched recipes'. This is far from being the case in Luke–Acts.

21. Weiss, *Biblical Theology of the NT* II, pp. 298f.

22. Rengstorf, *Lukas*, p. 60.

23. So Loisy, *L'évangile selon Luc*, p. 272.

24. Conzelmann, *Theology of St Luke*, p. 135; Bailey, *Traditions Common to Luke and John*, p. 31 n. 2.

25. Davies, *Magic . . . among the Hebrews*, p. 112.

26. See Fascher, *Jesus und der Satan*, 1949, for a review of the history of the interpretation of the temptation story.

27. See the seven spirits in Test. Sol. 8.1, and below pp. 103f.

28. This is the only place in the gospels where an illness is actually addressed by Jesus. For the description ἐπάνω αὐτῆς compare the similar instruction in *PGM* IV. 745, 1229 and 2735. Eitrem, *Demonology*, pp. 36f. n. 4, thinks Matt. 8.14, 'thrown on a bed', also indicates activity by the personified illness, but this is a more doubtful case.

29. This may be an important indication of the attitude of Jesus himself. Although his exorcisms were both at the time and in the history of the tradition interpreted in a magical context, Jesus himself appears to have been strangely indifferent towards magic. His own work as an exorcizer sprang from his perception of his role within the absolute demand of eschatological monotheism.

30. This story of the alien exorcist is not, as Manson (*Luke*, MNTC, p. 118) believes, 'an indictment of intolerance', but some practical advice about the warfare with Satan. Plummer (*Luke*, ICC, p. 259) contrasts the exorcisms of Acts 19, which he calls 'mere jugglery', saying that the sons of Sceva tried to use the formula as 'a charm'. But in Luke 9.49 'the exorcist was successful, and therefore sincere'. This is a misconception. Success in exorcism had nothing to do with sincerity, as the failure of the sincere disciples in Luke 9 shows, but was a question of technique. The exorcists in Acts failed to use the full and correct form of the name.

31. Plutarch, *De Defectu Oraculorum* 9 (*Moralia* V, 414E); *Pseudo-Clementine Hom.* 9.16.

32. Bonner however (*Magical Amulets*, p. 67) records but one amulet against fever and considers it surprising that there are not more. In the one he quotes, the sickness is addressed directly, just as in Luke. 'Plague and fever, flee from the bearer of this charm.'

33. See King, *Gnostics*, p. 57 fig. 3, where a seven-headed female demon is portrayed on a green gemstone. Legion is of course another example of demonic unity.

34. Conybeare, *JQR* 11, 1898, p. 18 n. 2.

35. This was not just because of the labour, but because of the water. The demon had already implored: 'I pray thee, King Solomon, condemn me not to go into water.'

36. For the way that dumbness is constitutional in a demon and not, as a rule, something that the demon chooses to inflict by a mere whim, see Test. Sol. 9, where the headless demon called Envy, having no eyes or voice of his own, takes those of men by damaging them when they are infants, making them dumb. Dumbness is thus driven to make dumb through envy of speech. The triple-headed spirit in Test. Sol. 12.2 says, 'I make them deaf and mute.' Obizuth, the female demon in ch. 13, says, 'I have no work other than the destruction of children and the making their ears to be deaf and the mouths with a bond . . .'. This demon like all the others does not do this from choice but from destiny. She cannot for example retire unsuccessful for a single night but must go on her terrible rounds. So convinced of her destiny is she that she doubts the power of Solomon's ring to prevent her activities.

37. The frequently asserted view that in Luke Jesus is portrayed as possessing prophetic power is in need of some clarification. The main point is not that Jesus is a prophet, but that the prophets and Jesus both had access to the

divine δύναμις, which provided the rationalization for the miracles of both Christ and prophets.

38. Bieler, Θεῖος ἀνήρ, pp. 79ff., shows the close connection between wisdom and power. The wisdom of the divine hero is revealed in his mighty works.

39. In Mark the exorcizing power of Jesus flows directly from his baptism, or rather from the authority conferred by the heavenly voice recognizing (or conferring?) the status which the demons subsequently recognize. The temptation is the first *use* of this power or, at least, the power's first use of Jesus ('the Spirit driveth him . . .'). There is, in the Marcan temptation, little sense of conflict and it is implied, not expressly stated, that Jesus conquered Satan. The angels, in Matthew present at the end of the temptations and in Luke absent altogether, are in Mark 'looking after him' in general during the period. But in Luke the exorcizing power flows directly from the conquest of Satan in the temptations, which is prepared for (*a*) by the dove, the direct indwelling bodily of the power, (*b*) by the bodily descent from God described in the genealogy. In Mark there is no particular connection between the defeat of Satan and the knowledge of the demons, but in Luke the testing of, then the confession of, the divine sonship (Luke 4.41) is the theme both of temptation and exorcism. The devils admit what previously their leader had unsuccessfully challenged.

40. In II Macc. 3.38 great care is advised in the selection of ambassadors to Jerusalem 'because there is some peculiar power of God about the place', cf. Luke 5.7. This is almost the only case in which δύναμις is used in the Lucan sense in Old Testament or Apocryphal writings.

41. Barrett, *Holy Spirit*, p. 72, remarks that, since Luke does not use δύναμις for the actual miracle, 'Luke seems to have had an objection to it – possibly because it did not belong to current Hellenistic or LXX usage.' But the use he *does* give to δύναμις is equally foreign to LXX usage. And δύναμις meaning 'miracle' *does* belong to Hellenistic usage. Bieler, op. cit., p. 81, gives examples. The explanation must be that Luke is working with another view of δύναμις, a view common in magic.

42. Preisigke, *Gotteskraft*, pp. 1–5.

43. Ibid., pp. 6ff.

44. Ibid., pp. 14f.

45. Ibid., pp. 15–17.

46. Ibid., pp. 17f., 16n.3.

47. Ibid., pp. 19ff.

48. Ibid., pp. 28–30.

49. Ibid., pp. 30–36; *Pistis Sophia* 61 (*NT Apoc.* I, pp. 257f.).

50. Bell et al., *Proc. Br. Acad.* 17, 1931, p. 254 line 9. The similarity of χάρις and δύναμις is met with frequently in magic.

51. Ibid., p. 257.

52. To what extent is the Lucan interpretation of ἐξουσία already found in Mark? Daube, *JTS* 39, 1938, has argued that the background to Mark's use of ἐξουσία is to be found in the rabbinic idea of teaching authority. C. K. Barrett, op. cit., pp. 81f., accepting this with reserve, suggests: '. . . Luke (perhaps because he was a Gentile and unfamiliar with the technical terms of

the Jewish schools) read Mark 1.27 so as to connect the ἐξουσία of Jesus with his exorcisms, and accordingly understood ἐξουσία as a term similar to if not synonymous with δύναμις.' But no Lucan misunderstanding is called for. Starr, *HTR* 23, 1930, had already shown that to Mark's Roman public ἐξουσία would have meant 'a mysterious superhuman force whereby demons were controlled and afflictions miraculously healed' (p. 303). Starr shows that of the ten cases of ἐξουσία in Mark, only one (13.34) is not connected with either healing or exorcism. The facts of the Marcan usage are thus heavily against Daube. Daube's view fails to account for the wonder of the crowd in Mark 2.12. One does not respond to a new doctrine or ethical precept, however novel it may be, by being 'beside oneself with utter amazement'. Yet Daube suggests (p. 49 n. 2) that since the standard of learning was low in Galilee, the people would indeed have been surprised. This misses the point. The people do not admire Jesus for his learning but for his power over the demons. Daube explains the connection of ἐξουσία with exorcism by pointing out that rabbis were famous as wonder-workers. But on p. 48 exorcism is not listed by Daube as one of the privileges of the rabbinic authority. So the ἐξουσία is not covered here by the rabbinical idea. Foerster has the same difficulties. The amazement of the crowd is due, he suggests (*TDNT* II, p. 569) to the fact that the rabbis were no longer prophets. Rabbinical teaching was now simply exposition. But if this is so, we have an example of the way in which Mark's use of ἐξουσία goes far beyond the idea of rabbinical authority. Foerster says the rabbis lacked ἐξουσία. How then can ἐξουσία be the same as the rabbinic idea of authority? For the rabbis hardly lacked a full possession of their own authority. The point is that Jesus did something the rabbis, as rabbis, did not do. What caused the early church the greatest difficulty, as Luke 11.19 shows, with its awkward connection with 11.20, was not that his ἐξουσία was like the rabbis' authority but that his control of the demons was like that of the Jewish exorcists, rabbis or not. The notion of authority is thus similar in Mark and Luke, but in Luke it is more systematic and is related to a total world-view.

53. The narrowing of ἐξουσία which we have found in Luke continues in Test.Sol. In every case it refers exclusively to authority over evil spirits, a remarkable confirmation of the Lucan study.

VII. Matthew: The Tradition Purified of Magic

1. Matt. 14.2 = Mark 6.14; Matt. 11.20-23 = Luke 10.13; Matt. 13.58 = Mark 6.5; Luke 19.37?

2. Mark 8.11f. = Matt. 16.1-4 and Luke 11.29-32 = Matt. 12.38-42.

3. If the transposition of the saying in Matt. 12.38 from its position in Luke 11.16, where it stands in the exorcizing context, is the work of Matthew rather than Luke, Matthew's purpose would be more clearly deliberate. But the difference in the outlook of the two gospels remains even if, as seems more probable, the shift in emphasis is the work of Luke. See Creed, *Luke*, pp. 159f.: 'His [Luke's] purpose is to shew that Christ's healings of the possessed have the force of a sign to those who can read them aright.'

4. Cf. Daube, *The NT and Rabbinic Judaism*, p. 41: 'In the Synoptics the term is employed only in depicting the attitude of the unbelieving who want visible evidence. To this, the passage about Herod who "hoped to have seen some sign done by Jesus", is not . . . an exception; we are here told about Herod's state of mind, the word "sign" is put from his, not from Luke's point of view'. But Daube is overstating the case. It is perfectly clear from Luke 2.12, 34, Matt. 24.2, 30 and elsewhere that σημεῖον has a rather broader connotation in the synoptics, than merely depicting the attitude of the unbelieving.

5. Cf. W. D. Davies, *The Setting of the Sermon on the Mount*, pp. 382–386 and note p. 386: '. . . the ethical teaching of Jesus in Q was preserved not merely as catechetically useful, and not only as radical demand, but as *revelatory*' (Davies' italics). That is to say that Jesus himself is revealed in his messianic significance. Q does not use the word 'sign', but the implication is there, and is wholly Johannine in character.

6. Allen, *Matthew* (ICC), p. 139, describes the puzzlement of Matthew at what he thought the Q version implied. 'How was [Jonah] a sign? Certainly not simply because he preached. His message of warning could in no true sense be called a sign.' That these questions presumably did not occur to Luke highlights the difference between the two evangelists.

7. The argument which results is incoherent. Matthew seeks to distinguish between Jesus and the Spirit, yet he records in the same context Jesus as saying that he casts out demons by the Spirit. As Allen says (op. cit., p. 137) 'How could the Pharisees be supposed to be able to distinguish between the Son of Man (= Christ?) acting as such, and the Son of Man driving out devils by the power of the Spirit?' The fact that in spite of this Matthew has used the saying and placed it in this context, a context which Luke avoids, illustrates his attitude towards the miracles – they are not wonderful pneumatic signs. (Whatever original misunderstanding or mistranslation may lie behind this verse makes no difference to its striking use here.)

8. T. W. Manson, *The Sayings of Jesus*, p. 94.

9. Ibid., p. 92.

10. The addition in John 12.28 of a heavenly voice is an inconsistent feature.

11. Lowther Clarke, 'The Rout of the Magi', *Divine Humanity*, p. 43, gives as examples *Barnabas* 20.1; *Didache* 2.2; 5.1; Hermas, *Mand.* 11.2; Ignatius, *Ephes.* 19.3.

12. E.g. Tatian, *Oration* 8.2; Justin, *Apology* 26.2; Justin, *Dialogue* 69.7; 78.9.

13. Smith, *Ante-Nicene Exegesis of the Gospels* I, pp. 258ff.

14. K. Stendahl in *Judentum, Christentum, Kirche*, pp. 97–100.

15. W. D. Davies, op. cit., p. 79.

16. T. Witton Davies, *Magic . . . among the Hebrews*, p. 4, points out that the magicians performed feats of power while the diviner specialized in knowledge. Although, as Davies points out, it cannot be pressed too rigidly, since the prophets' word was powerful, nevertheless the distinction is a real one.

17. Nock in Foakes-Jackson (ed.), *Beginnings* V, p. 181 n. 6.

18. Modi, 'Who were the Persian Magi who Influenced . . . the Essenes?', *Festschrift M. Winternitz*, pp. 208ff.

19. E.g. *PGM* I.62f., 73f., 243–7; *PGM* II.11–15; *PGM* XIII.14–20, 345ff., show that both myrrh and frankincense were associated with magical astrology.

20. Josephus, *Antiquities* III.197.

21. Bab. *Kethuboth* 67a (see also the note in Soncino ed., *Kethuboth* I, p. 408). Josephus, *Jewish War* VII.45, refers to the wealth of the Jewish community in Antioch.

22. Theophrastus, *Enquiry into Plants* IX.4.8 (see whole chapter).

23. Gen. 43.11 describes the myrrh given to Pharaoh, and I Kings 10.2 describes a foreign queen bringing gold and spices to a Jewish king.

24. E.g. McCasland, *The Finger of God*, p. 114, says: 'Matthew omits . . . those features from Mark's account, which might be taken to mean that he was attempting to obliterate evidences of magic in the procedure of Jesus. But he has also omitted much more from Mark's story, including the detailed description of the insane man's symptoms, and has preserved only the essential outline of the narrative. What his reason was for this abbreviation of Mark, no one can say, but it seems probably that he did not consider the sensational quality of Mark's story in good taste. . . . It did not seem fitting to preserve the record of resistance and efforts of defense made against the Messiah by demons.'

It can be shown, however, that Matthew omits in fact very little which is not connected with exorcism as such. McCasland refers to the symptoms of the man's insanity, but it hardly needs saying that to Matthew these details are not symptoms in the medical sense at all, but examples of the activity of the evil spirits with which the man was possessed. The details are given in Mark for the purpose of describing not the sickness of the man, but the type of demon about to be exorcized. It is certainly connected with the first rule of any exorcism – know your enemy! Matthew generally leaves out these examples of demonic identification. Note the way in which he changes Mark's 'He is possessed by a spirit which makes him speechless. Whenever it attacks him it dashes him to the ground . . . it has often tried to make an end of him by throwing him into the fire or into water' (Mark 9.17f., 22) into, 'He is an epileptic and has bad fits, and he keeps falling about, often into the fire, often into water' (Matt. 17.15). The characteristic behaviour of the demon is exchanged for a much briefer description. The same is true of the Gadarene madman.

McCasland thinks the details were omitted partly because of their sensationalism. This cannot be true. With the possible exception of the author of the Apocalypse, there is no author in the NT who loves sensationalism more than Matthew. McCasland also suggests that Matthew may have thought it unfitting that demons should be allowed to express violent defiance of Messiah. It is difficult to see why Matthew should have felt like this. He is not a squeamish author. No gospel describes in such violent colours the mutual antagonism between Jesus and his opponents. One only has to think of the massacre of the innocents, the indignant question following the cleansing of the temple, the additional words of insult on the cross (Matt. 27.43), to realize that Matthew often multiplies examples of Messiah meeting with abuse and defiance. Matthew contains the contemptuous remarks of the people of Nazareth, the scorn of the mourners of Jairus' daughter; when it comes to devils he retains the abusive defiance of the demons in 8.29 – but christologizes it. Matthew is not worried by resistance or opposition as such, but by details of the technique of devil-controlling exorcism.

25. Held, in *Tradition and Interpretation in Matthew*, pp. 173f., has drawn attention to Matthew's omission of the magical. He says the 'parallels in the papyri dealing with magic are most convincing precisely for these expressions' (i.e. the ones Matthew omits). 'When Matthew passes them entirely by and only uses the statement about the "coming", i.e. the mission of Jesus, it is clear that he does not wish to depict the demons as trying to exercise counter-magic, but he is putting a Christological statement into their mouths.' Held sees clearly what Matthew is *for* when he indicates the christological interpretation given, but he does not see equally clearly what Matthew is against. Held says, 'What he omits are the descriptive non-essentials' (p. 173). But he cannot understand in view of this the inclusion of Matt. 8.28b. He describes it as 'a brief and peculiar statement the meaning of which is not altogether clear' (p. 172). But surely the meaning is clear enough. It is a novelistic addition, although, by Held's account there should not be any! Matthew, in other words, was not trying to make the story less vivid or less apt for story telling; he was trying hard not to give an inch to those who might regard the incident as proof that Jesus was a strolling wonder-worker, an exorcist. Like John, he seeks to distract the reader from the technique to the significance of the person of Christ.

26. Bonner, *HTR* 20, 1927, pp. 174ff., gives details and examples.

27. Ibid, pp. 179f.

28. Held, op. cit., p. 171.

29. Bultmann, *History of the Synoptic Tradition*, p. 222.

30. W. C. Allen, *Matthew* (ICC), p. xvi, suggests that the story is left out because, in the first place, Matthew wanted a series of three miracles and preferred the centurion's servant because, as Luke's position indicates, it was already traditionally attached to the Sermon on the Mount. But this can hardly be the case since Matthew has broken the connection by inserting the story of the leper. He had to disrupt Mark's order to do this, and his use of Mark 1.27b (= Matt. 8.16b) makes it clear that he is selecting whatever he can from the Capernaum incident. Secondly, Allen suggests (p. xxxiii) that the continuation of the screaming after Jesus had spoken the word of power may have encouraged Matthew to omit it. This cannot explain the omission. If Matthew objected to one detail, he would simply have modified it as does Luke and as he himself does in all the other stories.

31. Quoted by Held, op. cit., p. 207.

32. See Daube, *The NT and Rabbinic Judaism*, pp. 224ff., and especially p. 234: 'There are several examples in Rabbinic literature of the belief that the hands of a saintly person might be possessed of a beneficent virtue.' An example of this is found in the case of the hand of Boaz discussed by Daube on p. 48. Note also p. 235: '. . . here and there we meet with the Old Testament notion, or more precisely, with extended applications of it, that a cure

may take place even if – instead of the miracle-worker taking action – the person in need touches the miracle-worker or something belonging to him.' Cf. II Kings 13.21. On the odd absence of any reference to touching in the epistles, Daube remarks '. . . this may be accidental. But it is quite possible that some writers found themselves in a situation in which, while far from opposing the practice, they did not want to encourage it' (pp. 235f.). Daube does not say what these situations might have been, although he thinks that Paul may have been worried about the limitation of God's grace implied by the practice of ordination by the laying on of hands (p. 241), but he is probably referring to the possibility of misunderstanding by the Hellenistic world of the nature of Christian healing. This possibility would be likely to arise because of the magical associations which the touch of blessing originally had. 'The idea no doubt was that by placing your hands on a person, some magic attaching to them took effect upon him. At a later stage, maybe your hands were conceived of as transmitting an influence from above, one might almost say, like conductors' (p. 225). Now if this is why the letters to the Hellenistic churches do not mention touching, nor in fact any detail of healing at all, it raises the possibility that Matthew had not been in contact with Hellenistic magic in detail; had he been in conflict with a magical therapeutic tradition in which the touch was a living item, and not merely a traditional gesture, he might have felt less happy about the inclusion of so many of Mark's touching incidents. Luke, who was certainly aware of the struggle with Hellenistic magic, actually multiplies the touching incidents, but that is because it is his aim to show not that Christianity has nothing to do with magic, but that Christians can outdo magicians at their own game.

33. Cf. the conclusion reached by S. V. McCasland after a brief study of the material: 'It is clear Matthew has made no effort to heighten or increase the phenomena of exorcism which he found in the sources. So far as the material found in Mark is concerned, Matthew has deliberately dropped many of the sensational features. He even omitted one of Mark's more important exorcisms. On the whole, the exorcisms are much less prominent in Matthew than in Mark . . . We must conclude, therefore, . . . that there was no tendency among the disciples of his time to build up legends about the exorcisms of Jesus' (pp. 48f.).

Three questions need to be asked about this.

(i) Is it going far enough to say merely that Matthew does not heighten the exorcisms? That he merely does not build up legends? Are the features he drops out merely sensational?

(ii) How far can Matthew be taken as representative of the typical interests of the disciples of his time? Luke does not seem to have his attitude towards exorcism.

(iii) If Matthew does not build up legends about the exorcisms of Jesus, why does he not? It is well known that Matthew's M is a 'wild source'; there is no richer vein of legendary tradition than that which contains the coin in the fish's mouth, Pilate's wife's dream, the flight into Egypt, and the resurrection of the saints. The elaboration which the synoptic tradition has received in the school of Matthew makes the lack of the exorcistic elaboration the more striking, and McCasland's conclusion does less than justice to the facts.

BIBLIOGRAPHY

Ancient authors have been cited where possible from the Loeb Classical Library or the Ante-Nicene Christian Library; some other editions and translations are included below.

Abt, A., *Die Apologie des Apuleius von Madaura und die Antike Zauberie*, Giessen 1908.

Ad-Damîrî's Ḥayât al-Ḥayawân, A Zoological Lexicon, ET by A. S. G. Jayakar, London 1906.

Aeschylus, *The Eumenides*, ET by Gilbert Murray, London 1925.

Alexander, W. M., *Demonic Possession in the New Testament*, Edinburgh 1902.

Alford, Henry, *The Greek Testament* I: *The Four Gospels*, London 1849.

Allen, W. C., *A Critical and Exegetical Commentary on the Gospel according to St Matthew* (ICC), ²1907.

Andres, F., 'Dämonen', Pauly-Wissowa, *Real-Encyclopaedie der classischen Altertumswissenschaft*, suppl. vol. III, Stuttgart 1918, pp. 267 511.

Apuleius, *Apologie*, ed. P. Vallette (Budé ed.), Paris 1924.
Apologia and Florida, ET by M. E. Butler, Oxford 1909.

Audollent, A., *Defixionum Tabellae . . . in Corpore Inscriptionum Atticarum*, Paris 1904.

Bailey, J. A., *The Traditions Common to the Gospels of Luke and John, Novum Testamentum* Suppl. 7, Leiden 1963.

Barb, A. A., 'The Survival of the Magical Arts' in A. Momigliano (ed.), *The Conflict between Paganism and Christianity in the Fourth Century*, Oxford 1963, pp. 100–25.

Barrett, C. K., *The Holy Spirit and the Gospel Tradition*, London 1947.

Bartlet, J. V., *St Mark* (Century Bible), Edinburgh 1922.

Baudissin, W. F. von, *Studien zur semitischen Religionsgeschichte* I, Leipzig 1876.

Bauernfeind, O., *Die Worte der Dämonen im Markusevangelium*, Stuttgart 1927.

Beare, F. W., *The Earliest Records of Jesus*, Oxford 1962.

Bell, H. I., Nock, A. D., and Thompson, H., 'Magical Texts from a Bilingual Papyrus in the British Museum', *Proc. Br. Acad.* 17, 1931, pp. 235–87.

Bernadin, J. C., 'A New Testament Triad', *JBL* 57, 1938, pp. 273–9.

Bidez, J., and Cumont, F. V. M., *Les mages hellénisés. Zoroastre, Ostanès et Hystaspe d'après la tradition grecque* I–II, Paris 1938.

Bieler, L., Θεῖος ἀνήρ. *Das Bild des 'göttlichen Menschen' in Spätantike und Früh-christentum* I–II, Vienna 1935–36.

'δύναμις und ἐξουσία', *Wiener Studien* 55, 1935, pp. 182–90.

Blau, L., *Das altjüdische Zauberwesen*, Strasbourg 1898.

Bonner, Campbell, 'Traces of Thaumaturgic Technique in the Miracles', *HTR* 20, 1927, pp. 171–81.

'The Technique of Exorcism', *HTR* 36, 1943, pp. 39–49.

Studies in Magical Amulets, chiefly Graeco-Egyptian, Michigan 1950.

'Amulets chiefly in the British Museum', *Hesperia* 20, 1951, pp. 301–45.

'A Miscellany of Engraved Stones', *Hesperia* 23, 1954, pp. 138–57.

See also under Youtie.

Bouché-Leclerq, A., *Histoire de la divination dans l'antiquité* I, Paris 1879. *L'astrologie grecque*, Paris 1899.

Bousset, W., *Kyrios Christos*, ET by J. E. Steely, New York 1970.

'Zur Dämonologie der späteren Antike', *Archiv für Religionswissenschaft* 18, 1915, pp. 134–72.

Boylan, P., *Thoth, the Hermes of Egypt*, London 1922.

Brandon, S. G. F., *Creation Legends of the Ancient Near East*, London 1963.

Branscomb, B. H., *The Gospel of Mark* (MNTC), 1937.

Breasted, J. H., *Development of Religion and Thought in Ancient Egypt*, London 1912.

Brewer, E. C., *A Dictionary of Miracles*, new ed., London 1897.

Brugsch, H. H., 'Über das ägyptische Museum zu Leiden', *Zeitschrift der Deuts-chen morgenländischen Gesellschaft* 6, 1852, pp. 250ff.

Grammaire démotique, Berlin 1855.

Budge, E. A. T. Wallis, *The Book of the Dead: the Chapters of Coming Forth by Day*, translation, London 1898.

Egyptian Magic, London 1899.

The Book of the Saints of the Ethiopian Church I–IV, Cambridge 1928.

Amulets and Superstitions, London 1930.

From Fetish to God in Ancient Egypt, London 1934.

Bultmann, R., *The History of the Synoptic Tradition*, ET by John Marsh, Oxford 1963.

Burkitt, F. C., *Church and Gnosis*, Cambridge 1932.

Charles, R. H., *The Apocrypha and Pseudepigrapha of the Old Testament* I–II, Oxford 1913.

Chifflet, J. (ed.), *Joannis Macarii Abraxas . . . Accedit Abraxas Proteus, seu multiformis gemmae Basilidianae . . . varietas*, Antwerp 1657.

Clarke, W. K. Lowther, *Divine Humanity. Essays on New Testament Problems*, London 1936, pp. 41–51, 'The Rout of the Magi'.

Clermont-Ganneau, C., 'Royal Ptolemaic Inscriptions and Magic Lead Figures from Tell Sandahannah', *PEFQS*, 1901, pp. 54–8.

Collingwood, R. G., 'Inscriptions on Stone and Lead', in Wheeler, R.E.M. and T.V., 'The Roman Amphitheatre at Caerleon, Monmouthshire', *Archaeologia* 78. v, 1928, pp. 155–9.

Conybeare, F. C., 'Christian Demonology', *JQR* 8, 1896, p. 576–608, and 9, 1897, pp. 59–114, 444–70 and 581–603.

'The Testament of Solomon', *JQR* 11, 1898, pp. 1–45.

Myth, Magic and Morals: a Study of Christian Origins, London 1909.

Conzelmann, H., *The Theology of St Luke*, ET by G. Buswell, London 1960.

Cook, A. B., *Zeus: a Study in Ancient Religion* I–II, Cambridge 1914, 1925.

Cormack, J. M. R., 'A Tabella Defixionis in the Museum of the University of Reading, England', *HTR* 44, 1951, pp. 25–34.

Cramer, F. H., *Astrology in Roman Law and Politics*, Philadelphia 1954.

Cranfield, C. E. B., *The Gospel according to St Mark* (Cambridge Greek Testament Commentary), Cambridge 1959.

Creed, J. M., *The Gospel according to St Luke*, London 1957.

Crum, W. E., *Coptic Ostraka from the Collections of the Egypt Exploration Fund, the Cairo Museum and Others*, London 1902.

Cumont, F. V. M., *Astrology and Religion among the Romans*, New York and London 1912.

L'Égypte des astrologues, Brussels 1937.

Dalman, Gustav, *Jesus Christ in the Talmud, Midrash, Zohar and the Liturgy of the Synagogue*, ET by A. W. Streane, Cambridge 1893.

Daube, David, 'ἐξουσία in Mark 1.22 and 27', *JTS* 39, 1938, pp. 45–59.

The New Testament and Rabbinic Judaism, London 1956.

David, M., *The Warren Papyri* (Papyrologica Lugduno-batava I), Leiden 1941.

Davies, T. Witton, *Magic, Divination and Demonology among the Hebrews and their Neighbours*, London 1898, reprinted New York 1969.

Davies, W. D., *The Setting of the Sermon on the Mount*, Cambridge 1964.

Dawson, W. R., *Magician and Leech*, London 1929.

Deissmann, G. A., *Bible Studies*, ET by A. Grieve, Edinburgh 1901.

'Heitmüller, *Im Namen Jesu*', *TLZ*, 1904, cols. 199–202.

New Light on the New Testament from Records of the Graeco-Roman Period ET by R. M. Strachan, Edinburgh 1907.

Light from the Ancient East, ET by R. M. Strachan, rev. ed., London 1927 (cited as *LAE*)

Delatte, A., 'Études sur la magie grecque: I. Sphère magique du Musée d'Athènes', *Bulletin de Correspondence Hellenique* 37, 1913, pp. 247–78.

Anecdota Atheniensia I–II, Liège and Paris 1927 and 1939.

Dell, A., 'Matthaus 16.17–19', *ZNW* 15, 1914, pp. 1–14.

Dibelius, M., *From Tradition to Gospel*, ET by B. Lee Woolf, London 1934.

Dieterich, A., *Abraxas: Studien zur Religionsgeschichte des späteren Altertums*, Leipzig 1891.

Eine Mithrasliturgie, Leipzig 1903.

Kleine Schriften, ed. R. Wünsch, Leipzig and Berlin 1911.

Diogenes Laertius, *La Vie de Pythagore*, ed. A. Delatte, Brussels 1922.

Dodds, E. R., *The Greeks and the Irrational*, Berkeley and Los Angeles 1951.

Doresse, Jean, *The Secret Books of the Egyptian Gnostics*, ET by P. Mairet, London 1960.

Dornseiff, F., *Das Alphabet in Mystik und Magie*, Leipzig and Berlin 1922.

Easton, B. Scott, *The Gospel according to Luke*, Edinburgh 1926.

Edelstein, Emma J. and Ludwig, *Asclepius. A Collection and Interpretation of the Testimonies* I–II, Baltimore 1945.

Ehnmark, E. J., *Anthropomorphism and Miracle* (Uppsala Universitets Årsskrift 12), Uppsala 1939.

Eitrem, S., *The Greek Magical Papyri in the British Museum*, Kristiania 1923.
(ed.), *Papyri Osloenses*: I, *Magical Papyri*, Oslo 1925.
'Kronos in der Magie', *Annuaire de l'Institute de philologie et d'histoire orientales*
(*Mélanges Bidez*) II, Brussels 1934, pp. 351–60.
Some Notes on the Demonology of the New Testament (Symbolae Osloenses
Suppl. 12), Oslo ²1966.
Eusebius, *Praeparatio Evangelica*, ed. and trans. E. H. Gifford, 4 vols. in 5,
Oxford 1903.
Fascher, E., *Jesus und der Satan: Eine Studie zur Auslegungen der Versuchungs-
geschichte* (Hallische Monographien 11), Halle 1949.
Festugière, A. M. J., *L'idéal religieux des grecs et l'évangile*, Paris 1932.
La révélation d'Hermès Trismégiste I–IV, Paris 1944–54.
(ed.), *Corpus Hermeticum* IV, Paris 1954.
Fiebig, P. W. J., *Jüdische Wundergeschichten des neutestamentlichen Zeitalters*,
Tübingen 1911.
Rabbinische Wundergeschichten des neutestamentlichen Zeitalters (Kleine Texte,
ed. H. Lietzmann, 78), Bonn 1911.
Foakes-Jackson, F. J., and Lake, K. (eds.), *The Beginnings of Christianity* I–V,
London 1920–33.
Foerster, W., 'ἐξουσία', *TDNT* II, 1964, pp. 562–75.
Föhrer, G., 'Prophetie und Magie', *ZAW* 78, 1966, pp. 25–47.
Frankfort, H., et al., *The Intellectual Adventure of Ancient Man*, Chicago 1946.
Frazer, J. G., *The Golden Bough. A Study in Magic and Religion*, 3rd ed., I.1–2,
The Magic Art and the Evolution of Kings, London 1911.
Frey, J. B., 'L'angelologie juive au temps de J. Christ', *Revue des sciences
philosophiques et théologiques* 5, 1911, pp. 75–110.
Fridrichsen, Anton, *La problème du miracle dans le Christianisme primitif*,
Strasbourg and Paris 1925.
Gaster, M., *The Sword of Moses, an Ancient Book of Magic*, London 1896.
Conjurations and the Ancient Mysteries, London 1932.
Gill, A. Wilson, 'Hysterical Aphonia in Soldiers', in A. F. Hurst (ed.), *Seale
Hayne Neurological Studies* I.3, London 1920, pp. 150–58.
Goodwin, C. W., *Fragment of a Graeco-Egyptian Work upon Magic from a Papyrus
in the British Museum*. Translation and Notes (Cambridge Antiquarian
Society Publications 2), Cambridge 1852.
Gould, E., *A Critical and Exegetical Commentary on the Gospel according to St
Mark* (ICC), 1896.
Grant, R. M., *Miracle and Natural Law in Graeco-Roman and Early Christian
Thought*, Amsterdam 1952.
Grenfell, B. P., and Hunt, A. S., *The Oxyrhynchus Papyri*, London 1898ff.
Grenfell et al., *Fayum Towns and their Papyri*, London 1900.
Griffith, F. Ll., 'The Date of the Old Coptic Texts and their Relation to
Christian Coptic', *Zeitschrift für ägyptische Sprache und Altertumskunde* 39,
1901, pp. 78–82.
Griffith and Thompson, H., *The Demotic Magical Papyrus of London and Leiden*
I–III, London 1904–9.
Grundmann, W., *Der Begriff der Kraft in der neutestamentlichen Gedankenwelt*,
Stuttgart 1932.

'δύναμαι', *TDNT* II, 1964, pp. 284–317.

'κράζω', *TDNT* III, 1966, pp. 898–903.

Harnack, A. von, *The Mission and Expansion of Christianity in the First Three Centuries*, ET London ²1908.

Heitmüller, W., '*Im Namen Jesu*', *eine sprache- und religionsgeschichtliche Untersuchung zum Neuen Testament* (FRLANT 2), 1903.

Held, H. J., 'Matthew as Interpreter of the Miracle Stories' in G. Bornkamm, G. Barth and H. J. Held, *Tradition and Interpretation in Matthew*, ET by P. Scott, London 1963, pp. 165–299.

Hopfner, Theodor, *Griechisch-ägyptischen Offenbarungszauber* I–II, Leipzig, 1921, 1924.

Hunt, A. S., 'An Incantation in the Ashmolean Museum', *JEA*, 1929, pp. 155–7.

'A Greek Cryptogram', *Proc. Br. Acad.* 15, 1929, pp. 127–34.

'The Warren Magical Papyrus', *Studies Presented to F. Ll. Griffith*, London 1932, pp. 233–40.

Hunter, A. M., *The Gospel according to St Mark* (Torch Bible Commentaries), London 1949.

Iamblichus, *Les mystères d'Égypte*, ed. and tr. E. des Places (Budé ed.), Paris 1966.

Life of Pythagoras, ET by Thomas Taylor, 1818, reprinted London 1965.

Jayne, W. A., *The Healing Gods of Ancient Civilizations*, New Haven 1925.

Jensen, A. E., *Myth and Cult among Primitive People*, ET by M. T. Choldin and W. Weissleder, Chicago 1963.

Justin Martyr, *Dialogus* in *Die ältesten Apologeten*, ed. E. J. Goodspeed, Göttingen 1914.

Keller, Otto, *Rerum Naturalium Scriptores Graeci Minores* I, Leipzig 1877.

Kemp, P., *Healing Ritual. Studies in the Technique and Tradition of the Southern Slaves*, London 1935

Kenyon, F. G., *Greek Papyri in the British Museum*. Catalogue with texts, London 1893.

King, C. W., *Handbook of Engraved Gems*, London 1866.

Antique Gems and Rings I–II, London 1872.

The Gnostics and their Remains, Ancient and Medieval, London ²1887.

Kittel, G., 'ἄγγελος', *TDNT* I, 1964, pp. 80–87.

Klausner, Joseph, *Jesus of Nazareth, his Life, Times and Teaching*, ET by H. Danby, London and New York 1925.

Knox, W. L., 'Jewish Liturgical Exorcism', *HTR* 31, 1938, pp. 191–203.

St Paul and the Church of the Gentiles, Cambridge 1939.

Knudtzon, E. J., *Bakchiastexte und andere Papyri aus der Lunder Papyrussammlung*, Lund 1946.

Koehler, L., *Hebrew Man*, ET by P. R. Ackroyd, London 1956.

Kuhn, H. B., 'The Angelology of the Non-canonical Jewish Apocalypses', *JBL* 67, 1948, pp. 217–32.

Lake, K., 'The Holy Spirit', in Foakes-Jackson (ed.), *Beginnings* V, pp. 96–111.

Lampe, G. W. H., 'Miracles and Early Christian Apologetic', in Moule (ed.), *Miracles*, pp. 205–18.

Lane, E. W., *An Account of the Manners and Customs of the Modern Egyptians*, enlarged ed. in 3 vols., London 1846.

Langton, E., *The Ministries of the Angelic Powers according to the Old Testament and Later Jewish Literature*, London 1936.

The Angel Teaching of the New Testament, London 1937.

— Legge, F., 'A Coptic Spell of the Second Century', *Proceedings of the Society for Biblical Archaeology* 19, 1897, pp. 183–7.

Lenormant, F., *Catalogue d'une collection d'antiquités égyptiennes rassemblée par M. d'Anastasi*, Paris 1857.

Lexa, F., *La magie dans l'Égypte antique, de l'ancien empire jusqu'à l'époque copte* I–II, Paris 1925.

Lindsay, T. M., *The Gospel according to St Mark*, Edinburgh 1883.

Loisy, A. F., *L'Évangile selon Luc*, Paris 1924.

The Origins of the New Testament, ET by L. P. Jacks, London 1950.

Loomis, C. G., *White Magic, an Introduction to the Folklore of Christian Legend*, Cambridge, Mass., 1948.

— Lowe, J. E., *Magic in Greek and Latin Literature*, Oxford, 1929.

Lowrie, Walter, *Jesus according to St Mark*, London 1929.

McCasland, S. V., *By the Finger of God: Demon Possession and Exorcism in Early Christianity in the Light of Modern Views on Mental Illness*, New York 1951.

McCown, Chester C., *The Testament of Solomon*, edited with Introduction, Leipzig 1922.

McDonald, A. H., 'Herodotus on the Miraculous' in Moule (ed.), *Miracles*, pp. 83–91.

MacRae, G., 'Miracle in *The Antiquities* of Josephus' in Moule (ed.), *Miracles*, pp. 129–47.

Malinowski, B., *Argonauts of the Western Pacific*, London 1922.

Magic, Science and Religion, and Other Essays, Boston, Mass., 1948.

Manson, T. W., *The Sayings of Jesus*, London 1949.

Manson, William, *The Gospel according to St Luke* (MNTC), 1942.

Marett, R. R., *The Threshold of Religion*, London ²1914.

Martroye, F., 'La répression de la magie et la culte de Gentils av. ive siècle', *Revue historique de droit français et étranger* IV.9, 1930, pp. 669f.

Maurice, Jules, 'La terreur de la magie dans ive siècle', *Revue historique de droit français et étranger* IV.6, 1927, pp. 108–21.

Menzies, A., *The Earliest Gospel. A Historical Study of the Gospel according to St Mark*, London 1901.

Meyer, H. A. W., *Critical and Exegetical Handbook to the Gospels of Mark and Luke*, ET of 5th ed. by R. E. Wallis, rev. by W. F. Dickson, New York 1884.

Michel, C., *Recueil d'inscriptions grecques* I–II, Brussels 1900 and 1912.

Micklem, E. R., *Miracles and the New Psychology*, London 1922.

Modi, J. J., 'Who were the Persian Magi who Influenced the Jewish sect of the Essenes?' in *Festschrift für M. Winternitz*, ed. O. Stein, Leipzig 1933, pp. 208–11.

Montefiore, C. G., *The Synoptic Gospels* I–II, London ²1927.

Montfaucon, B. de, *L'antiquité expliquée et representée* . . . I–X, Paris 1719–24.

Moore, G. F., *Judaism in the First Centuries of the Christian Era* I–III, Cambridge, Mass., 1927–30.

Moule, C. F. D. (ed.), *Miracles: Cambridge Studies in their Philosophy and History*, London 1965.

Moulton, J. H., *Grammar of New Testament Greek*, Edinburgh 1908.

Moulton and Milligan, G., *The Vocabulary of the Greek Testament*, London 1914–29.

Müller, C. O., Review of J. C. Reuvens, *Lettres . . . sur les papyrus bilingues et grecs . . ., Göttingische Gelehrte Anzeigen* 2, 1831, pp. 545–60.

Nilsson, M. P., 'Die Religion in der griechischen Zauberpapyri', *Opuscula Selecta* III, Lund 1960, pp. 129–66.

Geschichte der griechischen Religion (Handbuch der Altertumswissenschaft 5), Munich ²1961.

Nock, A. D., 'Greek Magical Papyri', *JEA* 15, 1929, pp. 219–35.

'Paul and the Magus' in Foakes-Jackson (ed.), *Beginnings* V, pp. 164–88.

Oesterreich, T. C., *Possession, Demoniacal and Other . . .*, ET by D. Ibberson, London 1930.

Oxé, A., 'Ein römanisches Fluchtafelchen aus Caerleon', *Germanica* 15, 1931, pp. 16–19.

Petrie, W. M. Flinders, *Hawara, Biahmu, and Arsinoe*, London 1889.

Amulets, London 1914.

Pistis Sophia, ET by G. R. S. Mead, London, reprinted 1947.

Plummer, Alfred, *A Critical and Exegetical Commentary on the Gospel according to St Luke* (ICC), 1896.

Plummer, Charles, *Vitae Sanctorum Hiberniae* I–II, Oxford 1910.

Preisendanz, Karl, *Papyri Graecae Magicae: Die griechischen Zauberpapyri* I–III, Leipzig & Berlin 1928, 1931, 1942 (cited as *PGM* with papyrus no. & line).

Papyrusfunde und Papyrusforschung, Leipzig 1933.

'Die griechischen und lateinischen Zaubertafeln', *Archiv für Papyrusforschung* 11, 1935, pp. 153–64.

'Zur Überlieferungsgeschichte der spätantiken Magie', *Zentralblatt für Bibliothekswesen*, Beiheft 75, *Georg Leyh Festgabe*, Leipzig 1950, pp. 223–40.

'Neue griechische Zauberpapyri', *Chronique d'Égypte* 26, 1951, pp. 405–9.

Preisigke, Friedrich, *Die Gotteskraft der frühchristlichen Zeit* (Papyrus institut Heidelberg Schrift 6), Berlin and Leipzig 1922.

Proclus Diadochus, *Commentary on the First Alciabiades of Plato*, ed. L. G. Westerink, Amsterdam 1954.

Psellus, Michael, *De Operatione Daemonum*, ed. J. F. Boissonade, Gr. Norinbergae 1838.

Dialogue on the Operation of Daemons, ET by Marcus Collisson, Sydney 1843.

Rad, Gerhard von, 'ἄγγελος', *TDNT* I, 1964, pp. 74–80.

Rawlinson, A. E. J., *St Mark*, London 1925.

Reitzenstein, Richard, *Poimandres. Studien zur griechisch-ägyptischen und frühchristlichen Literatur*, Leipzig 1904.

Hellenistische Wundererzählungen, Leipzig ²1922.

Rengstorf, K. H., *Das Evangelium nach Lukas*, Göttingen 1952.

Reuvens, J. C., *Lettres à M. Letronne . . . sur les papyrus bilingues et grecs . . . du Musée . . . de Leide*, Leiden 1830.

Riesenfeld, Harald, 'Remarques sur les hymnes magiques', *Eranos* 44, 1946, pp. 153–60.

Rivers, W. H. R., *Medicine, Magic and Religion*, London 1924.

Rohde, Erwin, *Psyche*, ET by W. B. Hillis, London 1925.

Ross, J. P., 'Some Notes on Miracle in the Old Testament' in Moule (ed.), *Miracles*, pp. 45–60.

Rougé, E. de, *Oeuvres diversées* III, ed. G. Maspero, Paris 1910.

Schubart, Wilhelm, *Die Papyri der Universitätsbibliothek Erlangen*, Leipzig 1942.

Schürer, Emil, *Geschichte des jüdischen Volkes im Zeitalter Jesu Christi* III, Leipzig, ²1898.

Simon, Marcel, *Verus Israel: études sur les relations entre chrétiens et juifs dans l'empire romain 135–425*, Paris 1948.

Smith, Harold, *Ante-Nicene Exegesis of the Gospels* I, London 1925.

Starr, J., 'The Meaning of Authority in Mark 1.22', *HTR* 23, 1930, pp. 302–5.

Stendahl, Krister, 'Quis et Unde? An Analysis of Mt. 1–2', in *Judentum, Urchristentum, Kirche Festschrift J. Jeremias* (BZNW 26), 1960, pp. 94–105.

Strack, H. L., and Billerbeck, P., *Kommentar zum Neuen Testament aus Talmud und Midrasch* I–IV, Munich 1922–28.

Svoboda, Karel, *La démonologie de Michel Psellos* (Spisy filosofické fakulty Masarykovy University v Brně 22), Brno 1927.

Sweet, J. P. M., 'The Theory of Miracles in the Wisdom of Solomon', in Moule (ed.), *Miracles*, pp. 113–26.

Swete, H. B., *The Gospel according to St Mark*, London 1898.

Sword of Moses, The, see Gaster, T.

Tait, J. G., and Préaux, Claire, *Greek Ostraca in the Bodleian Library at Oxford* II: *Ostraca of the Roman and Byzantine Periods*, London 1955.

Tavenner, Eugene, *Studies in Magic from Latin Literature*, New York 1916.

Taylor, Vincent, *The Gospel according to St Mark*, London 1952.

Testament of Solomon, The, see McCown, C. C.

Thompson, R. C., *The Reports of the Magicians and Astrologers of Nineveh in the British Museum* I–II, London 1900.

  The Devils and Evil Spirits of Babylon I–II, London 1903–4.

  Semitic Magic, its Origins and Development, London 1908.

Thorndike, Lynn, *A History of Magic and Experimental Science during the first Thirteen Centuries of our Era*, New York 1923.

Trench, R. C., *Notes on the Miracles of our Lord*, London ²1847.

Vogliano, A., 'Papiri Bolognesi', *ACME, Annali della Facoltà di Filosofia e Lettere dell'Universita' Statale di Milano* I, 1948, pp. 195–245.

Vouaux L., *Les Actes de Pierre*, Paris 1922.

Weinreich, Otto, *Antike Heilungswunder. Untersuchungen zum Wunderglauben der Griechen und Römer*, Giessen 1909.

Weiss, Bernhard, *Biblical Theology of the New Testament* I–II, ET by D. Eaton, Edinburgh 1882.

Weiss, Johannes, *Die Schriften des Neuen Testaments* I, Göttingen 1907.

Wessely, Carl, 'Griechische Zauberpapyrus von Paris und London', *Denkschriften der Akademie der Wissenschaften, Wien, phil.-hist. Klasse* 36.2, 1888, pp. 27–208.

Westermann, Anton, *Scriptores Rerum Mirabilium Graeci*, Brunswick 1839.

Wetter, G. P. von, '*Der Sohn Gottes*'. *Ein Untersuchung über den Character und die Tendenz des Johannes-Evangelium* (FRLANT 26), 1916.

Wilcken, Ulrich, *Griechische Ostraka aus Aegypten und Nubien* I–II, Leipzig and Berlin 1899.

Wiles, M. F., 'Miracles in the Early Church', in Moule (ed.), *Miracles*, pp. 221–34.

Wünsch, Richard, *Defixionum Tabellae Atticae* (*Corpus Inscriptionarum Graecarum* III.3), Berlin 1873.

Sethianische Verfluchungstafeln aus Röm, Leipzig 1898.

'Antikes Zaubergerät aus Pergamon', *Jahrbuch des Kaiserlich Deutschen Archäologischen Instituts*, Ergänzungsheft VI.

Antike Fluchtafeln (Kleine Texte, ed. H. Lietzmann, 20), Bonn ²1912.

Youtie, Y. C., and Bonner, Campbell, 'Two Curse Tablets from Beisan', *Transactions and Proceedings of the American Philological Association* 67, 1937, pp. 43–77.

INDEX OF PERSONS

INDEX OF REFERENCES

Papyri Graecae Magicae